D1359268

OPENNESS
IN ADOPTION

*This book is dedicated with gratitude
to all the participants in our study: adopted children,
adoptive parents, birthparents, other family members, and
adoption agency staff, who offered their perspectives
so that others touched by adoption now
and in the future might benefit.*

OPENNESS
IN ADOPTION
Exploring Family Connections

Harold D. Grotevant / Ruth G. McRoy

SAGE Publications
International Educational and Professional Publisher
Thousand Oaks   London   New Delhi

For information:

SAGE Publications, Inc.
2455 Teller Road
Thousand Oaks, California 91320
E-mail: order@sagepub.com

SAGE Publications Ltd.
6 Bonhill Street
London EC2A 4PU
United Kingdom

SAGE Publications India Pvt. Ltd.
M-32 Market
Greater Kailash I
New Delhi 110 048 India

Printed in the United States of America

Library of Congress Cataloging-in-Publication Data

Grotevant, Harold D.
   Openness in adoption : exploring family connections /
by Harold D. Grotevant and Ruth G. McRoy.
      p. cm.
   Includes bibliographical references and index.
   ISBN 0-8039-5778-5 (cloth : alk. paper)
   ISBN 0-8039-5779-3 (pbk. : alk. paper)
   1. Adoption—United States. 2. Open adoption—United States.
3. Adoptees—United States—Identification. 4. Birthparents—
United States—Identification. I. McRoy, Ruth G. II. Title.
HV875.55 .G757 1998
362.73'4'0973—ddc21   98-19745

98 99 00 01 02 03 04 10 9 8 7 6 5 4 3 2 1

Acquiring Editor:	C. Deborah Laughton
Editorial Assistant:	Eileen Carr
Production Editor:	Sanford Robinson
Production Assistant:	Denise Santoyo
Typesetter/Designer:	Marion Warren
Indexer:	Jean Casalegno
Cover Designer:	Ravi Balasuriya

CONTENTS

PREFACE

Adoption has received more national attention and debate in the 1990s than perhaps ever before in the United States. Changes in adoption practice from confidentiality toward openness have been provoked by broader changes in societal attitudes and shifts in population demographics. This book presents the results of a nationwide study designed to examine the impact of variations in openness in adoption on participants in the adoptive kinship network: adopted children, adoptive parents, and the children's birthparents. We have situated this research within the historical context in which it was conducted, and we report results, as well as recommend implications for adoption practice and policy. We hope this book will be useful to social scientists, practitioners in various human services fields, policymakers, and persons whose lives are touched by adoption.

Many individuals have assisted us in the process of interviewing participants, transcribing interviews, coding or preparing data, and performing statistical analyses. We express deepest thanks to Susan Ayers-Lopez and Deborah Lewis Fravel, who served as project managers at the Texas and Minnesota sites, respectively, during this phase of the study. Their orchestration and competent contributions at all levels contributed significantly to the success and integrity of this project.

We appreciate the substantial contributions made by our chapter coauthors: Susan Ayers-Lopez, Chalandra Bryant, Cinda Christian, Carol Elde, Deborah Lewis Fravel, Meredith Friedrick, Susan M. Henney, Julie K. Kohler, Steven J. Onken, Manfred van Dulmen, and Gretchen Miller Wrobel. Important contributions to the work reported in this book were also made by the following team members:

Timothy Balke, Phyllis Bengtson, Delaina Binnicker, Don Binnicker, Thomas Bohman, Adrienne Caffrey, Mary Cook, Jessica Cutrera, RoAnne Elliott, Amy Esau, Malinda Fennell, Deborah Fisher, Ann Furuta, Terrie Garcia, Claire Gibbert, Herb Grant, Isaac Gusukuma, Marilyn Gusukuma, Gayle Hasledalen, Vivian Jenkins, Susan Keskinen, Kathryn Kramer, Mary Ann Marchel, Lynn Marrs, Tai Justin Mendenhall, Susan Nordeen, Lloyd Potter, Nicole Ross, Tammy Schefelbine, Toni Schmitt, Mary Seabloom, Terry Shook, Anna Maria Signorelli, Chedgzsey Smith, Heather Stoerzinger, Tanya Thornberry, Reuel Tiesel, Vicky Weise, and Elizabeth Wilhelm. We also acknowledge the assistance of Anne Gillespie Lewis, who worked with us on a first draft of Chapter 1.

Most important, we thank the adoptive parents, adopted children, and birthmothers who opened their lives and their histories to us. We also thank the staff members and directors of the 35 cooperating adoption agencies who identified families, requested their participation for us, performed many of the interviews, and shared with us their experiences of changing agency practices.

We gratefully acknowledge funding for this project from the following sources: Office of Population Affairs, U.S. Department of Health and Human Services; National Institute of Child Health and Human Development; Hogg Foundation for Mental Health; William T. Grant Foundation; Lois & Samuel Silberman Fund; University Research Institute of the University of Texas at Austin; Center for Research on Interpersonal Relationships at the University of Minnesota; and Minnesota Agricultural Experiment Station.

Finally, we acknowledge the patience and encouragement of our acquiring editor, C. Deborah Laughton; the capable assistance of Sanford Robinson and Kassie Gavrilis at Sage Publications; and the support of our spouses, Susan Grotevant and Dwight Brooks.

Several chapters in this book are based on articles we have published in professional journals and/or papers we have presented at conferences. An abbreviated version of Chapter 2 (changes in agency practices) appeared in *Adoption Quarterly* (Henney, Onken, McRoy, & Grotevant, 1998). Earlier versions of Chapter 4 (child outcomes) were presented at meetings of the National Council on Family Relations in 1990 and 1992. Preliminary analyses of these data were conducted for the master's thesis of Meredith Friedrick, University of

Texas at Austin, Child Development and Family Relationships. Analyses of the data for the full sample were published in *Child Development* (Wrobel, Ayers-Lopez, Grotevant, McRoy, & Friedrick, 1996). Earlier versions of Chapter 5 (adoptive parent-birthparent relationships) were presented at the meeting of the International Society for the Study of Personal Relationships, Orono, Maine, July 1992; and at the meeting of the National Council on Family Relations, Orlando, Florida, November 1992. A version of this paper was published in *Family Process* (Grotevant, McRoy, Elde, & Fravel, 1994). An earlier version of Chapter 6 (birthmother adjustment) appeared in *Adoption Quarterly* (Christian, McRoy, Grotevant, & Bryant, 1997). An earlier version of Chapter 7 was presented in a symposium at the 1997 meetings of the Society for Research in Child Development under the title *Feelings and Perceptions About Face-to-Face Contact: Differing Trajectories for Adoptive Parents and Birthmothers?* (Grotevant, van Dulmen, & McRoy, 1997).

Communications about this work can be addressed to either of the coprincipal investigators: Harold D. Grotevant, Department of Family Social Science, University of Minnesota, 1985 Buford Avenue, St. Paul, MN 55108; or Ruth G. McRoy, School of Social Work, University of Texas at Austin, 1925 San Jacinto, Austin, TX 78712.

ACKNOWLEDGMENTS

We express appreciation to colleagues who served as coauthors on the following chapters:

Chapter 2   Susan Henney and Steven J. Onken

Chapter 4   Gretchen Miller Wrobel, Susan Ayers-Lopez, Julie K. Kohler, and Meredith Friedrick

Chapter 5   Deborah Lewis Fravel and Carol Elde

Chapter 6   Cinda Christian and Chalandra Bryant

Chapter 7   Manfred van Dulmen

1

OPENNESS IN ADOPTION

The Issues, the Debates, and Evidence to Date

Since the mid-1970s, adoption practices in North America and western Europe have changed dramatically, and the confidentiality maintained in the past is no longer the norm. The trend is toward "openness" in adoption, in which either mediated or direct contact occurs between the adoptive family and birthparent(s). However, openness in adoption is a continuing source of controversy and misunderstanding among persons touched by adoption, as well as among adoption agency staff, social services professionals, and the public at large. Although the increasing openness in the adoption process is merely one way the definition of family is changing, and although openness has many precedents throughout human history, the debate over openness in adoption has polarized the adoption community and fueled the development of frightening media portrayals of relationships in adoptive families. Unfortunately, the adversarial relationship between advocates and critics of openness in adoption has been exacerbated by the lack of empirical research. Few large-scale studies on the subject of openness in adoption had been done until our nationwide study of birthparents, adoptive parents, and adopted children in arrangements with varying degrees of openness, which is the focus of this book.

Because adoption practices and policies are so varied and are changing so rapidly, we want to clarify the boundaries of our research for our readers at the outset. Participants in the research reported in this volume were interviewed between 1987 and 1992 in the United States. Participants were all clients of private adoption agencies, and all adoptions involved placement of infants with adoptive families of the same race as the children's birthmothers. The research draws on personal interviews and questionnaires administered to birthmothers, adopted children (between the ages of 4 and 12), and adoptive parents. Funding and logistical constraints did not permit us to interview more than a few birthfathers. This book also includes data from adoption agency staff who were interviewed at two points in time, 1987 and 1993. This introductory chapter describes some broad historical trends in adoption practice and the social forces influencing them. It also reviews other studies examining openness outcomes and lays the groundwork for interpreting the results of our research.

THE CONTINUUM OF OPENNESS

The degree of openness in adoptions varies greatly, with frequency and regularity of contact between birthparents and the adoptive family falling across a continuum of openness and subject to change over time. The specific types of relationships evolving between adoptive and birthfamilies are almost as varied as the families themselves (McRoy & Grotevant, 1991).

Discussions of openness are further complicated because *open adoption* has been defined in different ways by different people. In our research, we conceptualize openness as a spectrum involving differing degrees and modes of contact and communication between adoptive family members and a child's birthmother. At one end of the openness continuum are *confidential* adoptions, in which minimal information is shared between adoptive and birthfamily members and is never transmitted directly; any exchange of information typically stops with the adoptive placement or shortly thereafter. In the middle of the openness scale are *mediated* adoptions, in which non-identifying information is shared between parties through adoption agency personnel, who serve as go-betweens. Sharing could include exchange of pictures, letters, gifts, or infrequent meetings at which full identifying information is not revealed. At the other end of the continuum are *fully disclosed* adoptions, which involve direct communication and full disclosure of identifying information between adoptive and birth-families. These adoptions may involve direct meetings in each others' homes or public places, telephone calls, letters sent directly, and sometimes contact with extended family members. Within both the mediated and fully disclosed categories of adoptions are those in which contact has stopped (*time-limited*) and those in which contact is continuing (*ongoing*).

The controversy over openness in adoption is one of many issues surrounding adoption that have elicited strong opinions from members of the adoption triad, as well as from the public at large. Indeed, the definition of *adoption* itself has been subject to continual reinterpretation and has changed over time. The traditional mid-20th-century definition of *adoption* in Western culture is

> a social and legal process whereby a parent-child relationship is established between persons not so related by birth. By this means, a child born to one set of parents becomes, legally and socially, the child of other parents, a member of another family, and assumes the same rights and duties as those that obtain between children and their biological parents. (Costin, 1972, p. 359)

After most adoptions were completed, the files were closed, and no further contact was made between birthparents and adoptive family; all information about the adoption was kept confidential by the adoption agency or the state.

In these confidential adoptions, the birthmother placed a child with an agency, a representative of the adoptive parents, or occasionally directly with the adoptive parents. Words such as *surrender* and *relinquish* were often used to describe the birthmother's role in the adoption process; these words, with their ring of finality, emphasized the seemingly irrevocable nature of confidential adoption.

After the birthmother's parental rights were terminated, it was assumed that she would be able to move beyond the difficulty of an unplanned pregnancy and "get on with her life," forgetting that she had ever given birth to a child. In the complementary half of this scenario, gaining a child through adoption enabled the adoptive parents to raise a child as their own in a nuclear family. This situation was thought to be an improvement over letting the child be raised by his or her birthparent(s). It was assumed that the adopted child would be better off in many ways—psychologically, socially, and economically—than if raised by a single, perhaps impoverished, birthparent and would grow up to be a well-adjusted member of society, with origins in and loyalties to only one family—the adoptive one.

The contrasting views of professionals in the field are illustrated by the following statements, which anchor the two most extreme positions. The first is from Baran and Pannor (1993), clinical social workers, who based their statement on more than 40 years' practice experience with adoption:

> Our decades of experience in counseling individuals affected by adoption suggest that requiring anonymity between birthparents and adoptive parents and sealing all information about the birthparents from the adopted child has damaging effects on all three parties. . . . We believe that confidentiality and anonymity are harmful and that adoptions should be open. (pp. 119-120)

A contrasting opinion is offered by Bevan and Pierce (1994):

> The sealing of adoption records and amending the adopted person's birth certificate ensures that all public documents about relationships show that the adopted person is part of his new family. This prevents any question of parentage and allows the family and the adopted person to choose when and with whom they want to share this personal information. (pp. 1-2)

BRIEF HISTORY OF ADOPTION

Although the current battle over how open or confidential adoptions should be has contributed to the public visibility of adoption, the practice of adoption is an ancient one. From the beginning of human history, alternative arrangements have been made for the rearing of children by other than their biological parents. One alternative, adoption, has served several functions: (a) to provide heirs or indentured servants, (b) to save children from harmful environments, (c) to meet the parenting needs of infertile couples, and (d) to provide solutions for birthparents unable to rear their children (Reitz & Watson, 1992).

Confidentiality and legality have not always been components of adoptions. In ancient Egypt, Greece, and Rome, adoption was an open, informal exchange that provided an additional parental relationship for the child, rather than a substitute relationship (Sachdev, 1989). More communal cultures, such as the traditional Hawaiian, have practiced openness in adoption for centuries (Baran, Pannor, & Sorosky, 1976).

In more highly individualistic societies, such as those in North America and western Europe, however, much more emphasis is placed on making the relationship a legally binding one and on keeping it confidential. The practice of permanently severing the relationship between a child and his or her biological parents (in other words, the pattern that is familiar today) was enacted into law in 1851 in Massachusetts. This law became the model for English-speaking North American states and for some western European countries (Sachdev, 1989). Confidentiality, espoused by social workers and the adoptive parents, gradually became an integral part of adoption. In 1917, Minnesota passed the first state law barring public inspection of adoption records (Watson, 1979), and by 1950, most states in the United States had passed legislation sealing adoption records.

Under the policy of closed and sealed records, agency personnel often tried to match the physical appearance of adoptive parents with the projected physical appearance of their baby (Sokoloff, 1993), thus minimizing questions that strangers might ask and discouraging adoptive family members, at least subliminally, from thinking of themselves as an adoptive family. Occasionally, adoptive parents did not inform their children of the adoption.

In more recent years, adoptive parents have been less and less likely to conceal the adoption from their children even though the adoption itself may have been a confidential rather than open one. The decision, adoptive parents found, became "how and when to tell," not whether to tell at all. (It follows, then, that in open adoptions, adoptive parents, as well as birthparents, must also decide "how much" to tell.) This increased candor with adopted children has in turn spurred more curiosity on the part of many children regarding their origins. Advances in the field of genetics have also played a part in stimulating adopted children to search for information about their birthfamilies' medical history, even when they do not desire a closer personal relationship, so that they can better deal with questions about their own biological heritage and medical conditions.

Some countries have moved toward granting adopted persons access to their birth records. For example, in 1975 Great Britain passed legislation allowing adopted persons free access to their original birth records, and New Zealand's Adult Adoption Information Act of 1985 permits adopted persons to receive copies of their original birth certificates and to begin searches for their birthparents when they reach the age of 20, unless a birthparent has placed a "contact veto" on his or her records (stated in the record that he or she does not want to be contacted). Likewise, birthparents can search for a child they placed when the child has attained the age of 20, unless the child has placed a contact veto. No similar law has been passed in the United States.

Despite the lack of empowering federal legislation, many adoption agencies in the United States have been changing their practices. In the 1970s, increasing numbers of adopted persons and birthparents returned to agencies, seeking additional background information, and more agencies faced the reality of the decreasing number of babies available for adoption. In response, some agencies began offering birthmothers and prospective adoptive parents a continuum of openness dependent on their needs and desires. Some agencies provided pictures of the children to birthparents, let birthparents select adoptive parents for their children, and arranged for birth and adoptive parents to meet at placement or after placement without sharing identifying information. Positive reactions to these new practices led many agencies to begin offering a wide range of openness options, including (a) exchange of pictures and non-identifying information between adoptive parents and birthparents, (b) meetings in which either non-identifying or identifying information is shared, and (c) ongoing direct contact between the parties involved (Sorich & Siebert, 1982). Our longitudinal study of changes in adoption agency practices between 1987 and 1993 found that many participating private agencies moved away from offering primarily confidential adoptions to offering a range of openness during that time. They cited client demand, competition from independent adoptions, and competition from other agencies that were offering open placements to birthmothers as reasons for their shifts (see Chapter 2, this volume, for further details).

This gradual movement toward some degree of openness has generated much discussion among practitioners involved in making adoptive placements, policymakers, theorists, and researchers, some of it very heated. Some adoption specialists with extensive experience making placements argue that fully open adoption should be standard practice because the secrecy of confidential adoptions has been harmful to all parties involved (Pannor & Baran, 1984). Although not all professionals believe that open adoption is best in all situations, many believe that open options (a) might help birthparents feel less pain and guilt (e.g., Chapman, Dorner, Silber, & Winterberg, 1986), (b) may eventually promote consideration of the adoption option (e.g., Cocozzelli, 1989), (c) ease adoptive parents' fear and questions, (d) provide adopted persons with biological continuity, and (e) "humanize" the adoption process (Sorich & Siebert, 1982). Moreover, advocates of open adoption believe that knowledge of one's past is a basic human need and that emotional problems may result when this knowledge is denied (Curtis, 1986; Silber & Dorner, 1990). Sorosky, Baran, and Pannor (1978) note that even though birthparents relinquish all their parenting rights and responsibilities and have no further physical contact with the child, they continue to have feelings of loss, pain, and mourning. Openness is also advocated by family systems theorists, who consider it important to include all family members—even those "absent" through adoption or only "psychologically present"—when seeking to understand how the family functions (e.g., Demick & Wapner, 1988; Fravel, 1995; Reitz & Watson, 1992).

Others, in contrast, have warned that the expectation of continued contact (a) may prevent closure on the birthmother's grieving process, (b) may prevent adoptive parents from feeling fully empowered to be their child's parents, and (c) may cause identity confusion among adopted children (Kraft, Palombo, Mitchell, Woods, & Schmidt, 1985; Kraft, Palombo, Mitchell, Woods, Schmidt, & Tucker, 1985; Kraft, Palombo, Woods, Mitchell, & Schmidt, 1985). Critics of openness in adoptions argue that it is experimental and potentially harmful (National Committee for Adoption [NCFA], 1989). Their view is that confidential adoption worked well, so why change it?

Along with such changing practices has come a more contemporary definition of adoption:

> We define "adoption" as a means of providing some children with security and meeting their developmental needs by legally transferring ongoing parental responsibilities from their birth parents to their adoptive parents; recognizing that in so doing we have created a new kinship network that forever links those two families together through the child, who is shared by both. In adoption, as in marriage, the new legal family relationship does not signal the absolute end of one family and the beginning of another, nor does it sever the psychological tie to an earlier family. Rather, it expands the family boundaries of all those who are involved. (Reitz & Watson, 1992, p. 11)

This definition is consistent with that of Silber and Speedlin (1982), who proposed that adoption involves accepting the responsibility of raising an individual who has two sets of parents. Pannor and Baran (1984), who called for the end of all confidential adoption in agency practice, define *open adoption* as the process whereby birthparents and adoptive parents meet and exchange identifying information. Although both sets of parents in an open adoption situation typically have continuing contact and access to knowledge about the child, the birthparents still, as in a confidential adoption, relinquish legal and child-rearing rights.

In the midst of this debate among professionals, the public has been inundated with media coverage of such cases as "Baby Jessica" and "Baby Richard," who were torn between competing sets of adoptive and birthparents (Chira, 1994). The parental rights of birthparents who have made adoption plans, as well as those of adoptive parents, have been questioned. Partially in response to the issues raised in these court cases, the National Conference of Commissioners on Uniform State Laws approved a draft of a Uniform Adoption Act in 1994 that is purported to expedite adoption placements, shorten time lines for birthmothers to make relinquishment decisions, further limit birthfathers' rights, and reverse the move toward open adoptions (Concerned United Birthparents [CUB], 1994). Debate continues on this proposed legislation in each state, and findings from this research may be particularly useful in providing empirical data on outcomes for families with varying openness arrangements.

Meanwhile, the types of openness options continually expand. Currently, some birthmothers and some prospective adoptive couples "advertise" to facilitate adoptions. After finding each other (with or without the assistance of a facilitator), they might go to an adoption professional or an agency to draw up the appropriate legal documents for the adoption. It is not unusual for prospective adoptive parents to know the birthmother while she is pregnant and even to attend the birth of the child. Some state legislatures are debating whether agreements about openness contact should be in writing and, if so, whether they are enforceable by the courts. Such practice, now enacted in the state of Washington, gives birthparent(s) enforceable rights to have contact with the child after the adoption is final. This is in contrast with the openness agreements among participants in our research, which are largely verbal, informal, and dependent on the mutual trust and goodwill developed among the parties involved.

FACTORS STIMULATING
CHANGE IN ADOPTION PRACTICE

Why have these dramatic changes in adoption practice occurred in recent years? Several factors, including important societal and demographic changes, insights of clinicians, and social science theory and research, are explored in the following section.

Societal and Demographic Change

According to the National Center for Health Statistics (1993), in 1992 more than 500,000 births to adolescents under the age of 20 occurred in the United States. About 30% of all nonmarital births in the United States occur to teenagers, and teenagers account for about half of all first births to unmarried women. Approximately 40% of all teen pregnancies end in abortion.

Although research findings on pregnant teens suggest that those who choose to parent are more likely to drop out of school, receive inadequate prenatal care, have a low birthweight baby, live in poverty, and rely on public assistance to raise their children, more teens choose to parent their babies than make adoption plans for them. In fact, adoption among unmarried teen mothers has been decreasing since the mid-1960s. At that time, an estimated 31.7% of babies born to unmarried women were placed for adoption (Cartoof & Klerman, 1982). Recent estimates suggest that about 3% of Caucasian, unmarried mothers and less than 2% of African American, unmarried mothers place their babies for adoption (Bachrach, Stolley, & London, 1992; Donnelly & Voydanoff, 1991).

This decline appears to stem from a variety of causes. With the sexual revolution of the 1960s came an associated decrease in stigma associated with childbearing out of wedlock, thus making parenting more attractive than adoption to many young women. The term *illegitimate child,* which had itself long since replaced pejoratives such as *bastard,* is seldom uttered now in reference to a child born outside a marriage. The accessibility of birth control and abortion, coupled with the provision of economic and educational supports for single mothers, has also been associated with a shrinking pool of babies available for adoption (Sokoloff, 1993). Many unwed mothers, however, never consider placing a child for adoption because of their uncertainty about the child's future and their fear of having to lose contact forever (Barth, 1987; Churchman, 1986; Mech, 1986).

Concurrently, the human potential movement in its various forms has made both birthparents and adult adopted individuals conscious of kinship connections they have lost in the process of adoption and has spawned support groups of individuals who help one another search for their birthparents or adopted children. In addition, clinical reports and empirical adoption research have also pointed out problems experienced by some individuals adopted with confidential arrangements.

In short, adoption agencies have had fewer babies to place, and birthparents, having become more keenly aware of the possibility of having at least some knowledge of their children's well-being as they grow up, have become far more visible and vocal than the silent partners they once were. For these reasons, agencies have found that openness options are attractive to birthparents who might place through them; many agency personnel also believe that openness is in the best interests of the child as well (see agency descriptions in McRoy, Grotevant, & White, 1988).

Recent changes in adoption reflect the changes in family structure in Western societies. The oft-cited nuclear family of the mid-20th century in North America, consisting of two parents of the opposite sex, still in their first marriages and living under one roof with their biological children, does still exist, but so do a myriad of other family types. Today's family may consist of a single parent with biological and/or adopted children, two same-sex parents with adopted and/or biological children of one of the parents, and "blended" families with parents of the same or opposite sex and children who may be a mix of both adopted and biological. In blended families, which form after remarriage that follows divorce or the death of a spouse, two nuclear families may be "yoked" through a child, who links the custodial and noncustodial families. Reiss (1992) defines *yoked families* as family units joined to one another because they have a person or relationship in common. In blended families, which are increasing in numbers, the children are sometimes designated as "hers, his, and theirs" to indicate their various parentages. The proliferation and acceptance of nontraditional family structures has contributed to the acceptance of open adoption.

Clinical Insights and Research Literature

The confidential adoption system dominated adoption practice in the United States from about the 1940s to the 1970s (Adamec & Pierce, 1991). Advocates of this system believed that confidentiality and secrecy were necessary for the healthy adaptation of adopted children, birthparents, and adoptive parents (NCFA, 1989). Outcomes for children of confidential adoption, however, were not always ideal. Only in recent years have problems that seem specific to confidential adoptions been acknowledged widely or been systematically studied by social scientists. A summary of the clinical and research literature on this topic follows.

Adopted children are referred for psychological treatment two to five times more frequently than their nonadopted peers. This finding has been replicated in countries such as Great Britain, Israel, Poland, Sweden, and the United States (e.g., Bohman, 1971; Brinich, 1980; Humphrey & Ounsted, 1963; Lifshitz, Baum, Balgur, & Cohen, 1975; Senior & Himadi, 1985; Simon & Senturia, 1966; Tousseing, 1962;

Ziatek, 1974). The children typically exhibit behavior characterized as impulsive, provocative, aggressive, and antisocial (e.g., Brinich, 1980; Eiduson & Livermore, 1953; Menlove, 1965; Offord, Aponte, & Cross, 1969). Results from an earlier retrospective study of emotional disturbance among adopted adolescents (McRoy, Grotevant, & Zurcher, 1988) revealed a variety of factors that might contribute to problematic outcomes.

Several causes of this higher rate of referral for mental health services have been proposed. Kirschner (1995) has identified a specific pattern of adoption-related psychopathology that he has called the *adopted-child syndrome*. He argues that this syndrome has psychosocial roots and needs to be distinguished from related *DSM-IV* diagnoses such as conduct disorder. This label is misleading, however, in that it attributes characteristics of some individuals in a group to the entire group; it is also stigmatizing. Other possible causes of the higher referral rate include adoptive parents' greater comfort with human services providers because of their experience in completing the adoption process and their typically higher educational level than that of the general population. Kirk (1995) noted that children currently available for adoption may come from backgrounds that put them at risk because of poor prenatal care, drug or alcohol exposure, or other health factors.

In nonclinical samples of adopted and nonadopted children, researchers have reported mixed findings about outcomes. Although some (Carey, Lipton, & Myers, 1974; Elonen & Schwartz, 1969; Hoopes, Sherman, Lawder, Andrews, & Lower, 1970) reported few differences between the two groups, Brodzinsky, Schechter, Braff, and Singer (1984) found that adoptive mothers and teachers rated adopted children lower on school achievement and social competence and higher on school-related problems than they rated nonadopted children.

A recent meta-analysis of 66 published studies revealed that adopted children had higher levels of maladjustment, externalizing disorders, and academic problems than nonadopted children (Wierzbicki, 1993). The effect sizes, though statistically significant, were modest in magnitude. Developmental level had a moderating effect: Relatively few differences typically were found between adopted and nonadopted children during infancy or preschool years, but by middle childhood and adolescence, differences began to emerge (Brodzinsky, 1993). Another study of socioemotional disturbance in adopted children found that one early risk indicator alone was not predictive of problematic outcomes but that two or more indicators were predictive of externalizing problems in the clinical range (Cohen, Coyne, & Duvall, 1993).

Virtually all the relevant literature, however, including the Search Institute study (Benson, Sharma, & Roehlkepartain, 1994) and the Colorado Adoption Project (DeFries, Plomin, & Fulker, 1994), involved confidential adoptions. It is possible that greater openness in adoption could buffer adopted adolescents from such problems because secrecy and uncertainty regarding their origins would be reduced greatly. For example, in a sample of adolescents from confidential adoptions, issues of attachment and entitlement were the best parental predictors of child disturbance (Cohen, Duvall, & Coyne, 1994). It is not known whether these processes would occur in the same way with more open adoptions.

Recent literature has also examined short- and long-term effects of adoption placement on birthmothers, with most studies being conducted with confidential placements. Several follow-up studies of birthmothers who placed children in confidential adoptions noted the following conditions: (a) prolonged feelings of loss and continued mourning (Sorosky et al., 1978); (b) depression (Burnell & Norfleet, 1979); (c) somatic symptoms, restless anxiety, anger, and loss reactions (Millen & Roll, 1985); and (d) intense attachment to and overprotection of children subsequently born to and raised by birthmothers after the placement of a child for adoption (Rynearson, 1982). Winkler and Van Keppel (1984) reported significant psychological impairment among birthmothers who were not participating in support groups 4 to 20 years after adoption. Nevertheless, in a comparative study of women who made the decision during adolescence either to place their children or to parent, no significant differences in negative psychological outcomes were observed (McLaughlin, Pearce, Manninen, & Winges, 1988).

Theorists differ on their beliefs about how open adoption arrangements may affect birthmothers' grief. Some believe that open arrangements may help facilitate healthy adjustment to grief and loss (Sorich & Siebert, 1982). Others argue that open adoptions are more difficult for the birthmother than confidential adoptions (Kraft, Palombo, Woods, et al., 1985). Kraft and colleagues believe that, in open adoptions, birthmothers cannot adequately grieve over placing their children and that therefore open adoptions may not be the best option. Silber and Dorner (1990), in contrast, argue that the relationships that develop between birthmothers and adoptive families in fully disclosed adoptions mediate the experience of grief and loss. They view openness as a process that allows a birthmother to confront her grief over the loss of the parenting role and to work through it in a supportive environment, which includes the adoptive parents and the child.

Similarly, research studies began to show that adoptive parents sometimes encounter postadoption difficulties. Adoptive parents were not always adequately prepared for dealing with the child's questions about his or her origins. Indeed, just a few decades ago many adopted children were not even told they were adopted. Many adoptive parents considered the adoption almost a shameful fact, to be hidden from the child at all costs. The adopted parents had to hope—and that hope was usually in vain—that no relative, friend, or neighbor revealed the truth of the adoption to the child. For an account of the cost of keeping such family secrets, readers are referred to *The Search for Anna Fisher* (Fisher, 1973), the autobiography of a woman whose adoptive mother swore other family members to secrecy over the adoption.

One social scientist who questioned some assumptions prevalent about confidential adoptions during the time when they were the norm in North America was H. David Kirk (1964, 1981, 1995), who advanced adoption theory and practice with his concept of *shared fate*. Speaking from his experience as an adoptive parent and his training as a sociologist, he argued that adoptive parents must acknowledge the difference between being a parent to a child by birth and to a child by adoption. Uncomfortable as it might be for both the parent and the child, a bond could be forged in this "shared fate," with their relationship being different from that found in the biological family norm. This acknowledgment, Kirk claimed, would lead to communication both within and outside the family about the differences and similarities and would ultimately benefit the adopted child.

Kirk's shared fate theory can well be applied to open adoptions because the concept can be broadened from a focus on adoptive parents and the children they adopt to include the children's birth-families. Such contact may seem an innovation to those familiar only with the confidential adoption system as it came to exist in Western nations, but it is the norm in many communally oriented cultures, in which the idea of shared fate often goes far beyond individual families and involves a larger community as well.

REVIEW OF STUDIES
EVALUATING OPENNESS OUTCOMES

The debate about openness has centered around several issues and concerns. One argument raised against open adoption has been that adoptive families would have attachment difficulties because the adoptive parents would perceive openness as a threat to the perma-nence of the adoption (Kraft, Palombo, Woods, et al., 1985). Another argument has been that agencies making open placements put the needs of birthparents ahead of those of adoptive parents and adopted children, thus sacrificing their rights to a secure family life (Kraft, Palombo, Mitchell, Woods, & Schmidt, 1985). Those on either side of the openness controversy, not surprisingly, say they have the best interests of the children in the adoption process at heart, that openness does not adversely affect adoptive families, and that the practice facilitates birthmothers' adjustment after the placement (e.g., Chap-man, Dorner, Silber, & Winterberg, 1987a, 1987b).

Although adoption professionals, advocates, and members of support groups of adopted individuals and birthparents hold passion-ately strong feelings about openness, scant research on open adoption has been available to guide adoption policy. This lack of research attention to openness in adoption has been reinforced because, until recently, most nonrelative adoptions in the United States have been built on assumptions of confidentiality and lack of contact between the adoptive family and the child's birthfamily, thereby promoting the invisibility of these families.

Empirical research is only beginning to document the inter-relationships among members in adoptive family systems. The few studies that exist suffer from such limitations as small sample size, biased sample recruitment, use of nonstandardized measures, and presence of many uncontrolled variables, such as age at placement and the different concerns raised by transracial, international, or special needs adoptions. For example, one study of *prospective* adoptive parents found that open adoption was unanimously considered undesirable because it represents a threat to the entitlement of the adoptive parents to act as full parents to the adopted child (Smith, 1991). Thus, prospective adoptive parents were perceived as losing in a competitive relationship with their child's birthfamily. A selection bias was evident in this study, however, because all couples participating in the study had selected adoption agencies that favored more confidential adoption practices. See Table 1.1 for a concise overview of research studies prior to the one reported in this book that have explored outcomes as a function of adoption openness.

Studies of adoptive parents actually involved in openness have been more positive toward openness (e.g., Dominick, 1988; Gross, 1993; Iwanek, 1987) and have begun to identify variables that contribute to effective functioning. Satisfaction with openness was found when openness agreements included clients' choice in the level of openness before matching, thorough preparation, and written agreements (Etter, 1993); and when the adoptive parents had planned for contact, the child did not have a history of maltreatment, the birthmother had completed more years of formal education, the contact was more direct, and the adoptive parents had talked with the birthparent(s) prior to placement (Berry, 1993a).

In a small exploratory study, however, Demick (1993; Silverstein & Demick, 1994) found no support for believing that a particular level of adoption is better or worse than another and that, in fact, open adoption may have both advantages and disadvantages. On the one hand, most parents in his open adoption group felt "an inner sense of peace and/or empowerment" that came from their personal knowledge of their children's birthparents and had fewer concerns about the attachment to their children than did parents in closed adoptions. On the other hand, adoptive mothers in open adoptions reported lower self-esteem, which the author thought related to their greater empathy for the birthmothers.

Several issues have emerged from an analysis of these reports. Some of these studies have directly or indirectly highlighted the importance of control over aspects of the relationship in determining the success of open arrangements, whether it be through informal contact (e.g., Berry, 1993a, 1993b; Siegel, 1993) or through written agreements (e.g., Etter, 1993). As a whole, the studies also consistently point out the flexibility required by more open arrangements (e.g., McRoy, Grotevant, & White, 1988). In addition, some (e.g., Dominick, 1988; Smith, 1991) have pointed to the important role that the attitudes of adoption workers play in shaping the attitudes of their clients. Several of these studies suggest that neither confidential nor open adoption is best for everyone and that the degree of openness should be decided by the participants themselves (McRoy, Grotevant, & White, 1988; Silverstein & Demick, 1994).

ORIGINS AND GOALS OF THE PRESENT STUDY

Some research on relationships among open adoption participants has been carried out and published in journals or books. Until our extensive, nationwide study of 720 participants in the adoption process (adopted children, adoptive parents, and birthparents), however, proponents and detractors of openness in adoption have had no extensive body of data against which to evaluate their arguments because scant relevant research had been done. The present study is a collaboration that developed between us when we were both on the faculty at the University of Texas at Austin. Although we had both conducted research with adoptive families for years, the initial impetus for this study of openness came from the vice president for social services of Lutheran Social Service of Texas, who in 1984 asked us to conduct a small-scale evaluation study of the agency's move toward openness.

Even with a small sample, we concluded that "the degree of openness desirable in any particular case is a highly individual matter. No one type of adoption can be regarded as 'best' for every family situation" (McRoy, Grotevant, & White, 1988, p. 125). Against that backdrop, however, we also noted that semiopen (mediated) adoptions appeared to maximize the benefit and minimize the risk to participants in adoption. Of course, these tentative conclusions were based on a small sample of adoptive families and birthmothers with

(Text continued on p. 21)

TABLE 1.1 Other Research Studies Exploring Openness in Adoption

Study	Sample	Conclusions	Weaknesses
Belbas (1987)	22 adoptive parents (APs) from 12 couples; "minimum," "moderate," and "maximum" contact with birthmothers (BMs); in Texas.	APs in greater contact groups did not view BMs as interfering and did not worry about reclaiming; 25% in minimum contact group worried about reclaiming. APs worried about openness diffs for siblings and how to help adopted child (AC) understand BM role.	Small sample, retrospective, no standardized measures.
Iwanek (1987)	17 adoptive couples and 14 BMs in New Zealand.	Following meetings at placement, agreements were made about future contact. As trust developed, most relationships became more open and flexible over time. APs did not think openness interfered with feelings of entitlement but rather enhanced them.	No comparison group with other levels of openness; small sample; no standardized measures.
Dominick (1988)	78 adoptive couples and 65 BMs in New Zealand; about half of APs had met BM at placement and half had not.	Attitude of social worker dealing with the parties had a strong influence on clients' attitudes about contact and on whether contact occurred. BMs thought meetings and pictures helped them adjust to placement. Nearly all APs felt that meetings with BMs were positive and satisfying. Many found meetings emotional, although they did not define that as negative. Not all parties thought their wishes about contact were taken into account. Many parties not in direct contact expressed the desire for some contact, although others wanted no contact.	No standardized measures; children too young to participate.
McRoy, Grotevant, & White (1988)	17 adoptive couples and 15 BMs, 1 birthfather (BF), 1 birthgrandmother from 3 Lutheran Social Services agencies in Texas (N = 51).	Confidential adoptions allowed APs to feel full parenting responsibility but was associated with lower acknowledgment of difference. Semiopen adoptions facilitated information sharing and kept communication lines open. Fully disclosed adoptions benefited children and BMs more than APs. BMs had reassurance about their children, but openness did not prevent feelings of loss. Open adoption does permit development of a realistic picture of all parties but also demands flexibility and willingness to negotiate boundaries.	Small sample, children young. This was a pilot study for the subsequent nationwide study reported in this book.

Blanton & Deschner (1990)	59 BMs: 18 open, 41 confidential; openness category determined by whether a meeting was held at placement.	BMs in open adoptions felt more isolated, felt more despair, had more difficulty with physical functions, and felt more dependency.	Only 39% return rate on questionnaires; openness category based only on meeting at placement; average time since placement = 2.3 years.
Smith (1991)	35 prospective adoptive couples approved for placement (N = 70) through agencies in Texas and Indiana.	Prospective APs were asked about preferences among confidential, semiopen, and open adoptions. 75% chose confidential; 25% chose semiopen; none chose open.	Likely selection bias of couples working with agencies whose philosophies did not advocate openness; no standardized measures; no discussion of the agencies' preparation policies for APs.
Berry (1993a)	1,268 APs in California; compared confidential and open.	Higher levels of direct contact associated with greater comfort with contact; key predictors of openness were APs planned for contact, absence of history of child maltreatment, BM level of education, direct contact, adoptive mother (AM) older age, APs talked with BMs prior to placement.	Limited to mailed survey; includes public agency and private agency adoptions, independent adoptions, and transracial adoptions.
Etter (1993)	Participants in 56 open adoptions (32 BMs, 4 BFs, 55 AMs, 38 adoptive fathers (AFs), 4.5 years after placement; all through one agency in Oregon.	APs and birthparents (BPs) who employed mediation services complied with written agreements; nearly all participants satisfied with open adoption, the mediation process, and each other.	All participants from one agency; no comparison group of participants who did not have written agreements.

(continued)

TABLE 1.1 Continued

Gross (1993)	Interviews with 32 APs and 16 associated BMs; questionnaires to 75 APs; all recruited from a private adoption agency.	In the interview sample, 72% of APs were "very satisfied" with contact with BMs, 19% were "basically satisfied" but had some reservations; 2 families were dissatisfied and had ceased contact. 15 of the 16 BMs were satisfied with contact. In the questionnaire sample, an association was found between higher degrees of satisfaction and more frequent contact. "Best" aspects of openness involved AP comfort knowing that they and their child would have the access to information and personal contact with birthfamily members they might want or need; "worst" aspects of openness were "none" and arranging the logistics of visits.	No standardized measures, no data from children; all placements from one private agency.
Siegel (1993)	21 adoptive couples; snowball sample.	Perceived advantages of openness: ability to adopt faster, felt some control over how they would deal with BM, liked knowing things about BPs, felt openness helped decrease fantasies and enhanced entitlement, felt relationship was "more natural." APs also saw advantages for ACs and BMs, although only APs were interviewed. Perceived disadvantages: uncertainty about long-term effects on children, lack of social norms, emotional demands of relationship with BM, feared rejection by BM. Overall, no regrets about openness; advantages seen as outweighing disadvantages.	Small sample; no standardized instruments; children and BPs not interviewed. Children were less than 2 years of age.
Silverstein & Demick (1994)	15 couples in confidential and 15 couples with some degree of openness ($N = 60$).	No difference between groups in life satisfaction, perception of stress, or perception of control; those with openness worried less about attachment to the children and saw their infants as less bothersome and demanding. AMs in open adoptions appear to have more empathic awareness for BMs. Suggest that open and confidential adoptions might be appropriate for different kinds of APs.	Small sample.

infants or young children, interviewed at a time when open adoptions were still uncommon. Recognizing the need to replicate and extend these findings, we applied for and received funding to conduct a nationwide investigation. Since its inception, we have received grant funding from several sources, whose assistance is gratefully acknowledged in the preface.

We believed that such an extensive study would add to the relatively thin body of research on adoptive families, particularly on families involved in open adoptions. To examine both practical and theoretical issues regarding these emerging family systems, we designed our study to focus on the consequences of variations in openness in adoption for all members of the adoption triad: birthmothers, adoptive parents, and adopted children. The study addressed the functioning of families varying along a continuum of openness in adoption ranging from confidential to fully disclosed. Our research questions focused both on development of the self (self-concept, identity, self-esteem) in each of the parties and on the nature of their interpersonal and family relationships.

The 720 study participants, recruited from 35 adoption agencies throughout the United States, included 190 adoptive families (which represented 190 adoptive mothers, 190 adoptive fathers, and 171 adopted children) and 169 birthmothers. We sought families with at least one adopted child, age 4 to 12 at the time of the interview, who had been adopted though an agency before the age of 1. In many cases, we were able to interview all members of an adoption triad (birthmother, adoptive parents, and adopted child), which gave us a unique opportunity to investigate how different parties perceived the same adoption experience. Details about the sample are included in Chapter 3.

We think it is important for us to state at the outset that neither the principal investigators nor the project managers are adopted persons, adoptive parents, or parents who placed children for adoption. At times, we have been criticized for this lack of direct personal experience with adoption. At other times, we have been praised for this because we do not have personal stakes in particular outcomes of the research. Throughout the study, we have maintained the stance of the social scientist, trying to understand the dynamics of family systems that vary in these interesting ways and hoping to inform public policy as an outcome of the work.

Our research teams have always been interdisciplinary, including colleagues and students from social work, family science, developmental psychology, sociology, child development, and clinical specialties such as school psychology and family therapy. We have also consistently included adoption triad members on our project staff, and we have consistently sought feedback about our research and our conclusions from other adoption professionals. Both of us have long been involved with national adoption organizations, and one of us (R.M.) has worked in the adoption placement process.

Our approach in conducting the study has been to examine the complexities in the dynamics of families across the spectrum of openness. We did *not* set out to determine which level of openness is "best" or to demonstrate that one particular type of openness is "best." We hoped to identify factors that differentiate which adoptive parents or birthparents might be better suited for different styles of adoption and to identify special issues and challenges associated with negotiating adoption arrangements with various levels of openness. We also sought to identify what kinds of supports are needed for parties in varying kinds of adoption arrangements. It is our intention to continue our research over time, following these families longitudinally as their children move through adolescence and young adulthood and into parenthood of their own.

OVERVIEW OF THE BOOK

To provide further context for understanding the recent changes in adoption practice in the United States, we report on our study of agency practices in Chapter 2. Details about the participants in our study and the measures they were administered are included in Chapter 3. The next three chapters focus specifically on outcomes for triad members: the adopted children (Chapter 4), adoptive parents (Chapter 5), and birthmothers (Chapter 6). In Chapter 7, we view openness from the perspectives of all participants simultaneously to understand points of convergence and difference in perspectives. In the final chapter, we summarize the general conclusions derived from the research and discuss implications of this work for adoption practice, public policy, and future research. We hope that the perspectives presented in this book will stimulate discussion of openness in adoption among policymakers and members of the public at large, as well as among social scientists, adoption professionals, and individuals who are personally involved in adoptive relationships.

2

CHANGING AGENCY PRACTICES TOWARD OPENNESS IN ADOPTION

With Susan Henney and Steven J. Onken

The halls of an adoption agency are the scene of a tremendous human drama. In these halls, one can observe the range of human emotions—grief, joy, anticipation, sadness, thankfulness, regret, acceptance, mourning, and awe. Adoption agencies and their staffs are both the context of, and participants in, this drama. Often, an agency may be likened to a stage on which the actors—birthfamilies, adoptive families, adopted persons, and professional staff—play out the very real drama of adoption. Birthparents face the pain of making an adoption plan instead of parenting a biological child, adoptive parents who experienced infertility realize the dream and desire of parenthood, and adopted children begin life in new families. The extent to which an adoption agency provides directions and props, in the sense of services, education, and support, directly affects the way the lifelong story of adoption unfolds for each participant. Agencies that provide competent, comprehensive, and proactive services to adoption participants provide a context in which each person's role in the adoption process is clearly understood and supported. Thus, the role and influence of the adoption agency in the life history of adoption should not be underestimated.

One of the many ways an adoption agency influences the course of the adoption experience for each participant is through its philosophy about, and practice of, openness. Unfortunately, the literature regarding the standard philosophies and practices of adoption agencies about openness is sparse. This chapter presents the findings from our study of private adoption agencies, which we initiated in the mid-1980s. The purpose of the study was to build knowledge about how agency practices had changed over time and to assess the influence of changing philosophies about openness on the services that were provided to adoption participants.

Because our focus was on the manner and extent to which openness was influencing evolving agency practices and philosophies, specific research questions included the following:

* How have the openness options offered by agencies changed over time?

* What factors motivate agencies to offer openness options? By what processes do agencies determine which openness options to offer, and what has been the evolution/history of these processes within agencies?

* Does the availability of open options increase the number of infants placed? Have some agencies moved toward open options because of competition from other independent adoptions in which these options are available?

* What is the role of adoption agencies in open adoption? What happens if problems arise, and how are agencies involved in openness mediation?

* What do agencies perceive to be the main advantages and disadvantages of each type of openness?

METHOD

Participants

Between 1987 and 1989 (Time 1), each of the 35 agencies in 15 states that had provided placement services to adoptive families and birthmothers in our research sample was contacted and invited to participate in a study of adoption agency practices (McRoy, Grotevant,

& White, 1988). At Time 1, a professional staff member from each of 31 of these agencies was interviewed. Interviews were conducted with knowledgeable staff members, including agency directors and executive directors, program directors, postadoption supervisors, and maternity caseworkers. During 1992-93 (Time 2), the 31 agencies were recontacted for participation. Two were unable to participate, however, because their infant adoption programs had closed and staff were not available to be interviewed. An additional two programs had closed, but staff were available to be interviewed. Five additional agencies that had not participated at Time 1 were interviewed at Time 2. Four of the five were agencies that had originally provided placement services for our research sample but had not participated in the agency interviews at Time 1. The fifth agency requested to participate in the research. Therefore, interviews were conducted with staff from 31 agencies at Time 1, 34 agencies at Time 2, and a total of 29 agencies at both points in time.

Procedure

All interviews were tape-recorded and transcribed verbatim. Interviews were designed to examine a wide range of topics that reflect the agency's past and present experiences with openness and the thoughts, feelings, and beliefs that motivate decisions about offering openness options. Among other topics, the interviews addressed the range of openness options offered; the history of the agency's adoption practices; economic, societal, or cultural forces affecting the agency's decision to offer openness; the process by which the degree of openness in a particular adoption is determined; the contractual arrangements surrounding the openness decision; the counseling, both pre- and postadoption, offered to clients; the agency's definition of openness and its particular philosophy of openness; statistical information on the open adoptions within the agency; and the impact that openness currently has on clients. Agencies only offering confidential adoptions were interviewed also about their choice not to offer open options.

The data we obtained from these interviews were rich and complex in both scope and depth of responses. Therefore, a system of coding was established that would adequately reflect the complex meanings and implications of the agency transcripts. The data were coded by using both profile and category coding. We determined that the best way to compare the results of the interviews from the two separate time frames was to develop profiles of the agencies at the time of each interview. Each profile was completed by a trained coder by using the interview transcript and tapes. Then a second coder compared the profile to the interview transcript to check for completeness and accuracy.

We also used category coding (classifying the narrative into discrete categories) to answer our specific research questions. To develop the categories for each scheme, coders read and recorded responses pertinent to each research question. The team leader then reviewed the records, combined similar responses into specific categories, and developed a code sheet for use with the profiles and transcripts. In each scheme, two trained research assistants read for the specific categories, completing a category code sheet on each agency for each time frame. The categories included, among others, option changes (How have agencies changed in terms of the type of adoption options they offer?), openness factors (What factors motivate agencies to offer openness options?), agency response (How does the agency address requests for changes in openness?), benefits and advantages (What benefits and advantages did agencies identify concerning openness options?), and problems and disadvantages (What problems and disadvantages did agencies identify concerning openness options?). Two research assistants separately coded the categories for all interviews, and intercoder reliability was checked regularly. Coders reached consensus for any differences, and these consensus decisions were reviewed and approved by the team leader.

While piloting our research instruments, we discovered that different agencies varied widely in the terminology they use to describe the various openness options. For example, what we term mediated adoptions may be called semiopen, part-open, open, or open sharing, depending on the agency. Therefore, we used the following openness definitions that were introduced in Chapter 1 as standard definitions in both the interview process and when coding the types of options that agencies offered at Time 1 and Time 2:

◈ *Confidential* adoptions occur when no information is shared between triad members (birthmother, adoptive parents, and adopted person) beyond 6 months after placement. Information may be given to update agency files beyond 6 months after placement but is not necessarily intended for transmission. Sometimes this option is referred to as closed or traditional.

◆ *Mediated* adoptions occur when the parties share information, and/or meetings, and/or telephone calls beyond 6 months after placement. Sharing is conducted through the agency or agency personnel, and triad members do not share fully identifying information. Information shared is intended for, and received by, the other party. This option is commonly referred to as semiopen.

◆ *Fully disclosed* adoptions occur when the parties share information, and/or meetings, and/or telephone calls and the sharing is conducted directly with the other party. Sometimes this option is referred to as full-open.

In addition, distinctions were made between options that were offered as standard practice and options that were available only on request. "Identified adoption," for example, occurs when prospective adoptive parents identify and recruit a birthmother and may or may not later adopt the child in a mediated or fully disclosed adoption arrangement. In a "birthmother request" situation, the specified adoption arrangement is provided only at the birthmother's request and is not considered standard practice by the agency.

RESULTS AND DISCUSSION

How Have the Openness Options Offered by Agencies Changed Over Time?

Since the early 1900s, adoption agencies in the United States have insisted on closed records. Once a child was placed, anonymity was maintained between birthmother and adoptive parents, and only limited, non-identifying information about each party might have been provided. Confidential practices of this type were assumed to be the best way to protect members of the adoption triad from emotional trauma (McRoy, Grotevant, & White, 1988). Confidential adoptions allowed birthparents to pretend they never placed a child for adoption, adoptive parents to behave as if the child never had another set of parents, and the child to feel as if she or he belonged only to the adoptive family (Sachdev, 1984). Agencies assumed that if anonymity of all parties was maintained, then the birthmother could more easily resolve her feelings about the placement, the child could become more easily integrated into the family, and the adoptive family and child would not have to deal with the stigma of illegitimacy. According to one agency staff member:

> The advantages [of confidential adoptions] are that . . . adoptive parents can feel that they are real parents in the sense that they're entitled to this child, that they're not just acting as a caretaker for the birthparent. They can approach parenting without the fear that there will be interference from a birthparent. They can parent the child and not have influences on the child from a birthparent who may show up. It really helps ease the minds of the adoptive parents that they might not be entitled or might lose the child in some way. That helps them, I think, to be better parents. With regard to birthparents, I think often birthparents want to have a child placed but don't want to be involved in an ongoing way.

In the 1970s, negative societal attitudes toward the children of unwed mothers decreased, and birthmothers and adopted adults returned to agencies in large numbers to seek additional information about their adoptions. Subsequently, agencies began to reconsider their original philosophy that confidential adoptions were best for adoption participants. Acknowledging that agencies had begun to move toward open contact between adoptive families and birthfamilies in older child and foster-adoptive placements, in 1976 Baran et al. called for agencies to consider openness as an option in some infant placements. One agency noted the advantages of contact as follows:

> We believe it's important that birthparents have participation in planning the future of the child, that they participate in selecting the family, that they're, in most cases, able to meet these people around the time of placement because there is an essential component in their ability to do the grief work . . . maybe they never totally resolve this loss, but that it can be more closely resolved and deal with that. On the adopting parents'

side, I think it is important that there is openness because in that way the adopting parents are not living in a fantasy that, "Oh, this is really our child"—that it's really a reality that this child has a birth heritage, that this child has another family out in the world, that they've met the mother or heard firsthand from the child's mother and father, you know, the circumstances around the relinquishment so that they communicate this to their adopted child. We believe that can be a preventive measure of the adopted child's life for not feeling rejected, as rejected, by birthparents. They can feel more of a connection to the birth family, and they can own that and that's all validated in this whole process.

Between 1987 and 1989 (Time 1), when the agencies in our sample were first interviewed, 9 (29%) offered the continuum of openness (confidential, mediated, and fully disclosed) practices; 16 (52%) offered only confidential and mediated, 2 offered only confidential adoptions, and 2 offered only mediated; and 2 agencies offered only mediated and fully disclosed adoptions, but 1 of these would offer confidential adoptions at the birthmother's request. Of the 31 agencies interviewed, only 1 agency reported offering identified adoptions, which occur when birthmothers and prospective adoptive parents find each other and contact an agency to facilitate the adoption (see Table 2.1).

Standard adoption options had changed considerably between Time 1 and Time 2. Whereas 20 agencies offered only confidential or mediated adoptions or both at Time 1, this number had dropped to 7 at Time 2. Of the 2 agencies that offered only confidential at Time 1, 1 agency had stopped offering confidential and at Time 2 offered mediated options and, on request, fully disclosed options. The other agency continued its practice of confidential adoptions but would offer mediated options when requested. Between Time 1 and Time 2, the most significant change in agency practices occurred among agencies that had moved away from offering confidential and mediated options as standard practice. Only 3 of the original 16 continued this practice. At Time 2, 5 offered mediated and fully disclosed adoptions as standard practice, with confidential arrangements offered only at birthmother request. Four offered all three options as standard practice. One offered mediated adoption options, with confidential limited only to birthmother request. The remaining 2 no longer offered confidential adoptions at all. At Time 2, 5 agencies were offering

TABLE 2.1   Options Offered as Standard Practice Among Agencies Offering Adoption Services

Year	Confidential Only	Mediated Only	Confidential and Mediated	Mediated and Fully Disclosed	Confidential, Mediated, and Fully Disclosed	Fully Disclosed Only	Total
1987/89	2	2	16	2	9	0	31
1993	1	3(1)	3(1)	9(2)	12(1)	1	29 {34}

NOTE: Five agencies were interviewed at T2 only. Numbers in parentheses refer to agencies that had T2 interviews only.

identified adoptions in which adoptive parents recruited birthmothers seeking to place children for adoption.

Only 11 (35%) of the original 31 agencies offered fully disclosed options as part of their standard practice at Time 1. Four to 5 years later, 22 (76%) of the remaining 29 agencies offered fully disclosed adoptions. The data thus reflect a growing trend toward offering some form of openness, which is reflected in the increase in agencies offering mediated and fully disclosed options as standard practice. For example, one agency noted:

> We did our first open placement in 1985, so we've become much more comfortable with it. We've become much more secure. I think it really is an integral part of our value system as a staff, and I think we impart those values to people differently than we did before. We work really hard at looking at how we are in the middle and where we can get out of the middle without giving up any professionalism. And, you know, still judging the clinical appropriateness of [it]. I think in the past, we probably had a lot of our practices designed around the exception rather than the rule. And I'll bet that's another way how we've changed, is that we now design our practices for the rule and make the exception when necessary. We were probably more leery early on. We were much more protective than we needed to be. Now we allow the parties to protect themselves. We just support them in that.

At Time 1, most agencies offered confidential adoptions as an option, and only 1 agency reported that the only time it would offer a confidential adoption was at the specific request of a birthmother. By Time 2, however, 13 (including 11 original agencies) said that the only time they would offer a confidential adoption was if a birthmother specifically asked for it. When factoring in agencies' willingness to provide an option at a birthmother's request, 24 (71%) of the 34 agencies interviewed at Time 2 allow all three options (confidential, mediated, and fully disclosed) to occur as part of their services. Twenty-one (72%) of the original 29 agencies still providing adoption services at Time 2 now fit into this grouping. Clearly, agencies moved away from confidential options as a part of standard practice but were willing to make exceptions for any birthmother who still wanted such an arrangement. One agency indicated that it offers fully disclosed adoptions as standard practice but will allow a birthmother to request mediated arrangements. One agency allowed birthparents or adoptive parents to request mediated options, and one agency allowed either party to request fully disclosed arrangements. Most agency personnel indicated that although confidential, mediated, and fully disclosed options are offered to birthmothers or allowed on request, they encourage birthmothers to choose mediated or fully disclosed adoptions. Adoptive parents are usually told that if they must have a confidential adoption, it is highly unlikely that they will ever receive a child because birthmothers rarely now agree to place a child in a confidential adoption.

At both points in time, agencies were also asked to distinguish between the types of adoptions they discouraged or encouraged. Most agencies encouraged mediated adoptions at Time 1, 9 were beginning to discourage confidential, and 11 discouraged fully disclosed. By 1993, 22 agencies discouraged confidential adoptions and 13 encouraged fully disclosed. At both points in time, no agencies discouraged mediated placements. Only 4 encouraged confidential adoptions in 1987/89, and 2 encouraged them in 1993. For example:

> Our problem is it's not a matter of offering, you know, saying, "We offer this kind of adoption, or this kind of adoption." It's really based on the adoptive parents and the birthparents and the agreement between the two. All of our adoptive parents, we tell them that we're not going to study a family unless they're open to an agency mediated. You know, they don't come in saying, "I only want a confidential adoption." They may

end up with one because their birthmother does not want to have contact with them, but any adoptive family coming through our agency is prepared for an agency mediated adoption.

In summary, by 1993, two thirds of the agencies offered the continuum of openness in adoption, from confidential to fully disclosed, whereas in 1987, most agencies offered only confidential and mediated adoptions. The types of adoptions currently offered actually ranged from confidential to cooperative or identified adoptions, in which both parties find each other and the agency facilitates the adoption. It is interesting to note, however, that the one agency offering only confidential adoptions in 1987 still offered only confidential adoptions in 1993.

What Factors Motivate Agencies to Offer Openness Options?

In the mid-1980s, agencies increasingly provided pictures of the placed child to birthparents, let birthparents select adoptive parents for the child, arranged meetings between birthparents and adoptive parents without sharing identifying information, and offered ongoing contact between parties (McRoy, Grotevant, & White, 1988; Sorich & Siebert, 1982). Pannor and Baran (1984) estimated that about 80% to 90% of adoption agencies offered information sharing and that about 20% had families participating in fully disclosed adoptions. Belbas (1987) noted that an infant shortage forced adoption agencies to reconsider the needs of the birthmother and her wish to be more actively involved in the adoption process. Prospective adoptive parents were told, "If you are not ready for contact, you're not ready for adoption" (p. 186). For example, one agency staff member noted at Time 1:

> [When] we go into that semiopen [mediated] meeting, I'll tell the family that it isn't that I don't care about them, but that my allegiance is with the birthmother because she's gone through the grieving and she's gone through the real tough time with the decision. And actually I've gotten closer to her usually than I have with the family. They've got each other, and they have a baby in hand. And when I sit down in that meeting, I usually sit right next to the birthmother. That's the biggest opportunity

for the adoptive family to really make the birthmothers human, which they are, and make them really sensitive to what they go through.

Berry (1991) reported from her survey of public, private, and independent adoptions in California that most adoptions involved some level of contact with birthparents. Bradbury and Marsh (1988) called for the linking of not only birth and adoptive families but also extended family members of each during preplacement counseling in infant placements. Similarly, the Child Welfare League of America's National Adoption Task Force (1987) reported that agency-mediated sharing of updated medical or social information or both should be encouraged and that the amount of additional openness in an adoption should be based on careful planning and mutual agreement among the agency, adoptive parents, birthparents, and older adopted persons.

Agency staff in the study were asked to identify factors that contributed to a change in agency principles and practices regarding openness. Among the factors most often mentioned as leading to offering greater openness options (see Table 2.2) were client demand, changes in agency values, and competition from independent adoptions and other private agencies that had begun offering openness in adoption placements. Closer analysis revealed that this demand for openness was primarily coming from birthmother clients. In fact, in 1993 the majority of agencies in the study stated that they viewed the birthmother as the primary client. The fact that very few agencies cited research as a factor leading to change in practice is noteworthy.

As more and more pregnant women began to demand ongoing contact, adoption agencies recognized the need to change practices in order to stay in business and remain competitive. At Time 2, 10 (27%) agencies indicated that their practices had changed to remain in business. More and more birthmothers refused to make adoption plans in which they would lose contact forever. For example, an agency staff member recalled one birthmother's poignant declaration:

> You want me to leave my baby with strangers? I wouldn't leave my child for 30 minutes with a sitter who wouldn't tell me her last name. How could I leave my child for a lifetime with someone I don't know?

Other agency staff members commented:

TABLE 2.2   Factors That Led to Changes in Practices

Factors	T1 (1987/89) Number of Agencies	T2 (1993) Number of Agencies
Response to demand	11	14
Response to problems or experiences of triad	6	7
Conferences and literature	5	7
Response to competition	1	10
Change in agency values	3	12
Change in societal values	1	4
Change in staff	2	1
Response to research	3	2
Tried openness and it worked	3	1
It's a right or entitlement	0	5

The marketplace, basically, is what it comes down to. We were only doing one or two adoptions in the traditional closed fashion. It didn't really even make sense to have an adoption program. Then after a series of really deciding that we really would like to have an adoption program, we decided to hire somebody new who had the idea of introducing the open program. I shouldn't say the marketplace. I think what first happened was the helping profession changed things based on what they began to say about adult adoptees having problems. Out of that, when the choice became available to birthparents to have more choice in their adoption versus not having choice, then, of course, birthparents as they became informed consumers were going to choose programs that allowed them to have choice. If you weren't one of them, then you weren't going to have an adoption program. So that's what I mean by the marketplace. The consumers, the birthparents, then began to demand choice.

The main factors that really encouraged the agency to [offer openness] were survival and quality of service. I know one thing is the fact that we are doing more adoptions. However, I am fully aware that in [state] there are some very good open adoption agencies that are doing the smallest number of adoptions they've done in years. So I see openness as no longer ensuring that your agency will remain open or growing. But I do know that openness is absolutely required if you're going to do adoption

. . . There is no doubt that maternity clients strongly prefer open adoptions.

The type and range of services offered by adoption agencies can play a crucial role in the appropriate resolution of adoption-related issues (McRoy, Grotevant, & Ayers-Lopez, 1994). Some agency personnel in our sample reported a change in their beliefs about the extent to which openness is related to good resolution of specific issues and difficulties encountered by adoption participants. The most widely held belief was that openness had an effect on the manner and speed in which birthmothers worked through the grief and loss associated with the relinquishment of a biological child. A range of grief reactions may be experienced by birthparents who have placed their babies for adoption, including an acute grief, mourning, self-doubt, and anger (Baran et al., 1976; Millen & Roll, 1985; Rynearson, 1982). Some evidence suggests that level of openness does affect grief resolution in birthmothers. As discussed in Chapter 6, we found that birthmothers with lower levels of openness (confidential and time-limited mediated) 5 to 12 years after placement tended to have more prolonged grief reactions than those with fully disclosed adoptions. Referring to mediated and fully disclosed adoptions, agency staff commented at Time 2:

I think [birthmothers have] a certain sense of peace with their decision. That's not to say without grief, but I think there's been a peacefulness about their decision in that, you know, they know that their child is in a loving home. They don't have to walk around with this ghost on their shoulder, and they don't have to wonder all the time. You know, peacefulness in that sense. What else? It allows them to confront their grief earlier on and to get on with their lives more fully sooner than the old system did.

Birthmothers have certainly benefited that their needs have been better addressed in that they do have more say and control . . . they will be able to live more comfortably with that decision than many mothers did 30 years ago when they had no say in that kind of thing, and a lot presented emotionally and psychiatrically and personally because of how adoption was 35, 40 years ago—for all the guilt that went into [it]. So we have to say that, from the birthmother's perspective, it has to be much more safeguarding of her feelings in helping her deal with the aftermath when she's released that child for adoption—and living with it and getting the sense that she can visualize where the child is and make sure that your child's well cared for. That's got to be a wonderful feeling to have 10 years later, and reaffirming that you did do the right thing at that time.

Ward (1979) suggested that the development of a sense of entitlement to the child and the development of appropriate family relationships are the two essential tasks of adoptive parents. She further noted that much of the work of family building must be accomplished after the placement of the child, even if competent preparation and education have been given to the adoptive parents. Thus, adoptive parents face tasks that constitute an ongoing process in dealing with the reality of adoption in their family. The agency has a role in this process well after the placement of the child and legal adoption. The agency can offer consultation, support, continuing education, and group and individual counseling for adoptive parents. When questioned about the impact that openness has had on adoptive parents, agency personnel tended to report that many adoptive parents initially found openness to be scary, intimidating, or overwhelming. Agency personnel also thought, however, that extensive education and particularly the opportunity to meet birthmothers and adoptive parents engaged in open adoptions (often in a panel format) often led to a change in adoptive parents' attitudes about openness. Many agency staff also reported that they perceived a positive impact of openness on adoptive parents' sense of entitlement, parenting behaviors, and thoughts and feelings about the birthmother as follows:

I think at first it was real hard for them [the adoptive parents]. [For] most of them, that [openness] was kind of a new concept and it was kind of scary. But I think with the education, most of our families are really pleased with that. Overall, I think the response has been very positive.

They're [adoptive parents] now more fully endowed to be the parents of the baby. They don't worry any more about the birthmother or birthfather being in the closet ready to jump out and grab the baby from them. Their biggest fears are decreased considerably. They're much more relaxed parents, much more confident parents. It decreases their need to be supermom and superdad to prove that they really did deserve a child because the very person who gave birth would have given this child to them. I just think it has to do with endowment. Unless she becomes intrusive and too demanding, that they feel very good [about the birthmother]. They have a lot more understanding of where she is coming from and what went into her decision. They have a lot more empathy for her and concern and sympathy for what she's gone through and what went into her decision.

An adopted person is faced with the task of becoming an integrated and fully functioning member of an adoptive family, which includes building a sense of attachment and entitlement to the adoptive family (Lawder, 1970). Although most adopted persons meet these challenges with success, others may experience emotional, behavioral, or family difficulties specifically associated with their adoptive status (McRoy, Grotevant, & Zurcher, 1988). For adopted adolescents, developmental tasks associated with identity formation may motivate a desire to gain additional information about the birthfamily, such as what birthparents look like or their reasons for placement, or to have contact with the birthfamily. Some agency personnel in our sample expressed concern over the eventual outcomes of openness for adopted persons, particularly because limited research has been available on long-term outcomes. Other agency personnel believed that openness contributes significantly to positive outcomes for adopted persons, especially in terms of identity formation and emotional health.

The children [of open adoptions] will probably be much, much more self-confident than other adoptees. I think the probability of an unplanned pregnancy amongst that population would be significantly decreased. They will be more self-confident and their self-esteem will then be higher because they know the truth. So, if you compare them with any other population that went through closed adoptions, I think there will be significantly higher levels of self-esteem. And the research will bear this out 20 years from now.

For some agencies, change could not happen until the philosophy of staff and board members changed. Addition of new staff and board members not wedded to the concept of confidentiality led to greater challenges toward confidential adoptions in some instances. Some agency personnel have found that openness "makes the choice of adoption more acceptable and more clear to the birthmother." Others have reported, as stated above, that their movement toward openness was a response to the many problems and experiences they found triad members encountering. Agency staff became aware of some postplacement problems of total secrecy as adopted adults returned to the agency to seek more information about their past, as adoptive parents brought adopted children in for counseling, or as birthmothers asked for help in searching for their birthchildren. These insights led some agencies to take another look at their values and practices:

> We've had openness now for probably 10 or 12 years. When we first went from totally closed adoptions to the semiopen that we have, we did it very slowly. We looked at each step along the way, and what we did was wait to get as much education as we could. We talked with other agencies, the social workers, with adoptive families, with adult adoptees—just got as much information as we could and slowly made one step at a time. We would decide on the next step, and we would wait for the social workers to get comfortable with it. We could then risk and start doing that and if it worked well, we would continue with that . . . After a few years of getting comfortable with it ourselves, it became imperative that we weren't going to have any adoptive parents that would have a totally closed unless the birthmother chose that.

Agencies are also well aware that their policies and practices occur against the larger backdrop of societal opinion and public policy. Societal perceptions of adoption, as well as state and federal legislation regulating adoption procedures, directly influence the way adoption agencies apportion and structure the provision of their services (DeWoody, 1993; Hollinger, 1993).

> Society in general in the last decade has changed a lot in sharing. We're much more open in general. We deal more with our emotions, with our emotional needs of people . . . There's much in the media too . . . There are more articles, more books written, more studies done. People are more conscious of adoption, that it's a different form of parenting . . . The more media exposure you have—when we first came out with our book [title], our author was interviewed by CBS. That was very positive because they had more things on open adoption where it's worked out. Those things, of course, are far-reaching and very positive. Some of them might consider adoption plans, "Well, that sounds like a sensible, healthy way to do adoption—I didn't think it could be that way." Media, I think, are quite influential.

Although various authors have decried the negative attitudes about adoptive relationships held by the larger society, indications are that these attitudes may be changing (Kirk, 1981). This may be, in part, because of greater attention being given to adoption at the statutory level. At the federal level, the Health Insurance Reform Act (§ 1028) of 1996 included special provisions making health insurance portable and the coverage of preexisting conditions mandatory for adoptive families. Adoption tax credits and exemptions were also enacted in 1996 as part of the Small Business and Job Protection Act (H.R. 3448). Although there is little consistency across states in the way adoption processes, particularly those relating to openness (searching, adoption records, postadoption contact, contact agreements), are handled, some efforts are being made to standardize state statutes via the Uniform Adoption Act. The fate of the controversial Uniform Adoption Act is far from clear, however, in part because it constricts the adopted person's right to information and does not clearly support the availability of openness options. Thus, individual states have been putting forth innovative and, at times, disputed legislation that in turn directly affects the services that agencies *can* offer.

I really think it's been the identified adoption law that kind of pushed [changes in openness] to the fore, whereas maybe, over time, they would have happened just in reaction to the whole adoption climate and what's happening socially . . . But once that law was enacted, it really opened the door to open adoptions and more face-to-face contact, whether it was names or not. Because now a law allowed these things to happen . . . If we had not had identified adoptions, it might have been a slower process to have perhaps more of this face-to-face business and sharing of information than what has happened now. It just accelerated it in [state].

Does the Availability of Open Options Increase the Number of Infants Placed?

The decline in the number of birthmothers choosing to make adoption plans may have contributed to the shift toward openness in adoption agency policy and practice. For example, in the mid-1960s, about 31.7% of women whose children were born out of wedlock

made adoption plans, whereas today only an estimated 3% of unmarried women make adoption plans (Bachrach, London, & Maza, 1991).
Many agencies began pondering whether offering birthmothers opportunities to receive updated information or contact with the
adopted persons or adoptive parents could make adoption a more
acceptable option (Borgman, 1982; Sorosky, Baran, & Pannor, 1984).

> I'd say maybe 4 years ago there was an increasing number of girls who
> wanted letters and pictures. It began to happen a little bit more. I regard
> the big punctuation mark as a girl [who] came in and said, "I will not
> give my baby to someone I cannot meet. And if you don't do it, I will
> take my business elsewhere." In the meantime other agencies in town
> were doing openness stuff more than we were . . . [Now] it's a standard
> option. To my astonishment, after that big barrier got broken and we
> could allow meetings, I thought there would be a great deluge of girls
> wanting that, and there hasn't been a deluge . . . Why did we decide to
> do it? I think it was a combination of all those pressures.

Regardless of how agency staff truly feel about openness, they
have had to move to offer this as an option to remain competitive.
This competition came not only from independent adoptions but also
from other adoption agencies that had begun to offer openness options
(Baran & Pannor, 1990). Not all adoption professionals, however, are
comfortable with contact as standard practice in adoption arrangements. Cocozzelli (1989) expressed caution about the availability of
open adoptions serving as an inducement to the adoption choice over
parenting. She suggested that, in these cases, the birthmother is not
able to make a complete relinquishment, as in confidential adoptions
in which there will be no further contact. Similarly, Baran and Pannor
(1993) warned that agencies should not use open options to encourage
placements because sometimes these promises for continuing contact
are broken after the consummation, when the agency may no longer
be involved with the family or birthmother. Agencies in our sample
appeared to be well aware of the potential difficulties raised by this
issue, as the following example illustrates:

> What used to happen was a sheet that they would sign about degree of
> communication they were comfortable with . . . Well, we stopped doing
> that simply because we began to see that [birthparents] were viewing that

as a legal and binding contract, and then if somebody didn't follow through, they might call up upset 3 years later or whatever and say, "I didn't get pictures and letters." The couples then felt, well, gee, we're not comfortable with that now . . . So what we do now is this gets discussed on both sides prior to and during the matching, and then, of course, after the baby is born. We make it very clear to the birthparent, however, that this has nothing to do with her deciding whether to relinquish or not because the court is never going to intervene if she says, "Well, gee, I only relinquished because you told me I was going to get to visit each year for the first 5 years."

For years, adoption agencies had emphasized the preparation, security, and confidentiality of their practices. However, with the decline in the number of women choosing to place for adoption, demands by birthmothers for a role in choosing parents for their offspring, and demands by both birthmothers and adult adopted persons to open previously sealed records, adoption agencies began to reconsider their previous total adherence to closed adoptions.

We found that our placements have been going down considerably in the last figures. We feel that it's because many birthmothers in the [city] area are choosing either private adoptions or something where they have more control over the placement, what happens in the placement. So part of it was that we thought we would be able to meet their needs better if we offered them some decision-making power about their child . . . It has some economic implications for us, but really it was just to see if we could give them some power.

Agency representatives were asked whether the actual numbers of birthmothers choosing to place through their programs had increased or decreased because of the availability of openness options. In 1993, 12 indicated that openness options increased the number of birthmothers placing infants through their agencies, and 13 indicated no increase had occurred because of openness. In some cases, staff reported decreased placements. Of the latter group, several respondents attributed decreases in placements to independent adoptions and to birthmothers' choices to parent rather than place. Others stated that their rates had remained stable, perhaps because of offering options. Respondents who attributed increase in placements to openness options suggested the following:

It's the reason they come to us.

I think perhaps, I can't prove this, but I think it makes the adoption more palatable to the pregnant girl.

I've had a lot of girls tell me that they don't think they could do it if they didn't have openness.

They're much more likely to go through with the adoption decision because they know where the baby is going. I think we're having a lot more clients.

Those agencies that had either a decrease or no increase in placements because of offering openness made such comments as:

We've had a decrease, but don't think it's related to openness or lack of it.

There's barely any women who want to consider placement, let alone follow through all the way to the end.

With fully disclosed being an option, there are far more birthparents and adoptive parents making matches through attorneys or independently and not through the agency.

Four of the original 31 agencies we interviewed at Time 1 had closed their adoption programs by 1993. When asked to provide reasons for the program closures, 1 agency could not provide specifics because it currently had no staff who had been involved in the infant adoption program. Another agency provided a letter from its board of directors stating that the program and alternatives to the program had been under careful study for 4 years prior to the closure, but it gave no specific reasons for the closure. The 2 agencies that had closed but participated in the Time 2 interviews both agreed that the low number of placements per year was the decisive factor in the closures; 1 agency said the combination of legalization of abortion, availability of independent adoptions, and societal acceptance of single mothers resulted in fewer placements; the other agency said it closed because it did not wish to facilitate identified adoptions, which had just been given legal sanction in the state. Additionally, many birthmothers from this state were going across state lines to make adoption plans with a large, private adoption agency whose practices were somewhat questionable, according to a news "exposé" (e.g., making promises to birthmothers that were not always kept). The 2 agencies said that the factors contributing to the low numbers of placements were not going to change in the near future and that it became too difficult to provide quality service and expertise for only two to four placements a year.

What Is the Role of Adoption Agencies in Open Adoption?

In the ever-changing world of adoption practice, adoption agencies continue to define and redefine their role in open adoption in relation to each of the participants. The role of the adoption agency usually begins sometime prior to the birth of the child. Once the child is placed in an adoptive home, however, the role of the agency does not cease. Agencies are well aware that they have an obligation to be careful and deliberate about the services they offer and, thus, the role they play in the lives of adoption participants. They are involved in actions, decisions, and choices that may affect the emotional, physical, and relationship-centered health of birthparents, adoptive parents, and minor children. This responsibility is in the forefront of most agencies' decisions about openness and the way they present these options. For example:

> We've had people call to say, "I don't want to go with that agency. They insist on openness, and I don't think I can deal with that." I don't think there's any way we can do adoption that is going to keep people from adopting children. I mean, if we say, "No, it doesn't have to be open, but you have to stand on your head every Thursday," the couples are so desperate, they would do that. I think that says to us that our responsibility is huge in asking only those things that are reasonable, because we have been so dependent upon the agencies. I don't think [openness] has prevented any adoptions. I just think for those agencies who insist upon it, they probably have had some people go to other agencies.

Agency personnel can assume a variety of specific roles in relation to openness, including educator, consultant, counselor, mediator of problems and disputes, negotiator of changes, and facilitator of information exchange or retrieval about other triad members. Agencies' philosophies about their role in openness, however, appear to be on a continuum of involvement. Agencies that move toward fully disclosed adoptions generally give up much of their power to adoptive parents and birthparents, and the latter are expected to play a major role in decision making. Agencies that prefer confidential or mediated arrangements tend to retain much of their decision-making power. In the latter case, agencies remain involved in all aspects of the adoption and, in mediated placements, negotiate all changes between birthfamilies and adoptive families.

As policies were changed, some agencies also began rethinking whom they defined as their primary client. In 1993, the majority of agencies interviewed indicated that the birthmother is the primary client. For years, agencies seemed to view their role as the protector of both the adoptive parents and the birthparents. Now, many agencies appear to be much less protective and are retreating from their policies of control and power. Instead, they are letting adoptive parents protect themselves and are letting adoptive and birthparents make joint decisions about what is best in their situation. Thus, considerable philosophical diversity is found in our sample about what role, in terms of both advice and services, as well as control and authority, the agency should have in openness processes between adoptive and birthfamilies.

One issue about which agencies uniformly agree is that they have a vital role in preparing birthmothers and adoptive families for the issues and challenges they will face in open adoption. Education about openness is a common element of adoptive parent preparation and birthmother counseling programs in all agencies offering openness. Agencies commonly sponsor panels of birthmothers and adoptive parents participating in open adoptions who share their experiences with prospective adoptive parents. Some agencies offer workshops or written materials about how adoptive parents can prepare themselves and, eventually, the adopted child for building a positive relationship with the birthfamily.

The most common form of openness offered by the agencies in our sample was some form of mediated adoption (albeit often in combination with other options). It is obvious that the role of the agency is essential to the provision of mediated adoption. The agency is placed in the "third party" or "intermediary" position between the adoptive family and the birthfamily. For mediated adoptions to work, cooperation is needed from adoptive parents, birthparents, and agency personnel. If contact is lost, birthmothers may experience a renewed sense of grief and loss. Similarly, adoptive parents may also experience disappointment if the birthparent fails to maintain contact. Much professional time and investment are required of agencies that offer mediated options. Some agencies continue to "screen" or monitor all correspondence that passes through to another triad member for identifying content. Others may copy the correspondence for the files and pass it on or may simply readdress the envelope or package. Most agencies are not compensated for this service and must pay for staff time and postage out of the normal operating budget. Agency staff note that, at special holidays, such as Christmas or Mother's Day, the influx of packages, letters, cards, and telephone calls tends to overwhelm agency resources. One staff member commented that the offices and hallways of the agency were so packed with gifts and correspondence during the Christmas season that it looked like "a Macy's warehouse before a big sale."

> Actually, one of the major disadvantages that jumps out at me is how much time professionally this new program is taking. When you begin to be a center where you exchange information, looking at the information, evaluating it sometimes when being asked to, looking at pictures, evaluating whether the birthmother is going to receive it or vice versa— this takes another piece of staff's professional time that we had not put into this. So it's adding a tremendous piece of service to the professional job.

In confidential and mediated adoptions or when the parties have lost contact in fully disclosed adoptions, the agency is often the most accessible repository of information about the adopted person. In cases of medical emergency or when the child is experiencing chronic medical or emotional difficulties, it may be essential for adoptive parents to obtain information from the birthfamily. In these situations, the agency might search its files for pertinent information or may contact the birthfamily for updated information. Thus, the agency's role in the adoptive family is accentuated in these circumstances, highlighting the fact that, indeed, a "third party" is involved in the dynamics of adoptive family life. Similarly, birthparents may contact the agency for updated information on the welfare of the child or to pass along necessary or newly acquired medical information.

Although these are probably the most commonly reported reasons why agencies may facilitate either open or mediated contact between birthfamilies and adoptive families, at times either party may be interested in initiating a new form of openness in the adoption. This may take the form of initiating contact between parties who have not previously had contact or may be a reduction or increase in contact that is already occurring. From interviews with birthfamilies and adoptive families, we were aware that, at times, one party will want to decrease contact, whereas the other party might want to increase contact or maintain the same level. We asked agencies whether they get involved in mediating differences between birthfamilies and adoptive families. Table 2.3 presents the results of this analysis.

The majority (60%) of agencies in the study indicated they have become actively involved in mediating difficulties between birthparents and adoptive parents. Others stated they would facilitate discussions, educate about options, but play a more passive role in actual negotiations. One agency was particularly concerned about disturbing the birthmother and indicated it would not get involved in adoptive parent requests for more openness but would if the birthmother wanted to change. Examples of responses are provided below:

> We help initiate contact in closed situations; set boundaries; encourage being truthful with each other; encourage them to deal with each other.

> Our role is to facilitate, educate, and help people understand the value of continuing contact.

> We mediate to ensure confidentiality is maintained. We counsel and advise people wanting to move to fully disclosed.

> We don't feel we have the right to change the initial openness agreement 2 or 3 years later.

TABLE 2.3 Agency Response to Requests for Mediation

Response	*Number of Agencies (34)*
Mediate difficulties/Negotiate/Help initiate contact	21
Facilitate/Educate	2
Will mediate but leave changes to triad	3
Don't deal with changing openness	2
Will only mediate if birthmother wants change to more openness; not if adoptive parent wants to	1
Keep letters and pictures in file, in case one party requests	1
Try to hold parties to initial agreement	1
Missing because of incomplete response	3

We facilitate changes if both parties request it. If only one requests it, we will call or write to the other party, and they will have to go through court.

Agency representatives were also asked to discuss how birthmothers and adoptive families negotiate increases or decreases in contact. Agencies vary in the extent to which they control this process. Some agencies directly negotiate the change, insisting that the agency is in the ideal position to protect the interests of both parties. Other agencies believe that the adoption participants are in the best position to negotiate their own joint decisions about openness. The majority of agencies, however, fall somewhere in the middle of this continuum, offering support, assistance, and advice when problems arise but generally allowing the parties to decide what is in their own best interests. Most agencies advise the parties to contact the agency first to process their desire for contact and to get advice about how to proceed. At this point, most agencies either advise the initiating party to write a letter requesting contact, which the agency will forward, or contact the other party directly on behalf of the initiating party. Some agencies attempt to evaluate the reasons why contact is desired and often refer to what they know about the other party's ideas about openness to guide the initiating party in these efforts. For example, one agency noted that it had received frequent requests from one birthmother about the possibility of letters or pictures from the adoptive family. On the receipt of the first request, the agency contacted the adoptive parents, who stated they were not comfortable with initiating contact and did not want to be approached with such a request in the future. The agency respected the adoptive parents' wishes, and thus its role changed from mediating openness to assisting the birthmother in processing the failure of her efforts to initiate contact.

Some agencies offering mediated adoptions are willing only to exchange communications between parties for 6 months or until the adoption is final. At that point, they notify birthfamilies and adoptive families that they will no longer be screening and de-identifying all information coming into the agencies. Therefore, if exchanges are to continue, participants must accept that identifying information may be transferred in the exchange process. In these cases, agencies may only become aware that the adoption has changed from mediated to fully disclosed or that contact has stopped completely as a result of the decrease or cessation of correspondence transmitted through the agencies.

Agencies that prefer that birthparents and adoptive parents negotiate changes through the agencies and/or through their own efforts gave the following types of responses:

> They contact the agency, which encourages them to write each other about the desired changes. Birthmothers often don't respond to the adoptive parents' letters.

> Sometimes changes are negotiated through the agency, but sometimes on their own, by just not communicating any more.

> Most changes people do themselves; some come to the agency for help and/or approval.

In cases in which negotiations occur without the agency, the following examples were given:

If they want to make a change to full disclosure, it must be on their own. The agency cannot be involved in these.

Whatever the parties agree on is fine with us. We don't put any limits on the relationship.

We may not know if families change their degree of openness. They may not feel it's necessary for the agency to be involved.

Agency staff who reported that changes are only handled through the agency stated:

We will contact the other party to see if they're willing to receive information. If the birthmother wants more, she's asked to present it to the adoptive parents in writing. The agency helps her think through the facets of her decision.

We will talk with both sides and try to come to a plan that is satisfactory. If it's a reasonable request, we will certainly think about it.

[Requests] generally would be discussed first between the birthparent and the maternity worker, and then in semiopen it would come to the adoption worker for discussion with the adoptive family. It is our responsibility to help people come to a good working arrangement and to understand what might lie in back of those requests.

What Do Agencies Perceive to Be the Main Advantages and Disadvantages of Each Type of Openness?

Along with changes in policy, agencies clearly have changed their perceptions of the advantages and disadvantages of each type of adoption during the past several years. Although some were still offering confidential adoptions, they were much more likely in 1993 than in 1987/89 to see them as preferable in only a few circumstances. Indeed, as agencies' philosophies regarding openness have changed, with more agencies *actively* encouraging openness and discouraging confidential adoptions, so have agencies' perceptions about the different types of adoption become more well defined and earnestly argued. The agencies in our sample were asked to delineate the advantages and disadvantages of each level of openness for each triad member. Because of the nature of the data, the following represents a qualitative analysis of their responses.

Confidential Adoptions

Advantages and Disadvantages for Birthmothers. On the whole, agency personnel were able to enumerate few advantages of confidential adoptions for birthmothers, in contrast with other options. The advantages cited were that confidential adoptions create real choices for individual birthmothers (in combination with openness options), allow for secrecy when birthmothers choose not to tell others of the relinquishment, protect birthmothers from the grief associated with seeing their children reared by others, allow for a sense of closure, and permit birthmothers to "move on" with their lives. As one agency staff member commented,

> The only advantage is that it does need to be available if a birthmother, for whatever her own personal reasons are, demands it. Then I think it absolutely must be available. So that's the only advantage I see is that it still needs to be available so that a woman never feels that she has no alternatives.

Most agencies in 1993 noted, however, that confidential adoptions hold real disadvantages for birthmothers. Agencies that reported disadvantages tended to focus on the detrimental effect of secrecy and lack of continuing information on birthmothers' grief resolution. Agencies also suggested that birthmothers in confidential adoptions were not able to "age" their children appropriately; lacked even basic "humane" information, such as whether their children were still living; and might have problems in later relationships with spouses or children because of denial or unresolved loss. For example,

> In some instances, [confidential adoption] continues the process of denial and maybe never allows oneself to grieve this, possibly at some point having a replacement child because this was never dealt with. Over and over, the older birthmothers are coming back and saying they've never really been able to put it aside. They didn't know if the child lived or died was their biggest question.

Advantages and Disadvantages for Adoptive Parents. For adoptive parents, the major advantage of confidential adoptions was that they would not have to share the child with a birthparent. In confidential adoptions, agencies believe there is no danger of "coparenting" of a child between birthparent and adoptive parents and no chance of birthparents "interfering" with the adopted child's upbringing. In some instances, confidential adoptions were seen as increasing the adoptive parents' sense of entitlement and attachment to the child, as in the following example:

> Adoptive parents can feel that they are real parents in the sense that they're entitled to this child, that they're not just acting as a caretaker for the birthparent. They can approach parenting without the fear that there will be interference from a birthparent. They can parent the child and not have influences on the child from a birthparent who may show up. It really helps ease the minds of the adoptive parents that they might not be entitled to or might lose the child in some way. That helps them, I think, to be better parents.

The majority of agency personnel, however, perceived these advantages to be a double-edged sword, which could and would operate to the disadvantage of the adoptive parents and adopted person in the long run. The denial of adopted family status; decreased ability to deal with infertility issues; increased fear of, and lessened empathy for, birthparents; and inability to deal with the child's questions about the birthparents were all common detriments attributed to adoptive parents in confidential adoptions. One staff member enumerated the following specific and general disadvantages:

> I really do not believe at all that it's an advantage for an adoptive family. They do not have access to medical information. They do not have access to that birthfamily if the child has questions, and if the child's need is to have information and contact, they are unable to do that for the child. In the long run, it's detrimental to the health and well-being of the entire family.

Advantages and Disadvantages for Adopted Persons. Again, few benefits were stated by the agencies for adopted persons in confidential arrangements. An unstable or emotionally disturbed birthparent was the most common reason to encourage confidential adoptions for the "best interests of the child." Most agency personnel, however, believed that the child loses a large piece of identity because she or he is limited to the background information contained on a piece of paper. Agencies note that adopted persons wonder about their genetic heritage and commonly ask questions such as, "Whom do I look like?" "Where did I get this personality?" or "Why did my parents give me away?" Agencies observed that confidential adoptions limit the adopted individual's access to information that others take for granted and pointed to the increasing search movement among adopted persons as an expression of a "fundamental, basic right and drive to know where we came from and who we are." A staff member commented on these disadvantages with an analogy:

> It seems like a very unnatural way to build a family system. I don't know that children need to lose a family to gain one. [Name of adoption educator] says it very well. She says that adoptees who grow up in a closed system kind of have become part of the victim-witness program in the country, where they're literally taken and removed and put in a new place with a new history and a new name and new legal pieces of paper—amended birth certificates to protect them in some way. What adoptees are never quite sure of is what they're being protected from.

Mediated Adoptions

Advantages and Disadvantages for Birthmothers. According to several agency representatives, mediated adoptions seem to be the safe middle ground because they allow for the advantages of contact without the agency relinquishing total control. One agency stated that, in general, mediated adoptions "allow for protection of all parties." Most agencies, however, suggested that this middle ground occupied by mediated adoptions implies that these adoptions have some of the drawbacks of confidential options while lacking some of the benefits of fully disclosed adoption. For birthmothers, some agencies consider that mediated adoptions may decrease the period of grieving, increase comfort with the adoption decision, and increase a sense of "peace" because of the continuing knowledge of the welfare of the child. Other agencies, in contrast, believe that mediated adoption represents a loss of a potentially positive full relationship with the adoptive family and may have implications for the birthmother's grief resolution, as is noted in the following example:

> The difficult side is the actual confrontation of one's pain. It's what I've come to call short-term pain for long-term gain because it does really rub their face in grief. The emotional process is more raw and requires more therapeutic support in an interesting way. The grief is much more palpable in those first couple of years. I think that surprises a lot of people because they assume that the openness would decrease the grief. I've certainly found that it increases it for a period of time, but it does allow for healing in a healthier fashion over time.

Advantages and Disadvantages for Adoptive Parents. In mediated adoptions, adoptive parents have the benefit of a greater sense of control over the openness process. Agencies state that adoptive parents' roles are more clearly defined in mediated adoptions, which increases their sense of entitlement and their acceptance of the parenting role. Adoptive parents also have an enhanced ability to address questions from the adopted person and to get information in the case of medical or psychological need. One agency commented as follows on the type of control experienced by adoptive parents:

> The agency-mediated area, what I hear is it feels like there is more control. They can stop or start. They can dictate more directly what can happen and can't happen. They can withhold or share at their own discretion. They don't have to worry about the child and the birthparents going off and having a relationship or talking about things that they're not privy to.

Other agencies, however, believed that even mediated sharing could be scary or intimidating to the adoptive parents and thus may interfere with parenting. Another disadvantage for adoptive parents proposed by the agencies was that adoptive parents miss out on the full richness of a relationship with the birthmother, which might include being present at the birth or having the birthmother directly available for questions. The impact of mediated sharing on entitlement was assessed by one agency in the following example:

Sometimes the adoptive parents have said initially that the birthmother's continued involvement has kind of troubled them in terms of their entitlement to the child. I would say that it doesn't happen often, but the birthmother's correspondence, pictures, and letters has been troubling some adoptive parents' feeling of entitlement to the child.

Advantages and Disadvantages for Adopted Persons. The advantages enumerated by the agencies for the adopted person include that the adopted person's questions about her or his genetic and birth history can be answered, the child knows that the birthparent cares and that she or he is valued by the birthparent, and the birthparent becomes a "real," rather than fantasy, person in the adopted person's life. Agencies suggest that each of these factors promotes positive adjustment in the adopted child and adolescent. It is important to note, however, that not all adoptive parents in mediated arrangements share the birthfamily's correspondence with the adopted child. One staff member stated that mediated adoptions are probably "not that much better than the confidential" if the adoptive parents are not sharing information with the child. The following example pertains to situations in which information is shared with the agency as an intermediary:

> In a mediated adoption, the advantage is that the child can get information. They can have access to reach the birthmother. They also have a social worker to help with that if they decide to meet or if they decide to have contact, that there is an intermediary to kind of smooth over the problems that might happen.

The suggested disadvantages for the adopted person centered around the loss or lack of information about the birthfamily and the harmful effects of family secrets. Loss of the potentially beneficial full relationship with the birthparents was a concern to some staff members, as in this example:

> There is a message that there is something to fear in each other, that in some way we're adversaries, that it isn't safe to know who we are, what our names are and where we live. I know very few adoptions, quite frankly, where that needs to occur. I think the message to the child is that

this isn't safe. It isn't safe for people to know who each other are. That to me is a major disadvantage.

Adoption professionals noted that the mediated contact adoption has drawbacks as well. Agency staff members found this arrangement particularly time-consuming because they were responsible for mediating all the correspondence, gifts, and other exchanges. Moreover, some indicated that this arrangement sometimes leads to a lack of trust toward the other party because all the information is handled through an intermediary and caution is taken to omit any identifying information. One agency commented as follows on the quality of the relationships formed in mediated adoptions:

Once again, there's just not the opportunity to really know each other as people. It's kind of a continuum, so it's better than closed. Birthparents can feel a greater sense of, "Oh, yes, this child's OK." And the child has a little more sense of who the birthparents are, but it's still so unreal. I mean, that's not what relationships are like in our lives. Real important people in our lives don't just send letters and pictures through a third party. It's just unreal.

Fully Disclosed Adoptions

By 1993, the majority of agencies had moved toward offering fully disclosed open adoptions as part of their services and could delineate benefits, concerns, and disadvantages to be addressed. As stated above, this move represented a strong value shift for most agencies, which resulted from clinical experience, education, and client demand, among other reasons. Some agencies still perceived fully disclosed adoptions as somewhat "experimental," and even though they were facilitating such adoptions, they were aware of the need for research delineating the long-term outcomes of such arrangements.

Overall, the agencies in our sample that offered fully disclosed adoptions perceived them to be more honest and truthful, to create trust among all adoption participants, and to create choices. Agencies also believed that fully disclosed adoptions are superior because of the quality and type of relationships that develop and because triad members become real to each other, cutting down on fantasies,

stereotypes, and "adoption myths." The general problems or disadvantages enumerated included boundary issues; lack of commitment
to openness arrangements; lingering fear or mistrust; cooperation,
communication, and/or negotiation issues; and availability of fewer
safeguards and more avenues for abuse of trust between the parties
(when one party violates a contact agreement). In terms of agency
participation, some agency personnel suggested that the agency's loss
of control is a negative, and they stressed the liability issues and
litigation potential in fully disclosed adoptions. In general, however,
agencies stressed that fully disclosed adoption involves a process that
requires hard work and commitment from all parties. Adoptive and
birthparents have to deal with both good and bad aspects of the
relationship that develops from their efforts.

> I have not known anybody who's an advocate for complete openness
> who would say that any of us believe that all the problems are going to
> go away. We're certainly seeing problems, but they're of a different
> nature. It moves a lot of the pain up front. There's more to deal with at
> the beginning—more fears, more grief. I think for everybody there's
> more to do up front. But I think that if there's any negative, it's that it
> takes much more skill, much more education, much more support to do
> a really fully disclosed adoption . . . The 1st year or so can be much more
> difficult for everybody, but as we watch it unfold over the next 3 or 4
> years, the kids in the families, birthfamilies, and adoptive families seem
> to be much more settled than the families in traditional agencies.

Advantages and Disadvantages for Birthmothers. Specific benefits
to birthmothers reported by agencies offering fully disclosed adoptions include an enhanced ability to deal with grief and/or loss issues
and to work through feelings, the peace of mind associated with
having firsthand knowledge of the adopted children's development
and welfare, and empowerment and a sense of control over decision
making. Fully disclosed adoptions also allow birthparents the ability
to have a more fully defined role in the postplacement adoption
process and to develop a uniquely fulfilling identity and self-concept
as a birthparent.

> Information and contact can help with grieving. I think for moms it can
> probably also help her have a realistic view of their child's growing up

rather than fantasy. If something bad happens, they can know about it. If something wonderful happens, they can know about it also.

Other agencies, however, reported that, as in mediated adoptions, fully disclosed arrangements may contribute to intensified grief reactions for birthparents. Agencies suggested that a significant danger exists when the birthmother is encouraged or pressured to meet a family very rapidly or very early in her pregnancy and is encouraged to form an emotional relationship with the adoptive parents. This may compromise her ability to change her mind about relinquishment and to decide to parent because she feels as if she "owes" this child to this family. One agency also suggested that when a relationship with the adoptive family is made, full disclosure can impede the birthmother from developing a full identity in addition to that of birthmother (i.e., of wife or mother of other children). Another disadvantage, outlined in the following example, reflects concern about incomplete relinquishment of the adopted child by the birthmother in the first few postplacement years.

> In her own mind, she's not really necessarily released this child for adoption because she's still hanging on. She's sort of halfway got the child up for adoption and halfway is parenting the child. So it's got to cause all kinds of emotional problems. As she gets more acquainted with what's happening, she may begin to disagree with the type of discipline the family might use. She might disagree with the kind of religious background that the adopting family is bringing the child up in or not bringing the child up in . . . There might be some surgery come along that's life-threatening and the biological mother might feel that she has to have a part in that decision, but the adopting family says, "No, you don't have a part in it." If she's tied up emotionally with . . . what's happening to the child, it could really be a drawback to her being all that she can be.

Advantages and Disadvantages for Adoptive Parents. Agencies indicated that the main advantage of full disclosure for adoptive parents was that it enhances and reinforces the adoptive parents' sense of entitlement to the child, particularly when the adoptive parents receive the child directly from the birthparent(s). In essence, agencies believe that the birthparents' message that "I trust you with this child, and I am doing this of my free will" has great meaning for adoptive parents' beliefs about their right to parent the child. Some agencies also mentioned the benefits of the genuine and authentic relationship that develops between birthfamilies and adoptive families. Other advantages included a reduced fear of the birthparents, a greater ability to make the birthmother "real" instead of a scary or worrisome fantasy figure, and empowerment of adoptive parents to "take charge" of their own adoption. As one agency staff member stated, full disclosure "takes away their fear of running into the birthmother at a mall or somewhere." Another agency that strongly encourages full disclosure said, "The more rapidly the adoptive parents can be encouraged to fully disclose, the better." Implications for entitlement and parenting are exemplified in this passage:

> We think that openness enhances the sense of entitlement because birthparents are selecting the parents and then handing the child to the adoptive parents . . . Adoptive parents will know that birthparents are making this decision of their own free will. No one is forcing them to do it. This naturally enhances the sense of security for the adoptive parents. They are more apt to feel, "Yes, this baby is really mine. This is not pretend, and I am not baby-sitting." This greater sense of entitlement has long-range implications in terms of parenting. They can do all those things that biological parents do, such as disciplining, without the subconscious worry that they really don't have rightful authority concerning the child.

Disadvantages of fully disclosed adoptions centered primarily around the difficulties associated with establishing clear boundaries and expectations about the roles of adoptive and birthparents in openness. For example, several agencies worried about the possibility of "coparenting" of an adopted child, in which the birthparent is seen as interfering with the adoptive parents' full ability to make decisions about, to discipline, or to otherwise parent the child autonomously. Also mentioned were issues associated with birthparents who have significant emotional, behavioral, or other problems. Establishing a productive and stable relationship with these birthparents is seen as a challenge for the adoptive parents and, perhaps, disruptive or disturbing to the adoptive family system. For example, it was suggested that some birthparents go to the adoptive parents for support and the adoptive parents end up taking care of the birthparents.

I guess the only disadvantage I could see would be if both sets of parents were not clear on their roles, and that might lead the child to not being clear . . . My observation is that parents who are not confused in their roles don't produce children who are confused in their roles. I am always presupposing that open adoption does not mean coparenting.

Advantages and Disadvantages for Adopted Persons. The central advantage of fully disclosed adoption for adopted persons was the direct access they have to the birthparents and, thus, to their own genetic and biological family heritage. Most agencies offering fully disclosed adoptions cited an increased sense of power for adopted persons, in which they are not dependent on adoptive parents or the agency for information because they have direct access to their birthfamilies. Eventually, an adopted person may have the additional advantage of not needing to search for birthparent(s) so long as contact is maintained. Agency personnel believed that this direct contact may help with identity issues in that the common questions of adopted persons ("Whom do I look like?" "Why do I have this medical problem?" "Will my own children have these problems?") have readily available answers. Other agencies stressed that adopted persons involved in full disclosure feel valued by, and important to, birthparents, which reduces feelings of abandonment and rejection. For example, several agencies noted that a birthparent had a greater ability to communicate that the placement was an "act of love" for the adopted child, which in turn reduces the "negative baggage" associated with the placement decision for the adopted person. Also mentioned was the fact that the adopted person forms a relationship in which the birthparents become real people, which reduces fantasies and stereotypes. One staff member summed up the benefits of this relationship as follows:

More subtle factors like personality, talents, those kinds of things, they can be celebrated in a different way. They can be acknowledged by birthparents at least from time to time, as well as by adoptive parents. I don't think anybody can ever have too many acknowledgments from people who care about them . . . With fully disclosed, I think that's the best of all worlds for everybody, especially the adopted person, because there's going to be more people who love and care about them and to express that directly to them. They will have direct access to the sources of information about their roots, either personalitywise or physically, and maybe develop some relationships with birthkin that they otherwise would probably not be able to—half-siblings, full siblings, cousins, whatever.

The agencies' concerns about fully disclosed adoptions for adopted persons tended to center around difficulties that may occur in the relationship between the birthfamilies and the adoptive families. Agency personnel were particularly concerned about the pain and confusion caused by birthparents who do not follow through with the relationship established in fully disclosed adoptions. Birthparents who have persistent personal or interpersonal difficulties or who stop or are inconsistent in their contact with the adoptive families can be distressing to the adopted persons. Difficulties in the relationship between the adoptive parents and birthparents, particularly when birthparents are seen as too intrusive or demanding, may also contribute to confusion, anger, or anxiety in the adopted persons. Other difficult issues included explaining the relationship with the birthparent(s) to other people (particularly peers) and the possibility of an adopted child playing birthparents and adoptive parents against each other or feeling torn between two sets of parents (a "loyalty conflict"). A few agencies mentioned that some adopted persons may be distressed by the information they do receive from the birthfamily regarding the circumstances of the birth, as in the cases of rape, incest, or other sensitive matters. According to two staff members:

> The disadvantage in the fully disclosed is if you had an adoptive family and a birthmother that really butted heads at some point or there was some real negative thing, that could really affect the child's perception. If the child had been involved in the meetings and the contact and all of a sudden it changed, like most kids whose parents get divorced, they assume it was because of something he or she caused. They'd either pick up real negative feelings or fears about the birthmother from the adoptive parents or maybe wonder if the birthmother had just disappeared and "rejected" them again.

> The fully disclosed adoption can be socially a liability for the child to have to describe who that other person is. A child does not have the sophistication to be able to put this into place and has to deal with the feelings of other peers. . . . Plus the fact that if they're needy birthparents,

I mean emotionally needy, socially needy . . . this can be an intrusion that is unpredictable for the future.

Although agencies identified potential risks in fully disclosed open adoptions, most still thought the advantages significantly outweighed the risks. One agency indicated that it had some concern that not enough research had been done on the outcomes of fully disclosed adoptions and thought this was essential before it would move from mediated adoptions to fully open.

SUMMARY AND IMPLICATIONS

During the past 5 to 10 years, many adoption agencies have moved fairly rapidly away from their traditional confidential adoption policies and practices and toward offering mediated and direct contact adoptions. Conservative estimates suggest that more than three fourths of all adoption agencies now offer mediated adoptions between birthparents and adoptive parents. Many agencies have moved toward greater openness without any empirical research on which to base their change in practice. The remainder of this book addresses this need for research by providing empirical data on outcomes for adoptive parents, adopted children, and birthparents.

The findings presented in this chapter suggest that agencies typically began offering more open options between 1987 and 1993 because of birthmother demand and competition from nonagency adoptions and other agencies offering openness, and changes in agency values. More than one third of agency personnel interviewed attributed increases in adoption placements to offering open options; the remainder thought openness had not increased or had decreased their placements. Four agencies had closed their adoption programs completely. The majority of agencies are actively involved in initiating contact and negotiating difficulties between birthfamilies and adoptive families in mediated and fully disclosed adoptions. Most agency staff believe that when changes in openness need to be negotiated, families should contact the agency for help, as well as make their own attempts to handle the changes. Agencies that identified many advantages of confidential adoptions in 1987/89 typically cited few advantages in 1993. By 1993, most agencies offered a continuum of openness options (confidential to fully disclosed) but gave clear preference to mediated or fully disclosed adoptions.

In addition, we have noted from our study that many considerations need to be weighed in selecting and negotiating the level of openness. In each type of adoption, problems or concerns may arise. For example, in confidential adoptions, adoptive parents may express fear that the birthmothers wish to reclaim the children. Also, adoptive parents, birthparents, and adopted persons sometimes return to the agency, seeking more information and perhaps contact with other parties. In agency-mediated adoptions, miscommunications can result from the indirect nature of the sharing, and adoptive parents sometimes experience problems deciding how and when to share information, gifts, and pictures with the children. In some mediated adoptions, one party may reject the other's request to move to a fully disclosed adoption. In fully disclosed adoptions, agency staff suggested that the following concerns or questions can arise: (a) determining at what age the child should be included in contact with the birthmother, (b) negotiating the birthmother's role in relation to the child, (c) helping triad members deal with their emotions if one party chooses to break off all contact, (d) helping a child who is having difficulty understanding the role of the birthparent, and (e) addressing sibling concerns in families in which children have different levels of openness in their adoptions.

Most agencies have moved away from their historic belief in confidential adoptions to offering openness options and, in some cases, to discouraging confidential adoptions. These shifts have been, in part, a result of competition from independent adoptions and birthmother demands for openness. In fact, most adoption agencies view the birthmother as their primary client. Agency authority and power in the matching of prospective adoptive parents and birthparents is now being shared. In cases of identified adoptions, birthparents and prospective adoptive parents self-select prior to coming to the agency. Birthmothers are now selecting adoptive parents not only on the basis of their personality and other characteristics but also on their willingness to participate in an open adoption.

Adoption agency personnel have found that ongoing contact between families increases their workload. They are performing the new roles of mediator, educator, and facilitator in openness negotiations. Staff are involved in transmitting correspondence, gifts, and other materials in the case of mediated adoptions. Expanded postadoption services are also being offered for all members of the triad. With increasing numbers of adult adopted persons and birthparents in confidential adoptions returning to agencies for more information or to seek contact, adoption agencies are having to increase staff and to develop fiscal procedures for costing out these new services. These emerging forms of open adoptions have a long-term impact not only on triad members but on the agency as well. It is our hope that the findings presented in this book will help adoption agency personnel weigh the advantages and disadvantages of each type of adoption in the light of research.

3

METHOD

PARTICIPANTS

Adoptive families and birthmothers were recruited for the study through 35 adoption agencies located across the United States. We sought families in which (a) there was least one adopted child (the "target child") between the ages of 4 and 12 at the time of the interview, who was adopted through an agency before his or her first birthday; (b) the adoption was not transracial, international, or "special needs"; and (c) both adoptive parents were married to the partners they had at the time of the adoption. We simultaneously sought birthmothers who made adoption plans for children placed with these families. Participants in the study were located in 23 states from all regions of the country, making this study the only nationwide one of its kind.

In 1986, we contacted approximately 40 adoption agencies across the United States to assess the range of openness arrangements they offered and their interest in participating in the study. Among our primary considerations in selecting agencies for participation was that the agency offer a range of openness options to families and that the staff was willing to follow a random sample process to select participants for the study. We also asked the initial agencies we contacted to nominate other agencies for involvement. After the initial contact, we sent agencies a research prospectus outlining the research design and asked their willingness to participate. The qualifying agencies that originally agreed to participate offered confidential, mediated, and fully disclosed adoptions or believed that some families for whom they had arranged mediated adoptions had subsequently fully disclosed to each other. As recruitment of participants progressed, agencies found that families and birthmothers with confidential adoptions were the most difficult to locate because they generally had not kept in touch with the agency. Therefore, to have a larger number of participants with confidential arrangements, we recruited several agencies specializing in confidential adoptions.

We asked each participating agency to select all children who met the criteria outlined above and then to sample randomly among them within levels of openness until it located a set number of families and birthmothers willing to be interviewed. A few families (12 of 190, or 6.3%) and birthmothers (20 of 169, or 11.8%) were recruited through advertisements in newspapers and periodicals. Data were collected between 1987 and 1992. Although this sample is not a fully random one, participants were specifically *not* recruited on the basis of their success with adoption or their having an interesting story to tell, which is often a problem in volunteer samples.

The study included 720 participants: both parents in 190 adoptive families, at least 1 adopted child in 171 of the families, and 169 birthmothers. Demographics of the sample are included in Table 3.1. The vast majority of adoptive parents were Caucasian, Protestant, and middle to upper middle class. Of the 190 adoptive couples interviewed, 177 identified themselves as Caucasian, 3 as Latino, 1 as African American, and 1 as Latino and Caucasian; 8 couples gave no indication of their race but were identified by interviewers as Caucasian. These couples reflect the population of families who are typically involved in formally adopting unrelated children, and birthmothers who tend to place their children for adoption. According to a 1987 national sample of women 20 to 45 years of age, the proportions of African American women and women of Latino origin who adopt unrelated children are lower than for Caucasian women (Bachrach, Adams, Sambrano, & London, 1990). Similarly, studies of pregnant African American adolescents reveal that they are very unlikely to place a child for adoption through official agency channels, choosing instead to place informally with a relative (Donnelly & Voydanoff, 1991; Sandven & Egeland, 1985). Virtually all adoptive parents in the study had adopted because of infertility. The average level of education was 16.2 years for adoptive fathers and 15.1 for adoptive mothers.

Adoptive fathers ranged in age from 32 to 53 (mean = 40.7) and adoptive mothers from 31 to 50 (mean = 39.1).

The average number of adopted children in each home was 1.9; 90 of the target adopted children were male and 81 were female; and their ages ranged from 4 to 12 (mean = 7.8 years). Target children in 19 of the 190 families were not interviewed: In 8 cases, the child was deemed too young to participate in a valid interview; in 9 cases, the adoptive parents requested that the child not participate; in 1 case, the child refused to be interviewed despite parental encouragement; and in 1 case there was equipment failure.

At the time of the birth of their children, the birthmothers ranged in age from 14 to 36 years (mean = 19.3). Almost two thirds of the birthmothers delivered when they were teenagers. At the time of the study, the birthmothers ranged in age from 21 to 43 (mean = 27.1), and the average number of years of education attained was 13.5. Income ranged from 0 to \$50,000+; the modal income range was between \$20,000 and \$29,000. In terms of ethnicity, 157 (92.9%) were Caucasian, 4 (2.4%) were Latino, 2 (1.2%) were Native American, 1 each was African American and Asian American, and 4 did not list their ethnicity. Half of the birthmothers were currently married, and they had from 1 to 5 children.

VARIATIONS IN OPENNESS

Families were sampled across the full range of openness in the adoption. Four major categories were used to differentiate among levels of openness:

1. *Confidential* (C) adoptions, in which no information was shared between birth- and adoptive parents after 6 months postplacement; (*N* = 62 adoptive families, 52 birthmothers)

2. *Time-limited mediated* (TLM) adoptions, in which information was relayed between adoptive parents and birthmothers by a caseworker at the adoption agency, but the information

TABLE 3.1   Demographic Information

		Adoptive Fathers		Adoptive Mothers		Birthmothers	
		N	%	N	%	N	%
Marital Status							
	Married	190	100	190	100	97	57.4
	Single	0	0	0	0	50	29.6
	Divorced	0	0	0	0	18	10.7
	Widowed	0	0	0	0	2	1.2
	Missing	0	0	0	0	2	1.2
Ethnicity							
	Caucasian	177	93.2	178	93.7	157	92.9
	African American	1	0.5	1	0.5	1	0.6
	Latino	4	2.1	3	1.6	4	2.4
	Asian American	0	0	0	0	1	0.6
	Native American	0	0	0	0	2	1.2
	Missing	8	4.2	8	4.2	4	2.4
Religion							
	Catholic	70	36.8	73	38.4	53	31.4
	Protestant	91	47.9	89	46.8	54	32.0
	Jewish	4	2.1	3	1.6	0	0
	Other	16	8.4	16	8.4	28	16.6
	Missing	9	4.7	9	4.7	34	20.1
Religious Activity							
	Extremely Active	20	10.5	25	13.2	8	4.7
	Very Active	48	25.3	58	30.5	22	13.0
	Active	54	28.4	56	29.5	42	24.9
	Not Very Active	41	21.6	31	16.3	47	27.8
	Inactive	15	7.9	7	3.7	34	20.1
	Not Applicable	4	2.1	5	2.6	7	4.1
	Missing	8	4.2	8	4.2	9	5.3
Income							
	< $20,000	1	0.5	(combined with		59	35
	$20-29,000	18	9.5	adoptive fathers)		50	29.6
	$30-39,000	28	14.7			21	12.4
	$40-49,000	29	15.3			17	10.1
	> $50,000	104	54.7			8	4.7
	Missing	10	5.3			14	8.3

	TABLE 3.1 Continued					
	Adoptive Fathers		*Adoptive Mothers*		*Birthmothers*	
	N	%	N	%	N	%
Was Adopted?						
Yes	2	1.1	3	1.6	15	8.9
No	175	92.1	167	87.9	153	90.5
Missing	13	6.8	20	10.5	1	0.6
Number of Birth Children						
0	139	73.2	137	72.1	0	0
1	32	16.8	34	17.9	69	40.8
2	8	4.2	8	4.2	49	29.0
3	2	1.1	2	1.1	39	23.1
> 3	1	0.5	1	0.5	12	7.1
Missing	8	4.2	8	4.2	0	0
Number of Children Adopted In						
0	0	0	0	0	167	98.8
1	49	25.8	49	25.8	2	1.2
2	107	56.3	107	56.3	0	0
3	19	10.0	19	10.0	0	0
4	6	3.2	6	3.2	0	0
> 4	1	0.5	1	0.5	0	0
Missing	8	4.2	8	4.2	0	0
Number of Children Placed for Adoption						
0	182	95.8	181	95.3	0	0
1	0	0	1	0.5	163	96.4
2	0	0	0	0	4	2.4
3	0	0	0	0	2	1.2
Missing	8	4.2	8	4.2	0	0
	Mean	*Range*	*Mean*	*Range*	*Mean*	*Range*
Age at Interview	40.7	32 to 53	39.1	31 to 50	27.1	21 to 43
Age at Placement	n/a	n/a	n/a	n/a	19.3	14 to 36
Years of Education	16.2	9 to 22	15.1	9 to 20	13.5	8 to 18

sharing had stopped by the time we interviewed the participants; ($N = 17$ adoptive families, 18 birthmothers)

3. *Ongoing mediated* (OM) adoptions, in which information
exchange mediated by the agency was continuing; ($N = 52$
adoptive families, 58 birthmothers)

4. *Fully disclosed* (FD) adoptions, in which direct sharing of
information occurred between adoptive parents and birthmother, usually accompanied by face-to-face meetings. For 57
adoptive families and 41 birthmothers, this contact was *ongoing* at the time of the interview; for 2 adoptive families, the
contact had ceased and the parties did not intend to resume
contact (*time-limited*).

We attempted to interview as many "fully corresponding sets" of
adoptive parents and birthmothers as possible (cases in which the
birthmother, her child by birth, and the family who adopted her child
were all interviewed). The sample included 77 fully corresponding
sets: 11 confidential, 36 mediated, and 30 fully disclosed.

Families were classified into the four main levels of openness
described above, although variations also occurred within each level
of openness. Families in C adoptions were the most homogeneous in
terms of openness because no communication took place between
adoptive family and birthmother. In some cases, adoptive parents or
birthmothers placed "updates" in their files at the agency, without
knowing whether this information would ever be shared with their
counterpart.

Families in mediated adoptions varied quite a bit more in terms
of type and frequency of contact. In the 17 TLM families, all contact
had stopped. In the 52 OM families, contact varied in terms of type
of contact arranged indirectly through the agency (letters, pictures,
gifts, telephone calls) and frequency of contact.

The frequency and intensity of contact in the FD families also
ranged quite widely, from occasional letters or telephone calls to
several meetings per year. The exchange of telephone calls, letters, and
holiday and birthday gifts was more typical. When the adoptive family
lived far away from the birthmother, visits were less frequent, although
letters and telephone calls may have been exchanged more frequently.

In some cases, contact with the birthmother was infrequent, but more contact with other members of her extended family took place. We conducted preliminary analyses to determine any confounding relations between sample demographic factors and levels of openness. No significant differences occurred by level of openness for the following: child's age or age at placement; adoptive parent's age or education; and birthmother's age, education, or age at which the child was placed (Grotevant & McRoy, 1997).

Choice Over Openness Arrangements

Assessing the degree to which adopting couples and birthmothers had initial choice over openness level was quite difficult. Agencies varied in the flexibility of their policies on contact between birthmother and adoptive family. Some prohibited direct contact, others permitted it, others encouraged it, and yet others required it. Some permitted confidential placements but suggested that the waiting time for a C adoption might be much longer than if the adoptive parents were willing to have contact with the birthmother.

Participants' knowledge about openness and options also varied. Some went to an agency not knowing anything about openness or the agency's policies. Others visited multiple agencies before finding one whose philosophy was compatible with theirs. Typically, adoptive parents had two priorities: (a) "getting a baby" and (b) minimizing the wait for a child because most infant placements in the 1980s did take a long time. The agency's policies often had a secondary role in its decision making. One adoptive father put it this way:

> I don't know of any [prospective adoptive parents] who would say, "No, I wouldn't do it," if it has to be an open [adoption]. I think again there is maybe a first choice, a second choice, and a third choice. Let's suppose that I go out to a restaurant to eat, and they have three entrees. They have good, better, and best. Now they're all good, but however, I might be able to get chicken for five dollars, steak for ten dollars, or lobster for fifteen dollars. If I have six dollars, I'm going to order the chicken and enjoy it.

Likewise, birthmothers were primarily interested in arranging good placements for their children. Most birthmothers in C adoptions, however, had that level of openness because it was the only option the agency offered or the only type of adoption with which they were familiar (see Figure 6.2b, p. 141).

For almost all participating adoptive parents and birthmothers, the agency that arranged the adoption had a formal and often elaborate preadoption process that socialized clients into the agency's perspective on openness. Although our data on this point are limited, it appears that some clients stopped working through some agencies if they perceived too large a gap between their philosophy about adoption and the agency's. Other participants proceeded with the agency's preparation program and had their philosophy shaped in the process. By the time an adoption placement was made, clients generally had been well socialized into the agency's philosophy about openness. Interviews with agency workers suggested that placements were generally not made to couples who were not able to work within the agency's placement framework.

To what degree did self-selection of adoptive parents or birthparents into differing levels of openness occur? As one can see from the discussion above, the actual amount of self-selection is unknown. It appears that some adoptive and birthparents played no role in choosing openness arrangements either because they were not aware of the options or because their desire to complete the placement overshadowed openness considerations. Others played a more passive role, perhaps accepting openness arrangements that might not have been their first choice in order to facilitate the placement. Yet others made proactive moves to ensure that certain arrangements were in place. How much did the self-selection of adoptive parents or birthparents into differing levels of openness bias the results of this study? We do know that demographic and background variables (e.g., age, education) were not related to openness arrangements. A fuller answer to this question is unknown. We cannot claim causal links between openness levels and outcomes because this is a correlational study and family members were not randomly assigned to different openness "conditions." Our data do suggest that, following placement, adoptive kinship members did evaluate their openness arrangements and make adjustments that they deemed appropriate, as we shall see next.

Change in Openness Over Time

Although this report is only from one wave of data collection, the interviews did include questions about participants' history with the adoption. Through these retrospective questions, we learned that almost two thirds of the FD adoptions in this sample did not start out that way: 51% began as mediated adoptions, and 14% began as C adoptions. In many cases, trust and mutual respect were established between adoptive parents and birthmother over time until a decision to share full identifying information was made.

The following case examples illustrate some changes in openness that occurred between placement and our first interview with the families. In some cases, the frequency or nature of contact decreased (see first example); in others, the contact increased (see second example). The changes were initiated in various ways: sometimes by the adoptive parents, the birthmother, the birthgrandparent, or the caseworker.

Now that she is married with children, it is not as easy for her to maintain the closeness we had before. She has tried to go on and make her own life, and she's more on the edge of our life than she was in the beginning. There's also a pretty good distance geographically between us now. (adoptive father, ongoing fully disclosed)

We've escalated the amount of openness after that first meeting. Our relationship has become more relaxed, natural, open, comfortable. We hadn't planned on any more meetings, but we broke some barriers as far as meeting again, meeting as the child got older, so we have increased our intimacy. We're in the process of deciding where to stop with that. (adoptive mother, ongoing fully disclosed)

Child's Perception of Openness and Inclusion in Contact

Interviews from adoptive fathers and adoptive mothers were coded separately for the kinds of information they had shared with the adopted child and whether the child had been included in any contact that was occurring with the birthmother. For families in which this type of sharing or contact occurred, each adoptive parent interview was coded as either including or excluding the child from the following types of openness activities: pictures from the birthmother, letters from the birthmother, and meetings with the birthmother. When discrepancies were noted between mother and father interviews, the code for the adoptive mother was used unless the adoptive mother's response was unclear and the adoptive father's response could be coded. The adoptive mother's code was used because, in most instances, the adoptive mother was the one who maintained contact with the birthmother and therefore had the most accurate knowledge of the child's participation.

Comparison of parents' and children's reports of openness revealed gaps between parents' participation in open arrangements and (a) their children's perception of openness and (b) the inclusion of the adopted child in the communication (see Tables 3.2 and 3.3). In C and TLM adoptions, most children said they had no information about birthparents or, at most, minimal non-identifying information such as nationality or talents. In OM adoptions, roughly one third of the children indicated they had no information, one third indicated they had some non-identifying information, and one third indicated they had been involved in some form of communication. Parents in all nine TLM families (for which data were codable) withheld from their children the information they received during their short period of information exchange. Almost half of the children in OM adoptions were excluded from the contact their adoptive parents had with their birthmothers, but most of these children were not aware of their being excluded. The anonymity associated with information exchange in mediated arrangements may make it easier to keep the birthmother psychologically distant so that information need not be exchanged when it is received. Some parents in mediated adoptions describe the information they possess as important to have available should their children indicate an interest in their birthfamilies' history at some unspecified future point. These adoptive parents do not feel a need for the children to participate actively in the information sharing, but they do want to be able to answer their children's questions as they arise.

In the FD group, 8 children reported having no information, basic information, or non-identifying information. Parents of 7 children in this group reported withholding information (see Table 3.3). Discrep-

TABLE 3.2 Correspondence Between Child's Perception of Openness and Family Openness Category

| Family Openness Category | Child's Perception of Openness | | | |
	No/Basic Information	Non-Identifying Information	Ongoing/ Direct Contact	Total
Confidential	36	18	1	55
Time-Limited Mediated	8	5	0	13
Ongoing Mediated	14	12	14	40
Ongoing Fully Disclosed	3	5	47	55
Total	61	40	62	163

NOTE: The child in the ongoing/direct contact group who has a confidential adoption is correct. This family knows recent information about the birthmother because the agency contacted the parents to find out whether they wanted to adopt a subsequent child from the same birthmother. The parents shared this information with the child in their decision-making process. Child's perception of openness could not be coded for 8 children.

ancies not accounted for by withholding information may be a result of a lack of comprehension of the information on the part of the child. In some FD adoptions, the young adopted children who meet with their birthmothers may not have been told that the women with whom they meet are their birthmothers or, if they have been told, may not fully understand what *birthmother* means. The children may perceive them as friends, relatives, or godmothers. Most of the children in FD adoptions (86%) were included in meetings with birthparents and were aware of the arrangements.

PROCEDURES

Each adoptive family was interviewed in their home in one session that lasted 3 to 4 hours. The session included separate interviews with each parent and with the target adopted child; administration of several questionnaires; and a joint couples interview with the adoptive parents. Each of the birthmothers was interviewed in her home, at the agency, or by telephone; they, too, completed several questionnaires.

TABLE 3.3   Adoptive Parents' Perception of Children's Inclusion or Exclusion in Openness

| | Family Openness Category | | |
Status of Child's Access to Information	Time-Limited Mediated	Ongoing Mediated	Ongoing Fully Disclosed
Inclusion	0	19	43
Exclusion	9	20	7

NOTE: Parental withholding of information was unable to be coded or did not apply for 16 children; 57 children had confidential arrangements and are not included in this table.

Adoptive Parent Measures

The following measures were administered separately to the adoptive father and the adoptive mother:

Demographic Questionnaire. This measure requested basic information about age, education, occupation, income, ethnicity, religion, and family composition.

Adoptive Parent Interview. The interview protocol included numerous questions concerning motivation for adoption, experience with adoptive placement, and experiences and feelings about level of adoptive openness.

Kirk Adoption Questionnaire. This measure assessed the amount of acknowledgment of difference, empathy, and communication in the adoptive family. Questions are answered on Likert scales, once pertaining to the period around 6 months after the child's adoption and once pertaining to the present (Kirk, 1981, as modified by McRoy, Grotevant, & Zurcher, 1988).

Child Adaptive Behavior Inventory (CABI). The CABI (Miller, 1987) is a 91-item questionnaire that each parent completed about the target child. It is organized in terms of 20 scales. Factor analyses of the 20 scales were conducted, and four summary scales emerged:

1. *Poor Emotional Control* (alpha = .92; hyperactive, antisocial, negative engagement, hostile, tension, fairness [reverse scored], calm response [reverse scored], and kindness [reverse scored])

2. *Social Isolation* (alpha = .88; apathy, introversion, depression, victim, extraversion [reverse scored])

3. *Symptoms* (alpha = .74; somatic symptoms, imitates, physical symptoms)

4. *Intellectual Engagement* (alpha = .90; intelligence, creativity, task orientation, distractibility [reverse scored])

Higher scores indicate higher levels of the quality indicated by the scale name.

Parenting Stress Index (PSI). The PSI (Abidin, 1986) is a self-report questionnaire administered to each parent; scales focus on aspects of the child, the parent, and their context that might contribute to parenting stress. The measure has been normed on both clinical and nonclinical samples of parents.

Twenty Statements Test (TST). The TST (Kuhn & McPartland, 1954) provides an open-ended and unstructured way for participants to describe themselves. The instrument allows researchers to observe in a systematic fashion aspects of the self based on social relationships (e.g., those involving adoption).

Adopted Child Measures

Child Interview. This interview was designed to elicit open discussion of the child's experiences and feelings about his or her adoptive family situation and knowledge of, and attitudes about, his or her birthparents; it covered general adoption issues, as well as issues specific to the level of openness of the child's adoption. Special training was provided for interviewers who worked with the children, and interviewers spent extra time developing rapport with each child before the interview.

Understanding of Adoption Scale. This scale (a) was administered as part of the child interview to examine children's understanding of adoption, nature of adoptive family relationships, motives underlying adoption, and adoptive placement and (b) was scored in terms of 6 levels of social-cognitive understanding of the adoptive family relationship, ranging from Level 0 (no understanding of adoption) to Level 5 (adoptive parent-child relationship is seen as permanent and based on the legal transfer of rights from birth to adoptive parents; Brodzinsky, Singer, & Braff, 1984).

Self-Perception Scale for Children. This measure assessed self-concept in children who were age 7.5 years and older; 36 items scored for 6 subscales: cognitive competence, athletic competence, social acceptance, physical appearance, behavioral conduct, and general self-worth (Harter, 1985). On this measure, a score of 1 represents low self-worth; 4, high self-worth. The measure is based on Harter's theory about the self-system (1983, 1984), which acknowledges the importance of assessing both domain-specific self-perceptions, as well as the child's overall sense of self-worth. In this study, the global self-worth (alpha = .78; Harter, 1985) scale is used because of our interest in the link between adoptive relationships and the child's global self-evaluation.

Twenty Statements Test. See above.

Birthmother Measures

Demographic Questionnaire. This measure requested basic information about age, education, occupation, income, ethnicity, religion, and family composition.

Birthmother Interview. This protocol included an extensive set of questions dealing with experience in making the adoption plan and the current adoption situation, including relationships with her birthchild, the adoptive family, her family of origin, and the placing agency.

Ego Identity Interview. These questions were administered at the beginning of the birthmother interview and examined exploration and commitment in the domain of career identity (Grotevant & Cooper, 1981).

Intimacy Interview. These questions followed the Ego Identity Interview and assessed levels of relationship maturity, from self-focused, to role-focused, to individuated-connected through questions addressing caring, commitment, and communication in close relationships (White, Speisman, Costos, Kelly, & Bartis, 1984).

Self-Perception Profile for Adults. This questionnaire included 12 subscales in which individuals make self-evaluations regarding competence and adequacy (Messer & Harter, 1986).

Health Checklist. This measure was a checklist for common stress-related physical symptoms (Pennebaker, 1982).

Twenty Statements Test. See above.

CODING PROCESS

To gain the most complete picture possible, self-report measures were complemented with ratings of data gathered through interviews. Coding schemes were developed to assess several issues of interest (described in subsequent chapters), and ratings for variables were based on the entire transcript of the interview of interest. Coders made judgments that required moderate to high levels of inference; therefore, all global coding was performed by graduate students, mature undergraduates in the social sciences, or the coprincipal investigators. Our general protocol was to train coders to an initial reliability of at least .80 on the system they were using (percent exact agreement) by using appropriate codebooks and criterion interviews. Interrater reliability was monitored throughout the course of coding. Each interview was coded independently by two coders; disagreements were resolved through discussion. Interrater reliabilities were calculated before consensus discussion. Percent exact agreement was used in reliability calculations because it required perfect agreement between coders and was therefore a stringent criterion.

IN THE WORDS OF THE PARTICIPANTS

Throughout this book, we use quotes from the participants in the study and vignettes written about them to let readers learn as much as possible from the words of the participants themselves. Quotations are cited verbatim from interview transcripts unless doing so would compromise the confidentiality we pledged to our participants. In these instances, to protect confidentiality, we changed certain details to de-identify the quotes without altering the basic meaning of the passage. After each quote, the role of the person in the adoptive kinship network and level of openness in the adoption is indicated.

4

OUTCOMES FOR CHILDREN

With Gretchen Miller Wrobel, Susan Ayers-Lopez,
Julie K. Kohler, and Meredith Friedrick

I n Chapter 1, we discussed the shifts occurring in adoption practice
in North America and the debates surrounding the shifts. Regardless of one's position on openness, most adoption professionals
contend that their viewpoint is "in the best interests of the child." We
argue that empirical research provides the strongest foundation for a
"best interests" argument; thus, the focus of this chapter is on outcomes for the adopted children in our study.

Although the professional debate about openness continues,
adoptive parents must make decisions now regarding the ways they
include their adopted child in the information sharing or contact with
the birthmother. The difficulty of this decision is exacerbated by
having no existing societal norm for this type of information sharing
(Siegel, 1993). It has therefore become important to examine not only
the impact of openness in adoption for the adopted child but also the
effect of the child's own understanding of, and participation in, the
openness arrangement.

Most research conducted on openness has reported perspectives
of the adults involved and not those of the children. In this chapter
on outcomes for children, we report both the self-reported perspectives of the participating children and the adoptive parents' perceptions of their children's adjustment.

The controversy about the effects of openness on children centers
around five issues: (a) quality of the relationship between the adoptive

parents and their child; (b) fears and unwelcome fantasies the child might have; (c) the child's understanding of adoption in general; (d) the child's self-esteem and emerging sense of identity; and (e) the child's socioemotional adjustment. The debate about each of these issues is explored, and then results relevant to these issues are presented.

QUALITY OF THE PARENT-CHILD RELATIONSHIP

Kraft, Palombo, Mitchell, Woods, Schmidt, and Tucker (1985) cautioned that openness in adoption could jeopardize the development of a secure attachment to the adoptive parents. These authors suggested that, in an open adoption, contact through letters or meetings with the birthparents could interfere with the adoptive parents' relationship with the child. Advocates of openness, in contrast, argue that adopted children are able to have high-quality relationships with multiple adults and that they do not become confused about who their parents are. Belbas (1987), in a small study of families participating in open adoptions, concluded that openness did not adversely affect parents' everyday lives or their sense of entitlement as parents.

FEARS AND UNWELCOME FANTASIES

Some (e.g., Kraft, Palombo, Mitchell, Woods, Schmidt, & Tucker, 1985; Rosenberg, 1992; Wieder, 1978) argue that telling children aged 6 to 8 about their adoption and providing information about birthparents could increase their fears and unwelcome fantasies because children are not yet cognitively able to understand the concept of adoptive permanence. Bevan and Pierce (1994) speculated that, in open adoptions, children could misinterpret information given to them about their birthparents. Advocates of openness (e.g., Silber & Dorner, 1990), in contrast, argue that open adoption allows a child to obtain answers to questions and to satisfy her or his curiosities without feeling disloyal to adoptive parents. "He also has a sense of belonging with his adoptive parents since he knows his birthparents selected them to parent him. This has tremendous implications for giving the child permission to develop bonds with his adoptive parents" (p. 15).

UNDERSTANDING OF ADOPTION

Children and adults in the adoptive kinship network bring differing levels of cognitive sophistication to bear in understanding and interpreting the information available to them. Brodzinsky and colleagues conducted empirical research with children in confidential adoptions and found that children's understanding of adoption undergoes a systematic developmental course that parallels their more general cognitive development (A. B. Brodzinsky, 1990; D. M. Brodzinsky, 1987; Brodzinsky, Schechter, et al., 1984; Brodzinsky, Singer, & Braff, 1984; Singer, Brodzinsky, & Braff, 1982). Silber and Dorner (1990) believe that openness facilitates the rate at which children understand the concept of adoption. For example, they believe that a child as young as 2½ years of age can understand the concept of "birthmother."

Children's understanding of adoption, openness, and related issues develops over time, along with the more general course of their cognitive and emotional development. Adults who use the services of adoption agencies are socialized into adoption through preplacement screening and education. These processes help adoptive and birthparents develop in their understanding of adoption and openness issues as well. For example, communication between birthmother and adoptive parents is influenced by what information they choose to share within their level of openness. Once information is exchanged between the adults in the system, the next decision is what shared information will be communicated to the adopted child. Regardless of how much available information is shared with the adopted child, she or he must use cognitive and environmental resources to construct a personal view of how much openness exists, which in turn influences the context in which the child's own development occurs.

Information is not necessarily shared equally among members of the adoptive kinship network, nor does contact necessarily include all family members. For example, parents might be concerned for an adopted sibling in the family who has a different level of openness. In a desire to equate the available information across children in the family, adoptive parents may withhold information from the child to whom it is potentially available. The parents might also think the child is too young to understand or handle the information or contact. They might also withhold information if they perceive that the birthmother's communication is troubled or that she is not doing well at the time.

Other professionals have suggested that outcomes for adopted children should be most positive when the children are able to have a positive image of their birthparents. Pannor and Baran (1984) suggested that adopted children who have pictures, personal contacts, or letters can gain a better understanding of their birthparents' situation and are therefore less likely to feel rejected by them.

SELF-ESTEEM AND IDENTITY

Advocates of confidentiality in adoption contend that such arrangements provide the child with a clear sense of who her or his family is, a clear sense of her or his place in the family, and a foundation for self-esteem. "Confidential adoptions provide opportunities for adoptive parents to nurture children as their own and in turn allow those children to internalize a single set of parental values. Open adoption allows the involvement of birth parents who may offer a differing set of values" (Byrd, 1988, p. 22).

The clinical literature, however, suggests differently—that the best outcomes for adopted children can be expected when the adoptive parents have provided a link for the children with their birthparents by giving them information about the relationship. Melina and Roszia (1993) believe that adopted children have a right to all available information about their origins and circumstances of their adoption. Provision of an information link is expected to give the children a greater sense of continuity with their personal history and thus to enhance their sense of self-esteem (Kirk, 1964, 1981).

SOCIOEMOTIONAL ADJUSTMENT

Much professional debate surrounds whether adopted children are at risk for developmental or emotional problems. Although many studies have noted an overrepresentation of adopted children (especially during adolescence) among clinical populations and have noted a small but consistent trend toward greater externalizing problems among nonclinical adolescents (see Wierzbicki, 1993, for meta-analysis), these studies have not examined possible connections between degree of openness in the child's adoption and socioemotional outcomes. Consistent with the rationales presented earlier in this chapter, critics of openness tend to believe that living in open arrangements would be confusing to children and cause them to have divided loyalties between their birthparents and their adoptive parents, thus causing difficulties in relationships and their sense of security. Advocates of openness argue instead that outcomes are better when adopted children have links with their birthparents that provide a greater sense of continuity and personal history, thus enhancing their senses of self-esteem and identity.

Given these varied viewpoints and the paucity of available research, the practices recommended by those writing in the professional literature need to be evaluated from a broad perspective that accounts for the development of the child within the context of relationships established by birth and adoption. Thus, to contribute better understanding of the link between the differing styles of communication found in various levels of openness and children's development, child outcomes relevant to the five issues outlined above are the focus of this chapter. These outcomes are viewed from three perspectives: (a) parental report of level of openness, (b) child's report of level of openness, and (c) degree to which adopted children were included in all applicable information sharing.

METHOD

Participants and Measures

Participants being considered in this chapter include the 171 adopted target children, 190 adoptive mothers, and 190 adoptive fathers described in Chapter 3. The children ranged in age from 4 to 12 at the time of the interview. The measures relevant to this chapter include the child and parent interviews, the Children's Understanding of Adoption Scale, the Self-Perception Scale for Children, and the Child Adaptive Behavior Inventory, all of which were also described in Chapter 3. Further details are next presented about some specific variables reported in this chapter.

Variables

Permanence of the Adoptive Parent-Child Relationship. Parent interviews were coded with respect to parents' perceptions of the strength of the parent-child relationship as it is projected into the future (PERMANENCE). Often, statements coded with regard to permanence were made when parents were discussing their willingness to help their children learn more about their birthfamilies or search for their birthparents when they were older. Permanence was coded on a 3-point scale: (a) strong concerns about permanence, (b) moderate concerns balanced by feelings of certainty, and (c) strong sense of permanence. Higher degrees of permanence were indicated by statements describing a parent's sense that her or his relationship with the child will endure despite whatever relationships the child might develop with birthfamily members. Permanence was coded independently of the positive or negative quality of the relationship itself.

Adopted Child Satisfaction With Openness. A child's satisfaction with, and desire for, change in openness level in the adoption arrangement was coded from the adopted child interview. Satisfaction with the degree of openness in the adoption was rated (interrater reliability = .64) on a scale where 1 represented *dissatisfied* (child stated a desire for a change in openness), 2, *neutral* (child did not report any feelings of being satisfied or dissatisfied), and 3, *satisfied* (child expressed satisfaction with current levels of openness).

Understanding of Adoption Scale. This scale (Brodzinsky, Singer, & Braff, 1984) was administered as part of the child interview to examine children's understanding of adoption, including the nature of adoptive family relationships, motives underlying adoption, and adoptive placement. The interview questions developed by Brodzinsky et al. (Brodzinsky, Pappas, Singer, & Braff, 1981; Brodzinsky, Singer, & Braff, 1984) were analyzed for children's conception of the "nature of the adoptive family relationship and the motives underlying adoption and adoption placement" (Brodzinsky, Singer, & Braff, 1984, p. 870). The interview was scored in terms of 6 levels of understanding of the adoptive family relationship:

Level 0, the child exhibits no understanding of adoption.

Level 1, the child fails to differentiate between adoption and birth, tending instead to fuse the two concepts together.

Level 2, the child clearly differentiates between adoption and birth as alternative paths to parenthood and accepts that the adoptive family relationship is permanent but does not understand why.

Level 3, the child differentiates between adoption and birth but is unsure about the permanence of the adoptive parent-child relationship.

Level 4, the child's description of the adoptive family relationship is characterized by a quasi-legal sense of permanence.

Level 5, the adoptive parent-child relationship is seen as permanent and based on the legal transfer of rights from birth to adoptive parents.

Descriptions of the levels were taken from Brodzinsky, Singer, and Braff's (1984) published work and represent degrees of cognitive sophistication in understanding the concept of adoption. The child received one numerical score for adoptive understanding level based on the Brodzinsky interview questions, using the entire interview as a source of information. Brodzinsky, Singer, and Braff reported interrater agreement equaling .85. Our interrater agreement, based on the entire sample, was comparable at .89.

Adopted Child Curiosity. A child's curiosity about birthparents was coded from the adopted child interview. The children's responses (interrater reliability = .82) were judged to fall into one of three broad categories: 1 represented *not curious;* 2, *curious;* and 3, *very curious.*

Socioemotional Adjustment. Variables assessing socioemotional adjustment were taken from the Child Adaptive Behavior Inventory

(Miller, 1987), which is a 91-item questionnaire organized in terms of 20 scales. Factor analyses of the 20 scales were conducted, and 4 summary scales emerged:

1. *Poor Emotional Control* (alpha =. 92; hyperactive, antisocial, negative engagement, hostile, tension, fairness [reverse scored], calm response [reverse scored], and kindness [reverse scored])

2. *Social Isolation* (alpha = .88; apathy, introversion, depression, victim, extraversion [reverse scored])

3. *Symptoms* (alpha = .74; somatic symptoms, imitates, physical symptoms)

4. *Intellectual Engagement* (alpha = .90; intelligence, creativity, task orientation, distractibility [reverse scored])

Higher scores indicate higher levels of the quality indicated by the scale name. Separate scores were derived for mothers' and fathers' perceptions.

RESULTS

The five issues of (a) quality of the parent-child relationship, (b) fears and unwelcome fantasies, (c) understanding of adoption, (d) self-esteem and identity, and (e) socioemotional adjustment were studied by using three perspectives. First, children were grouped according to the openness categories presented in Chapter 3 (called "family openness categories" in this chapter); second, they were grouped by child's perception of openness; and third, they were grouped according to the extent to which the adopted children were included in the communications occurring with their birthmothers (according to the adoptive parents' reports). The "inclusion" group consisted of children with whom parents shared all forms of contact that were applicable to their families (pictures, letters, meetings). The "exclusion" group consisted of children from whom the parents withheld one or more forms of applicable contact; for example, a girl may read her birthmother's letters but is not aware that the birthmother meets with her adoptive mother. The inclusion/exclusion analyses for self-perception, curiosity, and satisfaction with openness did not include the children in confidential adoptions, in which issues of inclusion are irrelevant. The degree of agreement between the family openness code and the child's openness code, and the inclusion of the child in the communication, were detailed in Tables 3.2 and 3.3.

Quality of the Adoptive Parent-Child Relationship

The key relationship quality issue raised in the adoption literature concerns security of attachment, one aspect of which is the sense of permanence of the relationship as it is projected into the future (see method section of this chapter for details about the permanence variable). For both adoptive mothers and adoptive fathers, the presence of a strong sense of permanence was the most frequently coded response across all levels of openness. Permanence was first examined from the perspective of the family openness code. These analyses revealed that feelings of permanence differed statistically across levels of openness for adoptive fathers but not for adoptive mothers. Scheffé tests revealed that fathers' sense of permanence in the fully disclosed families was significantly higher than in the ongoing mediated adoptive families. The highest proportions coded as "strong permanence" were in the fully disclosed adoptions for both mothers and fathers.

The same pattern (significant difference for fathers' perception of permanence but not for mothers') was evident when permanence was examined as a function of the child's view of how open the adoption was: Although "strong permanence" was the most frequent code across all levels of openness, fewer concerns about permanence were expressed in the families in which the children were aware of the nature of the openness. Finally, from the perspective of the child's inclusion in openness, a significant pattern once again emerged for fathers' perspectives on permanence ($\chi^2 = 7.44$, $p = .024$). For both mothers' and fathers' reports, approximately two thirds of the cases in which some concerns about permanence were voiced were among families in which the children were excluded from contact, and approximately two thirds of the cases in which strong permanence was registered were in families in which the children were included in the openness.

> When Mrs. Werner talked about the adoption of her son, it was clear that she feels a strong sense of permanence in their relationship. She told how she felt closely tied to the child immediately after placement, bonded by "the inseparable love of a parent to a child." Mrs. Werner has thought about her son's future well-being. She envisions herself and her husband as present and active in their son's life, through adolescence and into adulthood. She thinks of different circumstances in her son's life that might cause him to seek out his birthparents, but again in thinking of those circumstances she always imagines herself and her husband as part of the picture.

Fears and Unwelcome Fantasies

The issue of fears and unwelcome fantasies was evaluated by assessing children's satisfaction with the level of openness they were experiencing and their curiosity about their birthparents.

Satisfaction With Openness. Children's satisfaction with their current openness situation did not differ as a function of family openness category, child perception of openness, or parental withholding of information. Younger children were more satisfied than older children with their level of openness when viewed from the child's perception of openness ($F(1, 125) = 4.14, p = .04$). Younger children were also more satisfied than older children when viewed from the perspective of the family openness category ($F(1, 117) = 5.49, p = .02$), with the exception of children in the fully disclosed group. An openness by age interaction ($F(1, 117) = 7.80, p = .001$) revealed that older children, especially males, were more satisfied with their level of openness than younger children in the fully disclosed group only.

Curiosity. Children in all openness groups demonstrated curiosity about their birthparents. Curiosity about birthparents was not differentially related to the family openness category or to child's perception of openness. Girls were more curious than boys when openness was viewed by using the family openness category ($F(2, 113) = 4.53, p = .036$). This finding was supported by a trend in the same direction when child's perception of openness was used ($F(1, 123) = 3.89$, $p = .051$).

Here is an example of the questions asked by a child in a confidential adoption:

I (interviewer): What have you asked about your adoption?

R (respondent): Oh, I asked my mom how old was my birthmom when she had me, and she said, "17." And then I've been asking her how old she would be now, and she said, "Around 23 or 25." And I asked her what she looked like, and she said she doesn't really know because she hasn't met her.

I: How did you feel about asking those questions?

R: Well, I felt like, um, anxious to hear what—how old my birthparents were and if my mom ever saw her, my birthmom and my birthdad. And that's all. (age 9, confidential adoption)

Another child had many questions and actively sought answers:

My dad says, like, I kept on asking, you know, and asking all of my neighbors and teachers like, "Was it you?" but it was none of them. "I'm here; who did it; who was I?" I asked questions like what is the color of her hair, and I asked if I could have a picture. (age 10, fully disclosed adoption)

When asked what role his birthparents play currently in his life, the child replied,

They're just birthparents; they're not really anything but birthparents. They're just like people you know but you don't see. Actually, what I think in my mind is that I really have two families. I've got them in one of my families, and I've got my mom and dad in my other family. I kind of think of it that way, and it's easier to me that way. (age 10, fully disclosed)

For some children, issues of curiosity indicated fears they had about their birthparents:

> Sometimes I get scared that she [birthmother] will take me away. Mom says that she wanted me, but she just had to give me up because she didn't have any money. And I start thinking that she might get more money and come and take me away. (age 7, confidential adoption)

> Yeah, yeah. If they're dead, if they're alive, and um . . . I don't know. (age 8, time-limited mediated adoption)

Parental withholding of information ($F(1, 67) = 2.82, p = .10$) was not differentially related to curiosity, but there was an exclusion by gender interaction ($F(1, 67) = 4.39, p = .04$) and an age by gender interaction ($F(1, 67) = 4.13, p = .047$).

For both older and younger children, the included females were the most curious, with older females showing the highest levels of curiosity. In the excluded groups, younger males rated themselves as curious, whereas females rated themselves as closer to not curious. For the older children, excluded females were more curious than males but less so than included females. Older children were more curious than younger children when viewed from the family openness category, the adopted child's perspective, and parental withholding of information.

Understanding of Adoption

Descriptions of the levels of understanding of adoption (Brodzinsky, Singer, & Braff, 1984) are provided in Table 4.1, along with the number of children scored at each level, their mean age, and the age range of children scoring at each level. A strong linear relation ($F(5, 163) = 20.5, p < .001$) was found between children's age and level of understanding of adoption, which is illustrated in Figure 4.1. Only 33 of the 169 children with valid scores on this variable were at either Level 4 or Level 5, which indicate reasonably clear understanding of adoption.

Children in the study varied considerably in their understanding of the concept of adoption. At the youngest developmental levels, some children had no idea what the word meant. In responding to the question "What does the word *adopted* mean to you?" however, an older child answered:

TABLE 4.1   Levels of Understanding of Adoption

Level	Description of Level of Understanding	N	Mean Age	Age Range
Level 0	Children exhibit no understanding of adoption.	8	5.8	4.9–8.8
Level 1	Children fail to differentiate between adoption and birth; instead, they tend to fuse the two concepts together.	22	6.4	4.7–9.6
Level 2	Children clearly differentiate between adoption and birth as alternative paths to parenthood, and they accept that the adoptive family relationship is permanent but do not understand why. At best, they rely on a sense of faith ("My mother told me") or notions of possession ("The child belongs to the other parents now") to justify the permanent nature of the parent-child relationship.	75	7.5	4.7–12.9
Level 3	Children differentiate between adoption and birth but are unsure about the permanence of the adoptive parent-child relationship. Biological parents are seen as having the potential for reclaiming guardianship over the child at some future but unspecified time.	31	8.9	5.4–11.9
Level 4	Children's descriptions of the adoptive family relationship are characterized by a quasi-legal sense of permanence. Specifically, they refer to "signing papers" or invoke some authority, such as a judge, lawyer, doctor, or social worker, who in some vague way "makes" the parent-child relationship permanent.	19	9.5	6.6–12.6
Level 5	The adoption relationship is now characterized as permanent, involving the legal transfer of rights and/or responsibilities for the child from the biological parents to the adoptive parents.	14	10.5	8.0–12.1

SOURCE: Descriptions from Brodzinsky, Singer, & Braff (1984).

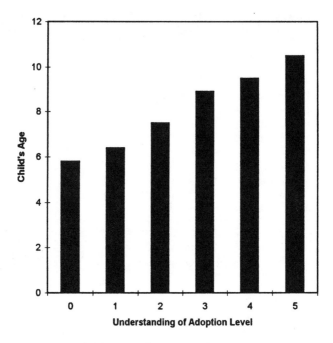

Figure 4.1 Mean Age of Children in Different Stages of Understanding of Adoption

Well, pretty much that it [the child] once had parents, well, they had me, and they couldn't afford or provide, you know, enough or whatever for me, so they, they had the heart to give me up, you know, to get, to be better in life. I mean, some people wouldn't do that. (age 12, fully disclosed adoption)

One issue differentiating among levels of children's understanding is the permanence of the adoption arrangement. Some children grasped the notion of adoption in part but did not understand its permanence:

I: What does the word *adopted* mean to you?

R: Adopted? It mostly means that I was not really like given up, but put into another parents' life for a while, you know.

I: Okay.

R: Those other parents still care for me, and they will come to me when the time is right. (age 11, ongoing mediated adoption)

In another case:

I: Suppose a man and woman want to adopt a child. Is that child theirs forever?

R: Unless they couldn't handle it just like the other person. (age 10, confidential adoption)

Another child responded differently:

I: Suppose a man and a woman adopted a child. Is that child theirs forever?

R: Yes.

I: How do you know that?

R: Well, it's like nobody can take it away 'cause one, it's adopted. It's like their real child, it's not like nobody can take it away 'cause even if the birthmother wanted it, I don't think that she could take it away 'cause it was officially adopted. (age 10, fully disclosed adoption)

Analyses connecting understanding of adoption with openness levels controlled for children's age statistically. The family openness category was not differentially related to understanding of adoption ($F(3, 166) = 1.07$, $p = .36$). Gender did interact with openness ($F(3, 166) = 3.98$, $p = .009$). As can be seen in Figure 4.2, the boys in ongoing mediated adoptions have the lowest level of understanding of adoption, falling between failing to differentiate between adoption and birth as alternative pathways to parenthood (Level 1) and differentiating between adoption and birth, accepting adoption as permanent (Level 2), but not understanding why.

A statistical trend linked child's perception of openness with children's understanding of adoption ($F(2, 160) = 2.84$, $p = .062$). The children's level of understanding increases as the children report having more information about their birthparents, with females in the

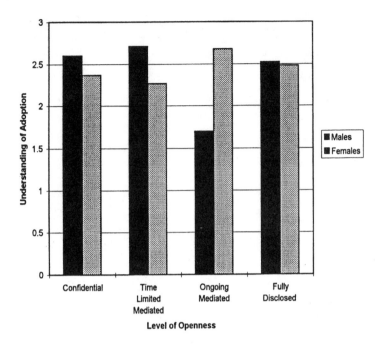

Figure 4.2 Adjusted Mean Levels of Understanding of Adoption by Level of Openness and Gender

nonidentifying information group having the highest understanding. When children were included in all forms of contact applicable to their situation, understanding of adoption was higher than when they were not included in the contact ($F(1, 97) = 8.61$, $p = .004$). The highest levels of understanding were reported by those in the inclusion group.

Self-Esteem and Identity

Children participating in all types of adoptions reported having adequate self-esteem, as described by the Global Self-Worth Scale of the *Self-Perception Profile for Children* (Harter, 1985). This measure was only administered to the 75 children in the sample who were age 7½ and older. The means for all groups ranged from 2.63 to 3.13, indicating positive self-worth. These scores are comparable with the range of 2.76 to 3.24 for third- through sixth-grade children reported in the manual of the *Self-Perception Profile for Children* (Harter, 1985). Global self-worth was not differentially related to the family openness category, adopted child's perception of openness, or child's inclusion in the openness.

Socioemotional Adjustment

Socioemotional adjustment was assessed by means of the four primary factors on the CABI. Separate MANCOVAs were performed for the four factors as perceived by the child's mother and the four factors as perceived by the child's father. Independent variables were child gender and adoption openness, and covariates were child age and age of placement. For mothers' perceptions, no significant relations were found between openness and the CABI factors, but a main multivariate effect for gender (Pillai's trace $= .086$, $p = .008$) was found, which was significant for the Poor Emotional Control scale only ($F(1, 156) = 7.22$, $p = .008$). Age of placement was not a significant covariate for any of the CABI scales for mothers. Child age was a significant covariate only on the Poor Emotional Control scale ($\beta = -.17$, $t = -2.09$, $p = .038$). For fathers' perceptions, a significant multivariate effect was found for family openness level (Pillai's trace $= .150$, $p = .024$) and for gender (Pillai's trace $= .069$, $p = .030$), but none of the univariate follow-up tests were significant, suggesting that these effects were not very strong. Neither age nor age at placement was a significant covariate on any of the CABI variables for fathers.

Presence of Siblings and Parental Choice to Withhold Information

A chi-square analysis was conducted by using families that had an adopted sibling of the target child to examine whether having a sibling with a different openness level would influence parental decision to exclude the target child from information sharing. Given the sometimes incomplete information provided by parents regarding the target child's sibling, the exact degree of difference in openness between the siblings could not be fully determined. The analysis was thus conducted by using the gross differentiation of same or different openness level between siblings. A trend indicated that when openness levels of the target child and a sibling are the same, parents are less likely to exclude the target child from information sharing and that when the openness levels of the siblings are different, parents move more toward exclusion from information sharing ($\chi^2(1) = 3.15, p = .076$).

Intercorrelations Among the Child Outcome Variables

Several child outcome variables were related to each other in intriguing ways. Taken together, the pattern of correlations suggests that as children mature cognitively and have a more complete understanding of adoption, they become more curious about their birthfamilies and less satisfied with their existing arrangements. A more detailed treatment of these intercorrelations can be found in Wrobel, Ayers-Lopez, Grotevant, McRoy, and Friedrick (1996).

DISCUSSION

The results provide an entry into understanding the perspective of the developing adopted child, who is growing within the complex adoptive kinship network in which members can hold differing perceptions about the openness being experienced. On an individual level, children in all types of adoptions in this study reported positive levels of self-esteem, curiosity about their birthparents, and satisfaction with their openness situation.

Although most groups of children reported being satisfied with their current openness situation, it cannot be assumed that the children understand the full range of possible openness situations and would still rate themselves as satisfied after a thoughtful comparison from an adult perspective. Even though children who were more curious tended to be less satisfied with their openness, other factors, such as what a child is curious about, must be taken into account when interpreting the relationship. Age was an important variable for understanding children's satisfaction and curiosity about their birthparents. Without exception, across all perspectives, older children were more curious. Older children were also generally less satisfied with their level of adoptive openness. Differing from this position were children in the fully disclosed group who were curious but also satisfied. The older children are approaching adolescence, at which time developing a personal identity becomes an important task. Information about one's past, which for these children includes birthparents, is important for developing this identity. The curiosity the children reported, coupled with less openness in the adoption, makes dissatisfaction with their level of openness more likely. Additionally, as children discover that they have been excluded from information provided by their birthmothers, their satisfaction with the current level of openness that contains exclusion of available information may be negatively affected.

Current satisfaction with their openness situation does not appear to reduce children's curiosity concerning their birthparents. The majority of children reported being curious about their birthparents. When openness was viewed from the perspective of the adopted child, girls were consistently more curious than boys about their birthparents. For younger children in the excluded group, males were more curious than females, whereas older females were more curious than older males. For both older and younger children, included females were the most curious, with older females showing the highest levels of curiosity. This gender difference may be explained by the important familial influences over gender role development that occur in middle childhood and early adolescence. Evidence for differential treatment of boys and girls in general is strong: Boys are allowed more freedom to be away from home without supervision and are encouraged in gross motor activities, whereas girls are encouraged to show dependency, concern for others, and expression of tender emotions (Huston, 1983). This emphasis for girls may lead to the role of mother becoming more strongly associated with being female at this age than the role of father becoming more strongly associated with being male. The differing emphasis in parental focus for male and female children, coupled with differences in the relevance of parenthood with gender identity, may be related to the differences in curiosity found among the adopted girls and boys. Girls in general may be more interested in what it means to be a mother, and adopted girls must incorporate two different models into their concept of motherhood. Thus, the meso-system of birthmother and female child becomes a vital source of important information for the adopted child as she looks for role models for being female. Nevertheless, because children did not have equal access to their birthmothers and birthfathers and because younger children did not equally understand the biological roles of birthmothers and birthfathers in reproduction, we cannot fully evaluate whether this pattern is a gender difference or whether it would also be apparent with boys if more contact with birthfathers had been available.

Although openness categories, as reported by adoptive parents or perceived by the child, and withholding of information were not related to curiosity, differences by openness category in what the children are curious about were found. Children with less information about birthparents tended to wonder about the birthparents' health and well-being and were most curious about what their birthparents looked like. One child, when asked what he would like to ask his birthparents, stated,

> I'd like to ask their names. 'Cause I don't really know their names. I want to know what they look like. I can't think of anything else.

Children with more information about birthparents tended to be curious about what the birthmother had been doing since they last had contact with her, when they will get to see her again, or meet her if they had not done so, and information about birth siblings. One child stated:

> Sometimes I wanted to meet her myself, and then Mom set up this rule, not until I'm 18. And I really wanted to meet her because, you know, my dad said I could and talked it over with my birthmother, and she would be glad if I met her. (fully disclosed adoption)

Another child who thought his birthmother "probably has a baby of her own" wanted to know "if she [birthmother] has a baby."

The lack of significant differences for self-esteem, curiosity, satisfaction, and socioemotional adjustment by openness level indicates that the results of this study are not compatible with assertions raised by critics of openness stating that such arrangements will damage children's self-esteem and cause confusion. But neither do these findings support the hypothesis that more openness enhances these outcomes. Future research must address under what circumstances openness in adoptive relationships is prudent and how to communicate available information about birthparents to adopted children in ways that are beneficial to their current and future development.

The results cited above address both direct and indirect effects of information exchange. Openness, by definition, is based on the amount of available information in the adoptive relationship. The main emphasis of the results is a direct effect model, but how the information is obtained by a child is an indirect effect based on the child's relationship with birth and adoptive parents. Adoptive parents who are withholding available information have qualitatively different relationships with their children than parents who are passing along all available information to their children. Future research should address what information is exchanged and what adoption issues are discussed in different periods of an adopted child's life, with emphasis on how communication influences parent-child relationships, which then influence the adopted child's development.

The most intriguing groups of children are those in the mediated and fully disclosed groups (primarily mediated) who report knowing no or basic amounts of information about their birthparents. Given the levels of curiosity reported by these children, how will they feel after discovering that information has always been available to their adoptive parents that was not shared with them? A total of 36 children in this sample were being excluded from some aspect of the information being received from the birthmother. Children from whom parents withheld information, for the most part, are not aware of their exclusion. On discovering that information has been withheld, these children may be less satisfied with their openness situation in the future and wonder whether all information in the adoptive parents' possession has been shared with them. This uncertainty was noted in the McRoy and Grotevant study on adopted adolescents in residential treatment after the children learned that the fact of their adoption had been withheld by their adoptive parents (McRoy, Grotevant, Ayers-Lopez, & Furuta, 1990; McRoy, Grotevant, & Zurcher, 1988).

Not surprisingly, the results make clear that having more information about a child's own adoption yields higher levels of understanding of adoption, provided the cognitive ability to grasp the concept is present. Results indicating that the family openness category was not related to understanding of adoption underscores the importance of studying the impact of openness from the perspective of the child. A trend indicates that when children were grouped according to their reports of known information, having more information was related to higher mean levels of understanding. A clearer picture of how information influences understanding of adoption can be seen when grouping children according to whether or not available information was shared with them. Children who were excluded from information had lower mean levels of understanding than those who were given known information.

Why parents choose to exclude their adopted children from information sharing is a provocative question. We speculated that having adopted siblings with different openness levels would promote excluding a child from information sharing concerning her or his adoption because parents would want to equate the amount of information each child has about her or his adoption. A trend based on a small number of families did indicate that when no difference was found in adopted sibling openness level, parents were more likely to include the target child in information sharing. This finding suggests that sibling differences should be considered in future studies to determine the degree to which parents include adopted children in information sharing. It will also be interesting to follow families who said they were withholding information because of the child's age, to see when they decide that the child is mature enough to have the information.

With respect to self-esteem, the Self-Perception Profile for Children (Harter, 1985) items that contribute to the Global Self-Worth Scale do not use any specific behavioral referents (e.g., some children are very happy being the way they are; other children wish they were different). This item format allows children to use whatever is important to them in deciding how good they feel about themselves. Adoptive openness status can contribute to this evaluation, but it does not appear to influence self-esteem in a negative way.

Overall, it does not appear that providing information about a child's birthparents will confuse the child about the meaning of adoption or lower the child's self-esteem, but neither will it move the child to levels of understanding that are beyond her or his cognitive capabilities to reach. Access to information gives adoptive parents an opportunity to facilitate their child's understanding of adoption.

Because many of the children were young when visited, a follow-up at adolescence will yield important information about longer-term openness effects, especially because less than 20% of the children had relatively mature levels of understanding of adoption (Levels 4 or 5) during our first interview with them. How will early understanding of adoption influence later relationships? Will the nature of curiosity about birthparents and satisfaction with openness level change at adolescence? What will be the impact of openness on the child's psychological adjustment at adolescence? How will changes in the access to information or changes in frequency of contact affect the child at adolescence? What are the implications when withheld information about birthparents is later presented? Continued research is necessary to help provide information that may further the discussion of the impact of openness in adoption on the development of adopted children.

5

ADOPTIVE PARENTS' PERSPECTIVES ON THEIR ROLES AND RELATIONSHIPS WITH BIRTHPARENTS

With Deborah Lewis Fravel and Carol Elde

amily systems theory has highlighted the importance of considering *all* members of a family when one wants to understand how
the family "works." Regardless of the amount of actual contact
between adoptive and birthfamilies, a systemic point of view would
consider it impossible to try to understand an adoptive family without
having the child's birthfamily be represented as part of the system (e.g.,
Demick & Wapner, 1988). As increasing openness is experienced, this
"hidden system" (e.g., Hajal & Rosenberg, 1991) becomes less hidden,
and personal relationships and more apparent subsystems emerge.
Goals may be articulated, rules may be made, and agreements may be
negotiated as all the individuals and subsystems attempt to function
in a way that is optimal for all members of the system. As in all systems,
conflict may arise when some individuals or subsystems have competing goals or needs. Critics of openness in adoption have emphasized
such conflicts, speculating about the harmful effects primarily on the
adoptive parents and on how connected they feel to their adopted
children. For example, in a psychobiological and psychoanalytic discussion of adoptive parenting, Kraft, Palombo, Woods, et al. (1985)
warned that attachment difficulties with adopted children may be
heightened if the adoption is open. Openness is seen as threatening to

adoptive parents' perceptions of the permanence of the relationship with the child and freedom from intrusion by the birthmother. The anxiety thus created by threats, either in reality or in fantasy, is deemed to have a disruptive effect on the adoptive mother-infant relationship and the infant's development. Kraft et al. contend that confidential adoptions may allay such anxieties. Furthermore, they assert that agencies advocating open adoptions put the needs of the birthparents above the needs of the adoptive parents and young child, sacrificing the rights of the adoptive parents to be full-fledged parents and to be free from the threat of interference from birthparents. Chapman et al. (1986, 1987a, 1987b) have argued that openness in adoption is in the best interests of all parties involved. Further details about this debate were presented in Chapter 1.

Four interrelated issues consistently raised by critics of open adoptions are directly addressed in this chapter. Two of them concern relationships between adoptive parents and birthparents (typically the birthmother): (a) the adoptive parents' fear that the birthmother would want to reclaim the child and (b) the adoptive parents' satisfaction with their sense of power/control over the birthmother's involvement in their family's life. The other two issues concern the relationship between the adoptive parents and their child: (c) the parents' sense of entitlement to act as the child's full parents and (d) the adoptive parents' feeling of permanence of the parent-child relationship as it is projected into the future. In addition, we consider adoptive family relationship issues that were highlighted in Kirk's (1964, 1981, 1995) theoretical work: acknowledgment of difference, empathy, and communication.

Specifically, the goal of this chapter is to explore the ways the above-mentioned family system issues vary as a function of level of openness in the adoption as seen through the perspective of adoptive parents. Critics of openness would hypothesize that fully disclosed adoptions are associated with greater fear of reclaiming, a reduced sense of power/control over the birthmother's involvement in their family life, and reduced feelings of entitlement and permanence among adoptive parents. Advocates of openness would hypothesize the opposite: that the personal relationships established between adoptive and birthparents actually reduce potential fear and enhance parents' sense of power/control over birthmother involvement, entitlement, and permanence.

METHOD

Participants and Measures

Participants considered in this chapter are the 190 adoptive fathers and 190 adoptive mothers described in Chapter 3. Data for this chapter are drawn from the adoptive parents' interviews, also described in Chapter 3.

Coding and Variables

A codebook (Grotevant, Fravel, Elde, Esau, & McRoy, 1995) was developed to assess several issues of interest, and ratings for variables were based on the entire adoptive parent interview transcript. Coders made judgments that required moderate to high levels of inference; therefore, all global coding was performed by graduate students or mature undergraduates in family science or the coprincipal investigators. Coders were trained to an initial reliability of at least .80 (percent exact agreement) using criterion interviews, and interrater reliability was monitored throughout the course of coding. Each interview was coded independently by two coders; disagreements were resolved through discussion. Percent exact agreement was used in reliability calculations because it required perfect agreement between coders and was therefore a stringent criterion.

The 10 variables examined in this study are described in Table 5.1. The first 5 variables, inspired by Kirk's (1964, 1981) work, focus on issues of communication with the adopted child (COMMUN/ CHILD), empathy toward the child (EMPATHY/CHILD) and the birthparent(s) (EMPATHY/BP), and acknowledgment that adoptive parenting is different from parenting by birth (AOD/FAMILY and AOD/CHILD). An example of the structure of one scale is given for the reader's benefit; information on other scales can be found in the codebook (available on request). The first variable, communication with the adopted child about the adoption (COMMUN/CHILD), was coded on a scale from 0 to 5. A rating of 0 indicated no communication beyond the simple telling to the child that he or she was adopted; 1 indicated "passive communication," in which parents responded to specific questions but did not initiate discussions; 3 indicated "active communication," characterized by answering the child's questions and initiating discussions about adoption and encouraging the child to talk about it; and 5, "excessive communication," the parent's overemphasizing adoption. Ratings of 2 and 4 were intermediate values. No mothers or fathers received the code of 5, and only 2 mothers and 2 fathers received the code of 4, so the scale is basically a linear one ranging from no communication to active communication. The next 4 variables address specific issues raised in the literature that are concerns in the debate about confidentiality versus openness in adoption: fear that the birthparent might try to reclaim the child (FEAR-RECLAIM), the adoptive parents' satisfaction with their power/ control over the birthparent's involvement in their family's life (SATIS-CONTROL), the adoptive parents' sense of entitlement to act as the child's "full" parents (ENTITLEMENT), and the adoptive parents' sense of permanence of the adoptive parent-child relationship as it is projected into the future (PERMANENCE). The final variable, narrative coherence, describes the degree to which the adoptive parents' philosophy about adoption, as expressed in the interview narrative, is internally consistent and free of contradictions (COHER-ENCE). Interrater reliabilities for each variable are also presented in Table 5.1.

RESULTS

First, descriptive statistics are reported for the 10 adoption variables described above. In this context, husband-wife correlations and differences are also reported. Second, correlations between background variables (see Chapter 3) and adoption variables and intercorrelations among the adoption variables are reported. Finally, mean differences in the adoption variables by level of openness, statistically controlling for family background variables, are reported.

TABLE 5.1 Variables Coded From Adoptive Parent Interviews

COMMUN/CHILD	Communication about the adoption with the AC beyond the simple telling of adoptive status. Higher ratings refer to active communication on the part of the parents, including initiation of discussions and encouragement of the child to talk about adoption. (.71)
EMPATHY/CHILD	Empathy for the AC connection to birthfamily and its importance for the child's self-understanding and identity. Higher scores indicate greater empathy for the child's desire to express curiosity about birthfamily or the child's potential feelings of grief or rejection regarding adoption. (.82)
EMPATHY/BP	Empathy for BP's difficulty of making the adoption decision, understanding the BP's need for information about the AC, and attempts to look at the adoption from the BP's perspective. (.83)
AOD/FAMILY	Acknowledgement of the family's status as an adoptive (rather than a biological) family and the particular issues that might be involved. (.69)
AOD/CHILD	Interest in the AC's history or background beyond medical information. Birthparents are considered part of the AC's background and history. (.79)
SATIS-CONTROL	Satisfaction with the AP's ability to regulate the birthmother's involvement in their family's life, either through preventing unwanted intrusion or through stimulating greater involvement, when desired. (.84)
FEAR-RECLAIM	Degree to which the AP currently fears that the birthmother might wish to reclaim the adopted child. (.69)
PERMANENCE	The AP's feelings of permanence in the parent-child relationship as it is projected into the future. (.83)
ENTITLEMENT	The AP's feeling of having both the role and responsibility to be the child's full parents. (.87)
COHERENCE	The consistency of the AP's "philosophy" about adoption, as expressed through their interviews. Higher ratings mean that the discussion of adoption is consistent within itself, that conclusions reached by the respondents match with the examples and episodes cited, and that emotional responses discussed in the interviews are congruent with the events to which they refer. (.91)

NOTE: AC = adopted child, AP = adoptive parent, BP = birthparent, AOD = acknowledgment of difference. Numbers in parentheses following descriptions are interrater reliabilities based on percent exact agreement between two coders before discussing discrepancies. All interviews were coded by two raters; disagreements were resolved through discussion.

Descriptive Statistics

In Table 5.2, descriptive statistics are presented for the adoption variables. The adoption variables are reported separately for fathers' and mothers' interviews, which were administered, transcribed, and coded independently of one another. In general, spouses' ratings were significantly but moderately correlated with one another (range: –.04 to .42). Significant differences emerged between spouses' ratings on all five adoption variables derived from Kirk's work: (a) communication with the child, (b) empathy toward the child, (c) empathy toward the birthmother, (d) acknowledgment of difference with respect to the family, and (e) acknowledgment of difference with respect to the child. In all these cases, adoptive mothers' ratings were higher than fathers', on average. It should be noted, however, that the actual mean differences did not exceed .25 of a scale point. No significant differences were found between spouses' ratings on the other scales.

Correlations were then computed between the background variables and the adoption interview ratings. Given the possibility of encountering significant correlations by chance, the $p < .01$ level (2-tailed) was used to assess statistical significance. By this criterion, only two correlations reached significance: (a) The number of other adopted children in the family correlated negatively with adoptive fathers' satisfaction with power/control ($r = -.21$, $p < .01$); and (b) adoptive mothers' education correlated with acknowledgment of difference toward the child ($r = .23$, $p < .01$). This largest correlation accounts for only 5.3% of shared variance. Intercorrelations among the adoption variables were also computed and are presented in Table 5.3.

Next, analyses of covariance were conducted, separately for adoptive fathers and adoptive mothers, for each of the 10 adoption interview variables by using degree of openness in the adoption as the independent variable and controlling for parental education, family income, number of birth children, number of other adopted children, and child's age as covariates.[1] Variance accounted for by the covariates was removed before the main effect of openness was assessed. Each of the 10 dependent variables had a coding option in which the rater could specify "unclear/can't code," and all variables with the

TABLE 5.2 Descriptive Statistics for All Variables

Adoption Variables

| | Adoptive Fathers | | | Adoptive Mothers | | | | |
Variable	Mean	Standard Deviation	Range	Mean	Standard Deviation	Range	Fa-Mo Correlation	Fa-Mo Difference
COMMUN/CHILD	2.38	1.02	0–4	2.63	0.79	0–4	.34***	–3.35***
EMPATHY/CHILD	1.84	0.37	1–2	1.91	0.31	1–3	.19*	–2.14*
EMPATHY/BP	1.90	0.41	0–3	2.02	0.44	1–3	.18*	–2.83**
AOD/FAMILY	2.74	0.55	1–4	2.93	0.40	2–4	.01	–4.09***
AOD/CHILD	2.73	0.68	1–4	2.85	0.56	1–5	.42***	–2.26*
SATIS-CONTROL	1.79	0.57	0–2	1.71	0.66	0–2	.40***	1.38
FEAR-RECLAIM	0.57	0.68	0–3	0.53	0.67	0–2	.35***	0.12
PERMANENCE	2.77	0.47	1–3	2.78	0.48	1–3	.24**	–0.13
ENTITLEMENT	2.87	0.37	1–3	2.87	0.35	1–3	–.04	–0.29
COHERENCE	3.79	1.09	1–5	3.93	1.04	1–5	.31***	–1.58

*p < .05; **p < .01; ***p < .001.

113

TABLE 5.3 Intercorrelations Among Adoptive Parent Interview Variables

	COM/AC	EMP/AC	EMP/BP	AOD/FAM	AOD/AC	SAT-CONT	FEAR	PERM	ENTITLE	COHERENCE
COMMUN/CHILD		0.44	0.25	0.35	0.51	-0.05	-0.23	0.25	0.05	0.42
EMPATHY/CHILD	0.52		0.47	0.26	0.62	-0.20	-0.21	0.12	0.01	0.24
EMPATHY/BP	0.27	0.57		0.13	0.42	-0.23	-0.07	0.06	0.00	0.23
AOD/FAMILY	0.33	0.40	0.29		0.44	-0.20	-0.28	0.22	0.20	0.18
AOD/CHILD	0.48	0.58	0.48	0.38		-0.22	-0.37	0.24	0.07	0.37
SATIS-CONTROL	-0.13	-0.11	-0.05	-0.17	-0.12		0.00	-0.01	0.02	0.01
FEAR-RECLAIM	-0.31	-0.51	-0.40	-0.05	-0.37	0.07		-0.45	-0.17	-0.55
PERMANENCE	0.31	0.35	0.21	0.18	0.30	-0.15	-0.38		0.22	0.30
ENTITLEMENT	0.17	0.20	0.14	0.11	0.04	-0.10	-0.22	0.46		0.34
COHERENCE	0.36	0.42	0.33	0.32	0.39	-0.24	-0.51	0.50	0.36	

NOTE: Intercorrelations for adoptive mothers above the diagonal; for adoptive fathers, below the diagonal. All adoptive parents across levels of openness included: Ns vary from 133 to 189.

exception of FEAR-RECLAIM and COHERENCE had a coding option for "mixed/ambivalent," to be used when the coder identified statements at both extremes of the continuum. Neither the unclear/ can't code nor the mixed/ambivalent statements are included in the analyses that follow because they are qualitatively different from the continuous scales. Thus, the total sample size for each variable (see Tables 5.4 and 5.5) differs because of missing data. Means, *F*s, and post hoc comparisons that reached statistical significance are summarized in Table 5.4 (for adoptive fathers) and Table 5.5 (for adoptive mothers). In only 7 of the 20 analyses were any of the covariates statistically significant. Therefore, to present the data by using the largest possible sample size, the analyses shown in Tables 5.4 and 5.5 are based on one-way analyses of variance for variables in which none of the covariates were significant and on ANCOVAs for variables in which at least one of the covariates was significant. Statistically significant covariates are listed in brackets in the tables.

Variations in Adoption Attitudes and Behavior by Level of Openness

Attitudes Toward Adoption. Analyses of variance were first conducted for the five variables describing adoptive parents' attitudes. Ratings for these variables are coders' evaluations of parent-child communication (for example) based on parents' statements in their interviews, rather than on direct observation of parent-child communication. For the first variable, *communication with the adopted child about the adoption* (COMMUN/CHILD), *F*s by level of openness were significant for both mothers and fathers. Scheffé contrasts indicated that the mean ratings for parents with fully disclosed adoptions were significantly higher than the mean ratings for parents with confidential adoptions; in addition, adoptive fathers in fully disclosed adoptions were rated higher in communication than fathers in time-limited mediated adoptions. The number of other adopted children in the family was a significant covariate (*r* = .16) for mothers only.

Examples of low and high levels of communication follow:

TABLE 5.4 Mean Scores by Level of Openness for Adoptive Fathers (N = 190)

Variable Name	Possible Range	Total N	Confid.	Time-Limited Mediated	Ongoing Mediated	Fully Disclosed	F	Sig Contrasts
Possible Number of Cases			62	17	52	59		
COMMUN/CHILD	0–5	181	2.13	1.64	2.44	2.74	6.81***	FD > C, TLM
EMPATHY/CHILD	0–3	178	1.70	1.53	1.90	2.00	12.14***	FD > C, TLM; OM > C, TLM
EMPATHY/BP	0–3	177	1.78	1.81	1.88	2.05	4.60**	FD > C
AOD/FAMILY	1–5	160	2.67	2.57	2.81	2.79	1.53, ns	[afed]
AOD/CHILD	1–5	168	2.36	2.53	2.78	3.09	13.28***	FD > C, TLM; OM > C [adch]
SATIS-CONTROL	0–2	173	1.74	1.88	1.93	1.67	1.76, ns	[adch]
FEAR-RECLAIM	0–3	140	1.10	0.80	0.68	0.19	17.85***	FD < C, TLM, OM; OM < C
PERMANENCE	1–3	182	2.70	2.80	2.65	2.93	4.09**	FD > OM
ENTITLEMENT	1–3	182	2.77	2.93	2.88	2.95	2.64, ns	
COHERENCE	1–5	189	3.54	3.41	3.58	4.36	8.67***	FD > C, TLM, OM

NOTES: C = confidential; TLM = time-limited mediated; OM = ongoing mediated; FD = fully disclosed.
Significant covariates: [afed] = adoptive father's education; [adch] = number of other adopted children in the family.
*p < .05; **p < .01; ***p < .001.

TABLE 5.5 Mean Scores by Level of Openness for Adoptive Mothers (N = 189)

Variable Name	Possible Range	Total N	Confid.	Time-Limited Mediated	Ongoing Mediated	Fully Disclosed	F	Sig. Contrasts
Possible Number of Cases			62	17	51	59		
COMMUN/CHILD	0–5	166	2.38	2.54	2.67	2.92	4.08**	FD > C [adch]
EMPATHY/CHILD	0–3	177	1.77	1.87	1.96	2.02	7.42***	FD > C; OM > C
EMPATHY/BP	0–3	174	1.83	1.93	2.08	2.16	6.24***	FD > C; OM > C
AOD/FAMILY	1–5	177	2.89	2.81	2.86	3.05	3.10*	
AOD/CHILD	1–5	166	2.59	2.62	2.91	3.13	10.04***	FD > C, TLM; OM > C [amed]
SATIS-CONTROL	0–2	170	1.70	1.93	1.72	1.65	0.68, ns	
FEAR-RECLAIM	0–3	125	0.94	0.56	0.67	0.23	9.03***	FD < C, OM [chage]
PERMANENCE	1–3	171	2.67	2.80	2.81	2.84	0.72, ns	[birthch]
ENTITLEMENT	1–3	183	2.92	2.75	2.84	2.89	1.17, ns	
COHERENCE	1–5	189	3.60	3.59	3.84	4.44	8.52***	FD > C, TLM, OM

NOTES: C = confidential; TLM = time-limited mediated; OM = ongoing mediated; FD = fully disclosed.
Significant covariates: [adch] = number of other adopted children; [birthch] = number of birth children; [amed] = adoptive mother's education; [chage] = child's age.
*$p < .05$; **$p < .01$; ***$p < .001$.

117

I: When did you tell Cindy[2] she was adopted?

R: Well, we really haven't told her—I mean we've told her, but she really doesn't know what it means. I don't think she does.

I: How do you plan to talk with Cindy about adoption?

R: Well, I think that any questions she has that she's not sure about, we can help her through it. We've tried to explain to her what adoption is all about, but at age five she doesn't know what it's all about now. (adoptive father, ongoing mediated adoption)

*   *   *

I: When did you tell Lars he was adopted?

R: Oh, I think he was very young. I think we started telling the kids when they were still babies, just talking to them because it seems to me there is no age at when they can't understand, and I assume any time from about 1 year of age and older.

I: How have you talked with your child about adoption?

R: Well, we have talked about the kids being adopted the whole time, and I think I would probably tell them the same thing no matter what age they were—that they were adopted and their birthparents loved them very much but they couldn't take care of them and they wanted someone that could take care of them and we've been very lucky that we ended up taking care of them. And then as far as other questions about their birthparents, I would be honest and tell them anything I knew. (adoptive father, confidential adoption)

The second variable assessed *empathy for the adopted child* and the importance of connection to his or her heritage in order to foster self-understanding and identity (EMPATHY/CHILD). One-way analyses of variance yielded significant differences by openness for both fathers and mothers. Scheffé tests indicated that, for fathers, those in fully disclosed adoptions were more empathic than those in confidential or time-limited mediated adoptions and that fathers in ongoing mediated adoptions were more empathic than those in confidential or time-limited mediated adoptions. Mothers in fully disclosed adoptions were more empathic than those in confidential adoptions, as were mothers in ongoing mediated adoptions.

In the following statement, an adoptive father weighs the advantages of different types of adoption, considering perspectives of adoptive parents and the adopted child:

> I'd say the advantage of a closed adoption is the security that it has. You don't worry so much about whether you'll be liked, whether you'll be appreciated, whether you'll be deemed appropriate for a child. You don't have to subject yourself to those stresses. I think the advantage to an open adoption is that there's more sharing and there's more sense of identity. If I had been adopted, I imagine that I would like to know more about my family history than my birth—or than my adoptive parents' family history. I would like to know if there were siblings that I had. If the degree to which I would like to include them in my life, I'd like to make that decision later upon reaching adulthood. But I see the advantage of an open adoption in that you have your sense of identity, your questions are answered, you know what your mother looks like, you know perhaps what your father looks like, and you no longer have to be concerned that you did not please your birthmother or father, that you were unacceptable to them and so they shipped you off somewhere else. And the flip side of that coin, the fact that your mother and father are not superheroes. (adoptive father, ongoing mediated adoption)

The third variable assessed *empathy for the birthparents' feelings* about making the adoption decision (EMPATHY/BP). One-way analyses of variance yielded significant Fs for both mothers and fathers; parents in fully disclosed adoptions showed more empathy toward their child's birthparents than did parents in confidential adoptions. Mothers in ongoing mediated adoptions also showed more empathy than mothers in confidential adoptions.

The following quotes from adoptive parents present contrasting views about concern for birthmothers' feelings:

> It must have been tough to make that decision, but once it's made, she needs to go on with her life.

I can have an appreciation for what it must take to have made a decision like that. And then if you have second thoughts about it, how it must come back to haunt you—painfully.

The fourth variable measured *adoptive parents' interest in or recognition of their status as an adoptive family* and its particular satisfactions, problems, and issues, as distinct from biological families (AOD/FAMILY). On this variable, the one-way analysis of variance was significant for mothers, but the differences between the means of specific groups were not significant at the .05 level. For fathers, the overall ANCOVA was not significant, but father's education did reach statistical significance ($r = .17$) as a covariate. The following adoptive father's view of adoption illustrates his acknowledgment of the special nature of adoption in his family:

> I have an extremely positive feeling about adoption. I don't argue with people about adoption because most people don't understand adoption that haven't been in the process. They don't know what they're talking about. I try to make a few points that we have a birthmother and that she didn't give the child up for adoption. She made a plan for the child. She was in the situation that she was aware that she couldn't provide for the child and what a child needed to be provided for. (adoptive father, confidential adoption)

The fifth variable assessed *acknowledgment of the child's interest in his or her history or background* beyond basic medical information (AOD/CHILD). The variable was rated along the same 1–5 scale as AOD/FAMILY. Analyses of covariance were significant for both fathers and mothers. In both cases, parents in fully disclosed adoptions were rated higher than those in confidential or time-limited mediated adoptions, and parents in ongoing mediated adoptions were rated higher than those in confidential adoptions. Significant covariates were number of other adopted children in the family (for fathers only, $r = .17$) and mother's education (for mothers only, $r = .23$).

> I'm not in favor of closed adoptions because I think sooner or later there's going to come a time to where the young man or young woman is going to want to know some things. To me, closed is where they bang their heads against a stone wall and nobody gives in, and I think they hurt. (adoptive father, ongoing mediated adoption)

Satisfaction With Power/Control Over Birthparent Involvement. Interviews were also coded for each adoptive parent's feeling of satisfaction with his or her ability to regulate the birthmother's involvement in the family's life, either through preventing unwanted intrusion or through stimulating greater involvement, when desired (SATIS-CONTROL). This involvement could include direct or mediated contacts by telephone, written correspondence, or personal visits.

It should be noted that the overwhelming majority of all adoptive parents indicated satisfaction with their power/control over birthparent involvement in their family's life. Across all levels of openness, from 80% to 95% of adoptive fathers and 70% to 79% of adoptive mothers were satisfied with their power/control over birthparent involvement. Satisfaction with power/control did not differ significantly by level of openness, perhaps because level of satisfaction was generally so high.

Responses were further examined for those cases in which the adoptive parent indicated a desire to change the level of contact with the birthparent. For adoptive mothers, 30 (15.9%) wanted *more* contact, and none wanted less. For adoptive fathers, 25 (13.2%) wanted more contact, and only 2 (both in ongoing mediated adoptions) wanted less. Those desiring more contact were spread across all levels of openness, from confidential through fully disclosed.

Adoptive parents in mediated or fully disclosed adoptions who were satisfied with their power/control over birthmother involvement generally cited their experience with the birthmother and their ability to develop a mutual understanding about the degree of involvement. Parents who were dissatisfied wanted more contact and typically thought the lack of contact was either a unilateral decision on the part of the birthmother or an adoption agency decision or policy. In several cases, the desire for more contact came about because of differing levels of openness for adopted siblings in the family. The following case examples illustrate issues involved with satisfaction over control:

At the time of placement, the Jones family was unable to meet their child's birthmother because she was afraid to come to a meeting. Within a month, however, she felt comfortable enough to do so. The Joneses proceeded cautiously, withholding their surname and address even after the birthmother provided hers. At that point, the Joneses anticipated that they would meet once, sharing letters periodically through the agency, and then not meet again until the child was near adulthood. Once they met the birthmother, however, they began to believe there were advantages in continued association with her. By their third meeting, the three adults seemed to agree that "no one was trying to take over," and the adoptive parents shared identifying information about themselves. For the members of this triad, control over openness appears to be based on mutual respect and an understanding that evolved over time.

Originally, the Brown family's adoption was confidential, but after experiencing more openness with a second adopted child, the Browns went back to their agency and requested a more open arrangement with the first child's birthmother. They are now sharing letters and pictures, with no identifying information, through the agency. Mrs. Brown confided that she and her husband share much more information with the birthmother than she does with them. However, Mrs. Brown expressed satisfaction with this arrangement. What matters to her is not so much having routine communication with the birthmother, but rather Mrs. Brown's sense that she can contact the birthmother through the agency if she needs or wants to.

This father in a confidential adoption addressed his satisfaction with control despite no contact with the child's birthparent(s):

> I think every set of circumstances, this one included, has its own particular set of problems which might be . . . present or future tense. I have no problem with any set of circumstances when I know what they are. The circumstance we had with the closed adoption is something I accept as a factual circumstance, and I'm very happy with our child and with the process, whatever it will bring and as it is. (adoptive father, confidential adoption)

Fear of Reclaiming. Interviews were coded in terms of the degree to which parents feared that the birthmother might try to reclaim the child. Specifically, coders were asked to indicate the degree to which an adoptive parent currently had fear of reclaiming concerning the particular target child (FEAR-RECLAIM). Most noteworthy is the changing distribution of coded responses by level of openness for both mothers and fathers. In general, the lowest degrees of fear at the present time were in the fully disclosed adoptions. In fact, 77.2% of adoptive mothers and 82.5% of adoptive fathers in fully disclosed adoptions indicated "no fear" of reclaiming. In response to the item concerning whether the parent had *ever* had such fear, "yes" was coded for 40% to 60% of adoptive parents across all levels of openness.

For both mothers and fathers, the difference across levels of openness in degree of present fear was statistically significant. Scheffé follow-up tests indicated that, for mothers, fear in the fully disclosed group was significantly less than in the ongoing mediated and confidential groups. The child's age was a significant covariate for mothers only ($r = -.19$). For fathers, the degree of fear in the fully disclosed group was significantly less than that in the confidential, time-limited mediated, or ongoing mediated groups; in addition, fathers in ongoing mediated adoptions felt less fear than those in confidential adoptions.

Coders also noted up to 4 reasons why adoptive parents were coded as either having or not having fear of reclaiming (see Tables 5.6 and 5.7). The reasons were drawn from a list of 15 possible reasons that had been compiled during the pilot phase of codebook development. Interestingly, the reasons for fear or no fear varied dramatically across level of openness and differed strikingly as a function of whether the adoptive parents had a personal relationship with the birthmother. In confidential and mediated adoptions, the most frequently cited reason for fear was "impressions about birthparents generally"; in other words, adoptive parents' stereotypes about birthparents developed from generalized experiences and knowledge. This logic is illustrated by a quote from an adoptive father:

> The disadvantage [of open adoption] is right back to this fear that I think all of us adoptive parents have that [the birthmother] is living here on the other side of Springfield. She comes and visits anytime, and you go visit her anytime. She loads up her car, comes gets the baby, and is in Los Angeles tomorrow morning. And like I say, it's not a problem if you're dealing with 100% rational people. You'll never run into these situations, but uh, . . . well, in our society we don't deal with 100% rational people all the time. (adoptive father, confidential adoption)

For a father with a mediated adoption, this fear dissipated after a meeting in which non-identifying information was shared:

> Well, the advantages of a fully disclosed adoption are many. Number 1, the fear that you have about the birthparents showing up at your

TABLE 5.6 Reasons Given for HAVING Fear of Reclaiming by Level of Openness

Reason	% Adoptive Fathers	% Adoptive Mothers
Confidential (N = 62)		
Impressions about birthparents generally	45.2	30.6
Other people's experiences with adoption (including "horror stories," court cases)	16.1	8.1
Time-Limited Mediated (N = 17)		
Impressions about birthparents generally	29.4	17.6
Other reasons (including episodic fear)	11.8	5.9
Ongoing Mediated (N = 52)		
Impressions about birthparents generally	28.8	15.7
Time-Limited Fully Disclosed (N = 2)		
Impressions about birthparents generally	0.0	50.0
Degree of openness selected	0.0	50.0
Adoptive parent projecting own attitudes onto child's birthparent	50.0	0.0
Ongoing Fully Disclosed (N = 57)		
Actual birthparent's life circumstances	5.3	10.5

NOTE: Items were included to which more than 10% of mothers or fathers in each openness category responded, not to exceed the highest three items for each openness level.

doorstep is dissolved. After you have a face-to-face meeting, you just get an understanding of who this person is, what makes her tick, you know, why they gave their child for adoption. In our case, both birthmothers we met, and we were just extremely comfortable. They were average people. They were people not to be feared. They were loving people. They loved us for taking their child and giving them a good home . . . They came from an imaginary face somewhere out in this world to be something that sits in front of you and talks and understands and is just a human being. And that for me, anyway, took away all my fears about ever losing our child. (adoptive father, ongoing mediated adoption)

The second most frequent reason for fear in confidential adoptions was "other people's experiences with adoption, including 'hor-

Table 5.7 Reasons Given for NOT HAVING Fear of Reclaiming by Level of Openness

Reason	% Adoptive Fathers	% Adoptive Mothers
Confidential (N = 62)		
Degree of openness selected	50.0	50.0
Adoptive parent control over information shared	16.1	21.0
Impressions about child's birthparent	6.5	12.9
Time-Limited Mediated (N = 17)		
Adoptive parent control over information shared	35.3	35.3
Degree of openness selected	29.4	47.1
Impressions about child's birthparent	17.6	29.4
Ongoing Mediated (N = 52)		
Impressions about child's birthparent	46.2	41.2
Degree of openness selected	40.4	33.3
Adoptive parent control over information shared	36.5	23.5
Time-Limited Fully Disclosed (N = 2)		
Impressions about child's birthparent	100.0	100.0
Legal reasons	100.0	0.0
Statements made by child's birthparent	50.0	50.0
Ongoing Fully Disclosed (N = 57)		
Impressions about child's birthparent	77.2	77.2
Actual birthparent's life circumstances	45.6	40.4
Statements made by child's birthparent	45.6	61.4

ror' stories, media portrayals, and court cases." In ongoing fully disclosed adoptions, however, indications of fear were based on the actual birthparent's life circumstances (and only 5.3% of adoptive fathers and 10.5% of adoptive mothers were coded for this reason). Reasons for *not* having fear of reclaiming also differed across levels of openness. Families with confidential and mediated adoptions cited "degree of openness selected" and "adoptive parent's control over information shared" as the primary reasons for having no fear. It appears that families thought the legal and social barriers inherent in their type of adoption protected them against reclaiming. For parents in fully disclosed adoptions, however, the reasons most frequently coded for not having fear of reclaiming were "impressions about the child's birthparent," "the actual birthparent's life circumstances," and "statements made by the child's birthparent." They often spoke of birthparents who specifically stated that they would never try to take the child from his or her adoptive parents. The following case examples illustrate changes in adoptive parents' fear of reclaiming as they develop a closer relationship with their child's birthmother.

> After watching several television shows that examined openness in adoption, the Hogan family decided to seek a fully disclosed adoption. Even though these adoptive parents admitted to some uneasiness prior to the first face-to-face meeting with the birthmother, their subsequent experiences with her allayed their fears. They now feel so comfortable with the birthmother that they invite her to spend nights in their home. The adoptive mother related that, for her and her husband, "whenever there is something that you don't know, it seems worse than if you know, bad or good . . . the unknown is more frightening . . . When you're involved in openness, you see every day that [reclaiming the child] is not the thought that is on [the birthmother's] mind."

> The French family has a fully disclosed adoption. Mrs. French stated that she has never feared that the birthmother would want to reclaim her child. However, the reasons for Mrs. French's lack of fear have changed over time. Initially, Mrs. French felt entirely protected by the "security blanket" of adoption laws. Gradually, however, as they became better acquainted, she realized that the birthmother was satisfied with her decision to relinquish the child and had no desire to reclaim her.

Permanence. In Chapter 4, we briefly discussed the adoptive parents' sense of permanence of the parent-child relationship as it is projected into the future because of its relation to security of attachment. Those findings are reiterated here because they also speak to adoptive parents' perceptions of their relationships and because they may vary by level of openness in the adoption.

Adoptive parents' interviews were coded with respect to parents' perceptions of the strength of the parent-child relationship as it is projected into the future. Often, statements coded with regard to permanence (PERMANENCE) were made when parents were discussing their willingness to help their children learn more about their birthfamilies or search for birthparents when they were older. Permanence was coded on a 3-point scale: (a) strong concerns about permanence, (b) moderate concerns that were balanced by feelings of certainty, and (c) a strong sense of permanence. These levels were coded independently of the positive or negative quality of the relationship itself.

For both adoptive mothers and adoptive fathers, the presence of a strong sense of permanence was the most frequently coded response across all levels of openness. Permanence was first examined from the perspective of the family openness code. These analyses revealed that feelings of permanence differed statistically across levels of openness for adoptive fathers but not for adoptive mothers. Scheffé tests revealed that the fathers' sense of permanence in the fully disclosed families was significantly higher than in the ongoing mediated adoptive families. The highest proportions coded as "strong permanence" were in the fully disclosed adoptions for both mothers and fathers. The following example illustrates how permanence is seen in adoptive families:

> When Mrs. Rankin discussed her adopted son, her comments often addressed his future. She makes plans for handling questions about his adoption as he grows older and thinks about what she can do now to makes things easier for him then. Her meetings with the birthmother are mediated, occurring at the agency. During one of those meetings, Mrs. Rankin shared with the birthmother the plans they have for their son as he is growing up, not necessarily plans for his adult occupation, but plans for what they would like him to be involved in and general ideas about what they envision for him as they raise him. (adoptive mother, time-limited mediated adoption)

Entitlement to Act as the Child's Full Parent. Interviews were coded in terms of each adoptive parent's sense of "entitlement" to act as the child's full parent (ENTITLEMENT). Reitz and Watson (1992) defined *entitlement* as adoptive parents having the "legal and emotional right to parent their child" (p. 125). Although the legal right is conferred by the courts, the emotional right must occur internally

(Reitz & Watson, 1992). Perception of entitlement did not differ statistically across levels of openness for adoptive fathers or adoptive mothers. For both mothers and fathers, the most commonly coded rating across all levels of openness was "very secure." Parents' perceptions of entitlement are illustrated in the following contrasting vignettes:

> Mrs. Larson related that some of her extended family members worried that adopting a child might cause her emotional distress. It turned out, however, that their worries were unfounded. Mrs. Larson shared that "from the time we brought [the child] home, she was ours. That was just it. [She] was ours. And I never felt any other way about it."

> The Hamms adopted a child after having several biological children, and Mrs. Hamm often struggles with conflicting feelings about raising the adopted child. On one hand, she feels that God gave her this child to raise and that she is "doing something good in my life for another human being." On the other hand, she often feels like a substitute mother or baby-sitter, thinking "this baby doesn't really belong to me, it belongs to this other girl . . . What if something happens to him? What will I tell her? What am I going to say?" Mrs. Hamm said she works to compensate for not having given birth to the child and that she sometimes thinks the birthmother is "raising" the child during their weekend visits. (adoptive mother, ongoing fully disclosed adoption)

Narrative Coherence. Narrative coherence of the entire interview was rated on a scale of 1 to 5 (COHERENCE). Higher ratings mean that the discussion of adoption is consistent within itself, that conclusions reached by the respondent match with the examples and episodes cited, and that emotional responses discussed in the interview are congruent with the events to which they refer. One-way analyses of variance were statistically significant for both adoptive fathers and adoptive mothers. In both cases, the narratives of parents in fully disclosed adoptions were rated as more coherent than ones for parents in confidential, time-limited mediated, or ongoing mediated adoptions.

DISCUSSION

The analyses presented above depict both similarities and differences in the dynamics of adoptive family systems across levels of openness.

In some ways, the similarities stand out: (a) Most adoptive parents feel secure in their roles and are not worried about the permanence of the relationship with their child, nor are they overtly fearful that the birthmother might try to reclaim the child as her own; (b) most are satisfied with their control over the birthmother's involvement in their family life. In the mediated and fully disclosed adoptions, the satisfaction appeared to be based on the adoptive parents' experience with the birthparent(s) and on their sense that the amount and type of contact was mutually negotiated. Overall, most ratings of the variables reported in this study fell within a moderate range for families across all levels of openness. Extreme responses were rare.

Clear differences were also evident, however, across levels of openness. The strong general pattern is that parents in fully disclosed adoptions demonstrate higher degrees of empathy about adoption, talk about it more openly with their child, and are less fearful that the birthmother might try to reclaim her child than are parents in confidential adoptions. When one focuses on the scales with significant Fs and on the significant contrasts within those scales, the ratings of parents with ongoing mediated adoptions tend to fall between those of parents with confidential and fully disclosed adoptions. Despite the concerns raised by critics of openness, the results of this study are not compatible with the hypothesis that openness necessarily produces undesirable outcomes for adoptive families with school-age children.

Differences across openness were sometimes not based on the degree to which a variable was present, but rather on the issues underlying the presence or absence of the issue. A striking example may be seen in the case of fear of reclaiming: Parents in confidential adoptions feel little fear because they feel protected by the type of adoption they have chosen and because they feel control over the information they share. Any fear they do show is generalized, based on negative stereotypes about birthparents and on "horror stories" sensationalized in the media. Parents in more open adoptions base their lack of fear on their personal relationship with their child's birthmother. Over time, they have built a relationship of trust. In many cases, the birthmother has explicitly stated that she would never think about trying to reclaim the child.

Thompson (1981) suggested that issues of control tend to center around a "unifying theme" of meaning and perception, incorporating the assurance that some undesirable issue/event will not exceed the participants' limits of endurance, the extent to which the event is associated with a desirable outcome, the extent to which people perceive order and meaning, and their interpretation of the motivation of others. In this study, we assumed that chosen levels of openness seemed to be an initially desirable outcome for these families. The measure applied in this study would have captured dissatisfaction had couples felt forced into a type of adoption, if that was, in fact, what had happened. Our findings suggest that that did not, in fact, happen or that if it did, it ultimately became acceptable and satisfactory for these families. The adoptive parents in this study are satisfied—so satisfied, in fact, that any dissatisfaction tends to focus around their desire for more, not less, contact with the birthparents. On the basis of analysis of family cases that involved an increase in level of openness over time (Mendenhall, Grotevant, & McRoy, 1996), we concluded that openness is often a process rather than a state and that it is a mutually evolutionary one; that is, the relationships appear initially to fall well within the participants' range of acceptability and that the relationship process toward greater openness is interactively determined by all those involved. At the same time, it should be noted that the perspectives discussed in this chapter are those of adoptive parents and that adoptive parents and birthmothers in general do not have equal power within their relationship to determine and negotiate openness arrangements. This issue is discussed further in Chapters 7 and 8.

These analyses have focused on aspects of adoptive parent-birthparent relationships and on aspects of adoptive parent-child relationships. It is significant to note that these relationships are all embedded within the adoptive kinship network and that they should not be viewed as independent. After all, the only reason that adoptive parents and birthmother have a relationship is there is an adopted child. The sense emerging from these interviews is that, among the variables coded for this report, the ones that seem highly salient to adoptive parents are their feelings of permanence and entitlement—in other words, in their connections to their child. They are maintaining a relationship with the birthmother because they believe it is in the best interests of the child. It should also be noted, however, that many relationships built between adoptive parents and birthparents have become friendships in their own right as well. Dealing with fear and control issues may be ways that adoptive parents think they can improve family relationships by achieving role clarity and not letting the parent-child relationship be triangulated by the birthparents. These insights will be tested more fully as we follow these families longitudinally.

The correlational analyses suggest at least two groupings of issues that must be considered in understanding the dynamics of varying degrees of openness. One grouping is quite reminiscent of the issues identified by Kirk (1964) more than 30 years ago: the intertwined issues of acknowledgment of difference about being an adoptive family and the consequences of that for empathy toward the child and the birthparent(s) and for communication about adoption. Kirk's model was developed during the time when adoptive parents often struggled with whether or not to tell the child he or she was adopted. Although those days have passed, the current struggle centers around communication and contact within the adoptive kinship network. With the trend toward greater openness in adoption, the "shared fate" theory needs to be expanded to include the birthfamily system. Today, the fate that is shared not only extends between adoptive parent and child but also reaches across the boundaries of the adoptive family potentially to birthmothers, birthfathers, and their extended families. Although most contact in our open adoptions is currently with the birthmothers, we predict that once these children reach adolescence or adulthood, contact will also be made with birthsiblings and the larger extended family networks.

A second grouping of intercorrelated variables includes permanence, entitlement, and coherence. Parents who have a clear sense of entitlement about the adoption generally tend to feel more confident that the relationship with their adopted child will endure across time (despite, or perhaps because of, contact with the child's birthfamily) and generally present a more coherent picture about the adoption in an interview. Daly (1992) suggested that resocialization of identity as an adoptive parent requires attention to the past, present, and future. The connections suggested by this grouping of variables imply that the transformation of these adoptive parents' identities from biological parents to adoptive parents is underway; that is, in the present, they feel entitled to be the parents of the adopted child, and as they look to the future, they sense permanence in the relationship. Transcending all this, the coherence in the narratives of these adoptive parents reflects their internal clarity about their new identity as adoptive parents.

As we have seen, spouses' ratings on the variables in this study tended to be significantly correlated but sometimes differed in systematic ways. We concur with Demick (1993) that studies such as these are strengthened when individual-, couple-, and family-level data are all included. In Chapter 7, we focus on the 77 of our families who are "fully corresponding"—in other words, for whom we have data from the birthmother, the child she placed for adoption, and the adopting family. These analyses permit us to discuss the congruence of the birthmothers' views with those of the adoptive parents in a more systemic manner.

These results of our study are fully consistent with Kirk's (1981) statements that were formulated during the era of confidential adoption:

> [E]mpathy and communication are key requirements for dynamic stability of families not regulated by tradition. By "dynamic stability" I meant social relationships which are both reliable and flexible, which provide a secure base for the small child's growth and development while making allowance for changes, for maturation, and the child's need to become an independent adult. (p. 40)

This perspective is illustrated well by a birthmother's response to the question, "Which of these three styles would make it easier for a birthparent to adjust to placing a child for adoption?"

> I'd have to say the open one, fully opened. But then again, I don't know. I think it's something that you have to work into. I think that's one reason why we have such a healthy relationship between one another. You know, it kinda gradually progressed. It wasn't all totally up—you know, out in the air and knowing everything about 'em. It was just like kinda putting together a puzzle. You just kinda got little pieces by pieces until now, you know, everything's there . . . So I would have to say, you know, starting from square one, with a little bit of information and then gradually moving on up. (birthmother, ongoing fully disclosed adoption)

In another ongoing fully disclosed adoption that was perceived to be functioning smoothly, the adoptive father made an important point: "Different adoptions fit different situations. I don't think every glove fits every hand." Each adoptive family system contains many individuals yoked by the adopted child. The adoptive parents' perspective is only one part of the system. If one carries the hand/glove metaphor a bit further, thinking of the adoptive family system as the hand and the type of adoption as the glove, it seems plausible that each glove, or perhaps even individual fingers of the glove, may need to be knitted for each family system. Additionally, the gloves may need to be hand-knitted, rather than mass produced, and made of natural fibers that breathe, grow, and change with the hand.

NOTES

1. We attempted instead to run a MANCOVA, including all 10 dependent variables and the background variables of parental education, family income, child age, and number of birth and adopted children as covariates. Some data were missing on the interview variables (see Tables 5.4 and 5.5 for Ns), typically because of transcripts coded as either "unclear/can't code" or "mixed/ambivalent." Other cases had missing data on one or more background variables. The net effect of the missing data was that the total sample size was reduced from 190 fathers to 92 and from 189 mothers to 93 because the analysis uses listwise deletion of cases; that is, the entire case is deleted if *any* variable is missing for that case. Because losing more than half the data was an unacceptable sacrifice, we instead conducted individual univariate analyses of variance for each dependent variable.

2. All names and places have been changed to protect identities.

6

BIRTHMOTHERS' ADJUSTMENT AND RESOLUTION OF GRIEF

With Cinda Christian and Chalandra Bryant

The previous two chapters focused on outcomes of the continuum of openness in adoption for adopted children and adoptive parents. In this chapter, we examine the birthmothers' experiences in varying types of adoptions, their role adjustment, and grief resolution 4 to 12 years after placement of a child in a confidential, time-limited mediated, ongoing mediated, or fully disclosed adoption.

Between 1987 and 1992, 169 birthmothers were interviewed. As mentioned in Chapter 3, each birthmother completed a series of standardized measures and an extensive tape-recorded interview conducted by telephone in her own home or at the agency. Our interviewers observed that many birthmothers preferred the telephone format because they were able to disclose personal feelings in a more anonymous manner. The birthmother interview included more than 300 questions dealing with education and career plans, close relationships, the general adoption process, the birthmother's experience with making an adoption plan for her child, and the birthmother's current experience with her adoption situation, including her relationships with her birthchild, the child's adoptive family, and the placing agency.

Fifty-two birthmothers (31%) were in confidential adoptions in which no information was shared among triad members beyond 6 months after placement. In some cases, updated information had been placed in agency files but had not been relayed to the other parties. Eighteen (11%) were in time-limited mediated adoptions in which only non-identifying information was relayed between adoptive parents and birthmothers by a caseworker at the adoption agency, but the information sharing had stopped by the time the participants were interviewed, and the parties did not intend to continue communication. Fifty-eight (34%) were in ongoing mediated placements, and the parties were continuing to share non-identifying information and/or meetings and/or telephone calls through the agency. Forty-one (24%) were in fully disclosed adoptions and were directly sharing information, usually accompanied by face-to-face meetings.

CHARACTERISTICS OF THE BIRTHMOTHER SAMPLE

As mentioned in Chapter 3, at the time of delivery, birthmother ages ranged from 14 to 36 years (mean = 19): 67% (n = 113) of birthmothers were adolescents ($\leq$ 19) at the time of the child's birth, and 33% (n = 56) were older ($\geq$ 20). The majority (92.9%) were Caucasian, and almost 91% of birthmothers (n = 153) reported being single at the time of delivery. At the time of the interview, birthmothers ranged in age from 21 to 43 (mean = 27.1) and had given birth to one to five children (mean = 1.96). The majority of birthmothers, 57%, were currently married; 18 (10.7%) were divorced at the time of the study; 2 were widowed; and 50 (30%) were single. Their mean educational level was 13.5 years, and 53% of the sample had an annual income between $10,000 and $29,000. Fifteen birthmothers (8.9%) were adopted persons. The majority of birthmothers in the sample reported no problems with alcoholism, schizophrenia, physical or learning disabilities, or depression. Most had successfully formed close adult relationships, and 62% had children other than the one who was placed for adoption (Grotevant, McRoy, Gusukuma, & Loera, 1993). At the time of the interview, 16 birthmothers (9%) were married to the birthfathers and 3 (1%) were involved in romantic relationships with the birthfathers.

BIRTHMOTHERS' EXPERIENCES WITH OPENNESS

Demographic Characteristics of Birthmothers and Openness

Analyses were conducted to compare demographic characteristics of birthmothers across adoption arrangements (see Table 6.1). Analysis of variance was used to assess any differences for birthmother age, birthmother years of education, and placed child's age between the four openness categories. Chi-square analysis was conducted on ethnicity, income range, marital status, and religious preference of the birthmothers by the four openness categories. No significant differences were observed for any of these demographic variables between the four openness categories (see also Grotevant, McRoy, Elde, & Fravel, 1994; McRoy et al., 1994).

Preliminary analyses were also conducted to examine differences in birthmothers' experiences and attitudes as a function of their age at the time of the child's birth or the age of the child at the time of the study. No significant differences were found, and therefore all birthmothers were combined for the following analyses. Statistical comparisons were made among birthmothers in the four adoption arrangements on the following variables: (a) reasons for choosing level of openness, (b) birthmother involvement in selection of adoptive parents, (c) satisfaction/regrets about choice to place, (d) attitudes toward child placed for adoption, and (e) problems with adoption arrangements.[1] The findings are presented below.

Reasons for Choosing Level of Openness

Many birthmothers in this study participated in confidential adoptions because they were not aware of the availability of open options. Birthmothers in confidential and mediated adoptions were significantly more likely than birthmothers in fully disclosed adoptions to learn about open options after placement, $\chi^2(9) = 23.3$, $p < .01$ (see Figure 6.1), and they were significantly more likely than birthmothers in any other form of adoption to report that they chose confidential adoption because it was their only choice, $\chi^2(6) = 59.2$, $p < .001$ (see Figures 6.2a and 6.2b).

TABLE 6.1 Birthmother Demographics by Adoption Arrangements

	Confidential N = 52		Time-Limited Mediated N = 18		Ongoing Mediated N = 58		Fully Disclosed N = 41		Total N = 169	
	n	(%)	n	(%)	n	(%)	n	(%)	n	(%)
Ethnicity	(n = 50)		(n = 17)		(n = 57)		(n = 41)		(n = 165)	
Caucasian	47	(94.0)	14	(82.4)	56	(98.2)	40	(97.6)	157	
African American	1	(2.0)	0	(0)	0	(0)	0	(0)	1	
Latino	1	(2.0)	1	(5.9)	1	(1.8)	1	(2.4)	4	
Asian American	0	(0)	1	(5.9)	0	(0)	0	(0)	1	
Native American	1	(2.0)	1	(5.9)	0	(0)	0	(0)	2	
Marital Status at Time of Interview	(n = 52)		(n = 18)		(n = 57)		(n = 40)		(n = 167)	
Single	18	(34.6)	5	(27.8)	16	(28.1)	11	(27.5)	50	
Married	26	(50.0)	11	(61.1)	35	(61.4)	25	(62.5)	97	
Divorced	6	(11.5)	2	(11.1)	6	(10.5)	4	(10.0)	18	
Widowed	2	(3.8)	0	(0)	0	(0)	0	(0)	2	
Parenting	(n = 52)		(n = 18)		(n = 58)		(n = 41)		(n = 169)	
0 children	23	(44.2)	9	(50.0)	23	(39.7)	20	(48.8)	75	
1 child	16	(30.8)	3	(16.7)	19	(32.8)	12	(29.3)	50	
2 to 5 children	13	(25.0)	6	(33.3)	16	(27.5)	9	(22.0)	44	
Religious Affiliation	(n = 36)		(n = 17)		(n = 49)		(n = 33)		(n = 135)	
Catholic	11	(30.6)	6	(35.3)	20	(40.8)	16	(48.5)	53	
Protestant	14	(38.9)	7	(41.2)	21	(42.9)	12	(36.4)	54	
Other	11	(30.6)	4	(23.5)	8	(16.3)	5	(15.2)	28	
Income	(n = 46)		(n = 16)		(n = 54)		(n = 39)		(n = 155)	
0–$19,999	22	(47.8)	5	(31.3)	18	(33.4)	14	(35.9)	59	
$20,000–$49,999	20	(43.4)	10	(62.6)	35	(64.8)	23	(58.8)	88	
> $50,000	4	(8.7)	1	(6.3)	1	(1.9)	2	(5.1)	8	
Mean Age (SD) at Interview Range: 21 to 43	27.5	(3.9)	27.5	(3.2)	26.8	(3.8)	26.8	(3.7)	27.1	
Mean Age (SD) at Placement Range: 14 to 36	19.3	(3.8)	20.0	(2.8)	19.2	(3.0)	19.3	(3.3)	19.3	

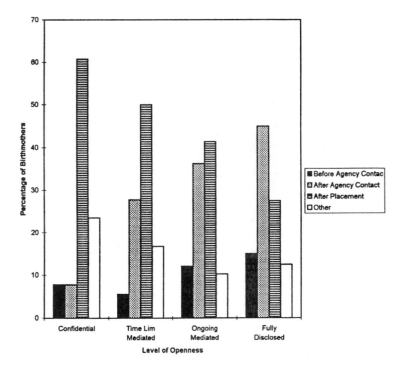

Figure 6.1 Timing of Birthmother's Awareness of Open Adoptions by Openness

Birthmother Involvement in Selection of Adoptive Parents

Thirty-one birthmothers (63.3%) in confidential adoptions and 6 (40%) in time-limited mediated adoptions had no role in the selection of the adoptive parents, compared with 13 birthmothers (22.4%) in ongoing mediated adoptions and 4 (9.8%) in fully disclosed adoptions. Birthmothers in ongoing mediated and fully disclosed adoptions were significantly more likely than birthmothers in confidential or time-limited mediated adoptions to select the adoptive parents for the child, $\chi^2(6) = 56.2$, $p < .001$. Twenty-eight birthmothers (48.3%) in ongoing mediated adoptions and 31 (75.6%) in fully disclosed adoptions selected the adoptive parents, compared with only 4 (26.7%) in time-limited mediated adoptions and 2 (4.1%) in confidential adoptions (see Figure 6.3).

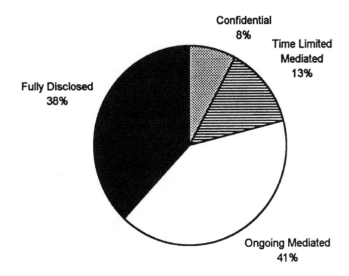

Figure 6.2a Adoption Arrangement Chosen Was Not the Only Option Given

Satisfaction/Regrets About Choice to Place

No significant differences were found among openness types on birthmother satisfaction with choice to place the child for adoption. At the time of the interview, the majority of birthmothers were satisfied with their choice to place. Only five birthmothers (four from confidential, one from an ongoing mediated adoption) reported dissatisfaction with placing the child for adoption.

Birthmothers were also asked whether they ever regretted the choice to place: 12% of birthmothers in fully disclosed adoptions, 24% of birthmothers in ongoing mediated adoptions, 22% in time-limited mediated adoptions, and 22% in confidential adoptions at some point in time had regretted the choice to place. Some of these birthmothers expressed their feelings of regret about making an adoption plan in the following ways:

> I regret it everyday. I wish I could have seen into the future. My child is gone—I thought about his first day at school, first steps—that makes me feel close to him and the adoptive parents—but he's gone. (ongoing mediated adoption)

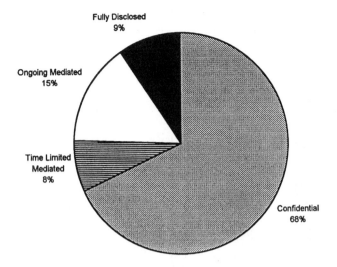

Figure 6.2b Adoption Arrangement Chosen Was the Only Option Given

I made a mistake—I should have kept her. (confidential adoption)

I'm satisfied but sometimes regret it. Now that I have children and see how I've made it, I know I could have made it with her too. (time-limited mediated adoption)

Although some birthmothers regretted their choice at some point, at the time of the interview only two birthmothers in the entire sample (one in a time-limited mediated adoption, one in a confidential adoption) expressed dissatisfaction with the quality of the adoptive family situation.

Birthmother Perceptions in Confidential Adoptions

Birthmothers in confidential adoptions received only limited non-identifying information until finalization of the adoption, about 6 months later. In a few cases, updated information on the birthmother or the adopted child might be placed in the agency files for future reference, but it was not intended for immediate transmission by the agency to either party. When these birthmothers were asked what kind

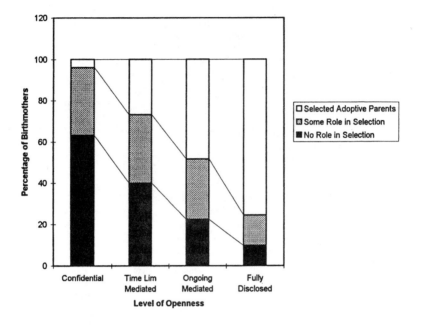

Figure 6.3 Birthmother's Role in Selection of Adoptive Parents by Openness Arrangement

of information they thought birthmothers should have, typical responses were as follows:

> Information about the child's personality, his looks, his interests.

> When he entered high school, how he did, if he was sports oriented, what career he had chosen.

> If he died; if he was healthy; if he had a birth defect that was noticed afterwards or a terminal illness; if the family was trying to adopt another child.

> Things about my child that would satisfy my peace of mind—but at the same time would not be too revealing so that I could find out who he

was or where he was. I wouldn't want to know too much, just enough to make me feel happy.

Most birthmothers in confidential adoptions indicated they would be pleased if the adoptive parents wished to give them updates through the agency on the child's development and activities. Many believed, however, that confidential arrangements are really better for the child because it causes less confusion. For example, one birthmother stated:

> I feel like the child would be confused, especially when they find out they're adopted and who their birthmother is. I think this would be a very confusing relationship for them. I feel like for me I've given up my rights as a mother in the fact that I placed him for adoption. And if I was to associate with him every day or on a regular basis, I think it would be too hard on me to keep leaving that child there, knowing that he was mine. (confidential adoption)

Another birthmother in a confidential adoption stated:

> A child doesn't have to go through the conflict of there being an extra person. My child, when he's 18 years old, can find out who I am. All he has to do is go over here and ask. At that point he'll be an adult, and it'll be his choice what he wants. It'll never be forced on him. And I like that. (confidential adoption)

Birthmother Perceptions in Mediated Adoptions

Birthmothers in time-limited mediated adoptions typically shared information with the adoptive families for only a few years after placement. Birthmothers in ongoing mediated adoptions, however, planned to share at least until adulthood, and most planned to share indefinitely. Only 13 birthmothers (17%) in mediated adoptions had written agreements, and 15 (20%) indicated they thought they had verbal agreements concerning sharing. Two birthmothers (3%) in ongoing mediated adoptions expressed concern that sharing might have a negative impact on their spouses, and two (11%) in time-limited and two (3%) in ongoing mediated adoptions thought there could be a potential negative impact on the adoptive parents.

Fourteen birthmothers (24%) in ongoing adoptions and three (16%) in time-limited mediated adoptions had face-to-face meetings with the adoptive parents. Only one thought the impact had been negative for her, and none thought the impact had been negative for the adoptive parents. Also, 50% of birthmothers in mediated adoptions indicated that the meetings with adoptive parents occurred after placement and that most took place at the agency. About 70% of birthmothers recalled having mixed or ambivalent feelings during the first meeting. They felt a combination of sadness as well as feelings of reassurance about the child's well-being. The following quotes illustrate the various feelings birthmothers recalled about initial meetings:

I was very nervous and extremely obnoxious at the first meeting. I told the adoptive parents that I wanted them to put it in their will that if anything ever happened to them, I wanted the child back. They [adoptive parents] straightened me out right away. (mediated adoption)

I was a basket case at the first meeting. It was much harder than I thought it would be—the meeting was a shock in itself. I had no idea it would hurt so much. When I placed my child in their arms [at placement] and walked away, the reality hit me for the first time. (mediated adoption)

I met my child's adoptive family and [birth child] when [adopted child] was 5 years old. She just climbed in my lap and showed me her baby books. She was so cute and she just loved me, you know. I felt real good, better than I have felt anywhere in a long time because the parents are so neat. (mediated adoption)

I felt relieved about the whole situation when I met them [adoptive parents]. They made me feel comfortable about it. I was nervous until they got to the hospital. Then I wasn't nervous anymore. (mediated adoption)

I was excited during the meeting. I was, you know, kind of nervous too, not really knowing. Afterwards, it was real weird because until I found out that he really was with good people, that he was safe and happy, then I could relax. Afterwards, he was still in my prayers, but it wasn't something that just consumed me all the time, thinking about it and wondering. (mediated adoption)

Clearly, the meetings seemed to help many birthmothers resolve some pain, hurt, guilt, and sad feelings over the placement of their children. Others were confronted with the reality of their loss for the first time. Seeing that their children were happy and in loving homes allowed these birthmothers to begin to accept the decision and loss of their children. They seemed to enter these meetings with a great deal of fear and anxiety but left feeling quite satisfied and positive about the adoptive families.

Birthmothers' Perceptions and Experiences in Fully Disclosed Adoptions

The majority of birthmothers in fully disclosed adoptions had their first meeting at the adoption agency sometime after placement. However, 9 met before the birth, 10 after the birth but before the placement, and 9 at placement. After the first meeting, 28 (68%) decided to have ongoing direct contact as a result of the first meeting. Attitudes toward contact are conveyed in the following statements:

> Contact reassures me about my decision, and I plan to keep in touch for this reason.

> I think it is healthy for me—it has allowed me to heal and not be so consumed with the relinquishment. His adoptive parents think this is good. They initiated the face-to-face contact, and I now visit their home occasionally.

> Contact will give Susan, my birthchild, a sense of her own self—a sense of self-acceptance. I think the more she understands where she came from, the better her sense of self and the more balanced she will be emotionally. I also think the meetings solidify a bond between me and the adoptive parents.

All but two birthmothers perceived the relationship with the adoptive parents to be positive. One birthmother felt in competition with the adoptive parents, and one thought the adoptive parents were in competition with her. The majority thought the impact of the meetings on their children, on the adoptive families, and on themselves was positive and would continue to be positive as the children matured. All but three birthmothers in fully disclosed adoptions stated that their placed children referred to them by their first names, and 92% of birthmothers in fully disclosed adoptions stated that their placed children referred to their adoptive mothers as "Mother" or "Mom."

When birthmothers considered the impact of contact on themselves and their spouses and future children, diverse responses were given. Among the birthmothers who responded, 30% thought the future impact would be positive, 30% thought the impact would be mixed, 10% thought the impact would be neutral, and 5% predicted the impact would be negative (25% of the responses were not codable). All birthmothers with fully disclosed adoptions who were married at the time of the interview had told their spouses of the adoption and the sharing/contact with the adoptive families. Although most spouses were supportive of the openness arrangement, very few took an active role in the contact regardless of whether the spouse was the birthfather or not. In some cases, however, when the birthmother had married the birthfather, the spouse tended to prefer that they "put the adoption behind them." This seemed to be especially true when painful circumstances surrounded the adoption, such as cases in which the birthfather had wanted to parent rather than place the child. In other cases, birthmothers indicated that their non-birthfather spouses did not wish to be involved in the contact because it was hard to be reminded that the birthmother had given birth to a child who was fathered by another man.

Some birthmothers had not shared the fact of the adoption with the children they were currently parenting and were worried about when and how to disclose this information. For example, one birthmother mentioned the difficulties of explaining her own teenage sexual activity and earlier pregnancy to the daughter she is parenting. Another expressed concern that the children she was raising may compare their family's lifestyle with that of the adopted child.

Birthmothers' Relatives'
Involvement in Ongoing Contact

A majority (56%) of birthmothers in fully disclosed arrangements indicated that other relatives were involved in the interactions with the placed children and their adoptive families. A few commented as follows:

My brother and sister-in-law have gone with me to meet Angie's adoptive parents. Other family members have seen her picture. (fully disclosed adoption)

Almost always at Christmas, my mom goes over and brings presents to Rodney [adopted child] and brings presents to Melissa [adopted child's sibling, not related to this birthmother] too. I think Melissa calls my mother "grandmother" too. They [adoptive family] were invited to my sister's wedding. (fully disclosed adoption)

Attitudes Toward Child Placed for Adoption

Birthmothers in all types of adoptions were asked a series of questions focusing on their attitudes toward the children they placed for adoption: 94% of birthmothers indicated they think about the children they placed for adoption on special occasions such as birthdays, Mother's Day, and other holidays. Regardless of adoption arrangement, all but two birthmothers (who were in ongoing mediated adoptions) thought the adopted children truly belonged to the adoptive families. Two other birthmothers (one in time-limited mediated adoption, one in fully disclosed adoption) thought the children only belonged "to some degree" to the adoptive families; both of these women acknowledged that the children fully belonged to the adoptive families yet also believed that, in some way, the children also belonged to them by bloodline or by the love they held for the children.

About 40% of birthmothers in the study fantasized about meeting or visiting with the child: 22 (13%) fantasized about having an ongoing relationship with the child at adulthood but not necessarily having a mother-child relationship (8 of these were in fully disclosed, 10 were in ongoing mediated, 1 was in time-limited mediated, and 3 were in confidential arrangements). No statistically significant differences were found for any of these items by level of openness.

Four of the 41 birthmothers in fully disclosed adoptions indicated they had at some point wished they could reclaim their children. As noted below, although they had a desire at some point, they still felt very ambivalent about the idea of reclaiming:

> Sometimes I'd like to have her back because I want to be a parent. It is still in a lot of ways your child, 'cause you gave birth. In some ways I do have some concerns, but I really feel OK. (fully disclosed adoption)

> I mean, I'd love to have her, but no way. That would just tear her apart. She would hate me. For her sake, no, because I just couldn't imagine what that would do to a child. (fully disclosed adoption)

Problems With Adoption Arrangements

Slightly more than half (60%) of the birthmothers identified problems with their adoption arrangements: 31 of these were in confidential, 7 in time-limited mediated, 32 in ongoing mediated, and 22 in fully disclosed adoptions. Problems with confidential adoptions included a desire to have more information about the adopted child and anxieties and worries about the child. Some birthmothers in time-limited mediated adoptions worried about the child and expressed their desire to have more information as well. Birthmothers in ongoing mediated adoptions expressed concern that adoptive parents might eventually cease contact. They were also anxious for several reasons: (a) information they knew about the child or family, (b) delayed or interrupted transmissions of information through the agency, and (c) having to wait for the adoptive parents to respond. Birthmothers in fully disclosed adoptions expressed concern about the following: (a) having shared too much personal information with the adoptive mother, (b) comparisons of the birth and adoptive families by the adopted child, (c) the way the adoptive parents were raising the child, (d) their obligation to keep in contact with the adoptive family even if the they preferred not to, (e) fear of jeopardizing the relationship with the adoptive parents, and (f) the birthmother's own role with the adopted child.

Counseling had been sought by 37% of birthmothers in the sample, but no significant differences by adoption arrangement were found on this variable: 17 (34%) confidential, 7 (38.9%) time-limited mediated, 24 (42%) ongoing mediated, and 13 (32%) fully disclosed birthmothers had sought counseling. Of all the birthmothers, 31 (18.8%) indicated they sought help for problems related to the adoption. Examples of adoption-related issues included "working through guilt feelings about having placed a child and my anxiety over how she was doing" and "being a mother and having your body go through all these changes and [having] no baby to relate all these feelings to."

Summary of Experiences of Birthmothers

The majority of birthmothers in the study did not choose to place a child for adoption because of their awareness of open options. In fact, the majority had never heard of open options prior to agency contact, and most birthmothers in confidential adoptions typically selected this form of adoption because they were unaware of any other option. Many who were having contact with adoptive families, however, said they would not have made an adoption plan if it had to be completely confidential with no contact. Some birthmothers even mentioned they would have changed agencies if necessary in order to have an opportunity for contact with the adopted child.

Most birthmothers were generally satisfied with their adoption choices and with the quality of the adoptive family situation. Although some critics of openness have suggested that fully disclosed adoptions may lead to competition with the adoptive parents, problems in later adjustment, jealousy toward the adoptive parents, and possibly regret about the decision to place, the majority of birthmothers in this study who were engaged in direct contact with the adoptive families did not express these feelings. Contrary to critics' predictions, the opportunity to see the child with the adoptive family seemed to have a "healing effect." Many claimed they were able to better accept their decision to make an adoption plan once they knew the child was happy.

The desire for information about the child was relieved in the case of mediated and fully disclosed adoptions. These birthmothers knew the locations and situations of their birthchildren and seemed to have developed positive relationships with the adoptive families. The non-significant trend was for birthmothers in ongoing mediated and fully disclosed adoptions to anticipate a continuing relationship with their children with higher frequency than birthmothers in confidential and time-limited mediated adoptions. The latter may have found ways to accept the fact that they may never see their children again, whereas birthmothers who have contact see the possibility for ongoing relationships. Birthmothers with fully disclosed arrangements seemed to view their relationships with their children realistically and assess their openness arrangements at this point as being mutually beneficial.

The following section provides a conceptual and empirical analysis of role adjustment and grief resolution issues that birthmothers reported in this study.

BIRTHMOTHER POSTPLACEMENT ROLE ADJUSTMENT AND GRIEF RESOLUTION

Role Adjustment

Roles typically refers to "the behavior expected of individuals who occupy particular social categories" (Zurcher, 1983, p. 11). Generally, roles are learned during the process of socialization (Bush & Simmons, 1981). In many instances, individuals learn a role by observing the behaviors of other people in that role and also by observing the expectations of others regarding individuals in that role. *Anticipatory socialization* refers to the role learning that takes place in advance of the opportunity to take on a particular role (Riley, Foner, Hess, & Toby, 1973). Often, expectations for filling a future role are communicated to individuals from others already in that role, although the expectations need not be explicitly stated. An example of this phenomenon is a child learning about her expected future role of parent during the process of the relationship with her own parent. Conversely, *role ambiguity* is experienced when there are no clear expectations of performance in a given role or no "role model" has been established. This is illustrated by the relatively new "birthmother" role being experienced by women placing their children both in fully disclosed adoptions and in mediated adoptions.

Traditionally, confidential adoptions were considered the best (and only) option for the birthmother because it allowed her to save herself from the embarrassment of an unplanned child, to put the past behind her, and to go forward with her life. In theory, confidential adoptions would provide the birthmother freedom from new roles to adjust to; without the physical reminder of the child, the birthmother might be more likely to return to her life and the roles within it as it existed before the pregnancy. Kraft, Palombo, Woods, et al. (1985) suggest that the birthmother in a confidential adoption is provided the opportunity to grieve the placement of the child and then, in effect, move on. In the cases of fully disclosed and mediated adoptions, however, the birthmother may experience considerable "role strain," which is the difficulty in fulfilling her newly acquired role obligations (Goode, 1960). Not only must she adopt the new role of birthmother to the child she placed for adoption, but she also has had absolutely no socialization for this role. It is unlikely that, as she grew up, there were any role models of this type for her to observe and learn from, nor are there currently any specific societal expectations from which she can draw information about her role. As a result, the birthmother is left in an ambiguous situation, unclear of what others (the adoptive family and child in particular) expect of her and, in fact, unclear on what she should even expect of herself.

A birthmother who chooses a fully disclosed or mediated adoption fills a role in which she has demonstrated concern and responsibility by the desire to observe her child develop despite being unable or unwilling to fully take on the role of mother. Role conflict, whether between distinct roles that an individual occupies or between the individual's self-concept and a particular role, can cause considerable personal stress (Zurcher, 1983).

Role Enactment. Factors other than type of adoption may also influence the amount of role strain experienced by the birthmother. For example, it may be possible for birthmothers to have improved adjustment to role strain over time. According to Zurcher (1983), humans are active role enactors, able not only to conform to role expectations but also to interpret, organize, modify, and *create* them. Perhaps the birthmother in the situation involving openness will modify and create expectations for herself as "birthmother" after she has had more experience in the situation. Thus, she would no longer be in an ambiguous situation. In addition, she may also be able to come to terms with the potential mother/birthmother role conflict with increased experience in the role. In effect, birthmothers who have had more experience in the role (longer time since placement) should have less role strain than those for whom it is still relatively new territory.

Adolescent Adjustment Issues. As mentioned earlier, the majority of birthmothers were adolescents at the time of the births. Adolescent birthmothers may be facing an additional set of difficulties when making decisions about placing a child for adoption. According to Piaget, an adolescent is only beginning to function at the level of formal operational thought. The adolescent's newly formed abilities to think logically and to anticipate future consequences to particular actions are not well established. "In times of stress, the need for immediate gratification may not be delayed. The normal adolescent's cognitive level will vacillate between childlike and adultlike levels of functioning from moment to moment" (Kraft, Palombo, Woods, et al., 1985, p. 17). For the adolescent birthmother, this means the task of making decisions regarding placement may not be consistent with her capabilities; she has the disadvantage of being unprepared to weigh the choices with which she is confronted. As a result, later adjustment to her role as birthmother may be hampered by her poor foresight at the time of placement regarding the impact this decision will have on her later life.

Grief Resolution

Grief is defined as the range of feelings, behaviors, and thoughts that may occur in response to a loss; these responses may include anger, crying, withdrawal, guilt, sadness, anxiety, or numbness (Dominick, 1988; Raphael, 1984; Worden, 1982). Several theories addressing the grief cycle have been applied to birthmothers placing children for adoption. Watson (1986) suggested five sequential stages of grief: (a) shock and denial, (b) guilt, (c) anger or depression, (d) sadness, and (e) acceptance. Watson noted that the denial process is emphasized in confidential adoptions and that birthmothers are encouraged to forget their placed children ever existed. Millen and Roll (1985) applied Parkes's (1972) six-phase theory of grief and loss, which was originally concerned with the experience of widows, to explicate the experiences of a clinical sample of birthmothers who were characterized by pathological mourning. The researchers suggested that birthmothers deal with grief through a "process of realization" that the loss is permanent. The six phases are (a) a state of alarm in which the birthmother may think the world is no longer a safe place, (b) a search for a mental image or fantasy about the child, (c) anger and guilt for not preventing the placement, (d) feelings of emptiness, (e) identification with the child, and (f) gradual acceptance of the placement. D. M. Brodzinsky (1990) outlined a model for adaptive grieving that included the following five criteria: (a) a safe place to be; (b) freedom to express feelings; (c) proximity, empathy, and warmth of loved ones who can express "some measure of 'knowing' what has occurred"; (d) rituals of passing; and (e) opportunity for reorganization in which an understanding of the situation and roles of everyone involved is eventually gained. Brodzinsky noted that these criteria, though necessary for adaptive grieving, are not always available to women who have placed children for adoption.

Silverman (1981) suggested that, regardless of specific stages, a birthmother's feeling of loss should be viewed as healthy and appropriate, given the circumstances of placing a child for adoption. Resolution of this feeling results in the birthmother forming a new, integrated identity in which the past is not denied. Instead, past events become a connected part of her new self-perception.

The extant research on birthmother grief focuses primarily on confidential adoptions. Several follow-up studies of birthmothers who placed children in confidential adoptions noted the following conditions: (a) prolonged feelings of loss and continued mourning (Sorosky et al., 1978); (b) depression (Burnell & Norfleet, 1979); (c) somatic symptoms, restless anxiety, anger, and loss reactions (Millen & Roll, 1985); and (d) intense attachment to and overprotection of children subsequently born to and raised by a birthmother after the placement of a child for adoption (Rynearson, 1982). Winkler and Van Keppel (1984) reported significant psychological impairment among relinquishing mothers who were not participating in support groups 4 to 20 years after making an adoption plan for a child. Similarly, a survey of women who had relinquished infants for adoption in confidential adoptions reported a strong correlation among birthmothers' feelings of guilt and shame about the decision to relinquish, their perceptions about the decision to relinquish, their perceptions of coercion by others, their lack of an opportunity to express their feelings about the relinquishment, and their unresolved grief (DeSimone, 1996). Nevertheless, in a comparative study of women who made the decision during adolescence either to place the child or to parent, no significant differences in negative psychological outcomes were observed (McLaughlin et al., 1988).

Theorists differ in their beliefs about how open adoption arrangements may affect birthmother grief. Some believe that open arrangements may help facilitate healthy adjustment to grief and loss (Sorich & Siebert, 1982). Others argue that open adoptions are more difficult than confidential adoptions for the birthmother (Kraft, Palombo, Woods, et al., 1985). Kraft, Palombo, Woods, et al. (1985) believe that, in open adoptions, birthmothers cannot adequately grieve over placing their children because there is no closure, and therefore open adoptions may not be the best option. Silber and Dorner (1990), in contrast, argue that the relationships that develop between birthmothers and adoptive families in fully disclosed adoptions mediate the experience of grief. These authors view openness as a process that allows a birthmother to confront her grief over the loss of the parenting role and to work through it in a supportive environment, which includes the adoptive parents and the child.

Relatively limited empirical attention has been given to the issue of birthmother grieving in open adoptions. Two studies conducted in New Zealand and Australia have reported mostly positive outcomes for birthmothers in open arrangements. Iwanek (1987) observed 14 birthmothers who were involved in open adoptions for 7 to 12 years. These New Zealand birthmothers reported that knowledge about the well-being of the children for whom they made adoption plans facilitated their coping with grief. Iwanek recommended that "secret" adoptions cease and be replaced by open adoptions, while acknowledging that these arrangements may not be easy or problem free.

Dominick (1988) interviewed 65 Australian birthmothers who had made adoption plans for their children 2 to 4 years earlier. Two thirds of the birthmothers had met the adoptive parents after the birth of the babies, and most were having ongoing, indirect contact. Nearly all the birthmothers thought the meetings did not hinder their adjustment to adoption. The majority of birthmothers who did not have a meeting, however, anticipated that having a meeting would have caused them difficulties about the decision to relinquish. Birthmothers who met the adoptive parents did not experience significantly more unresolved grief than birthmothers who had not met. Of the 21 birthmothers (32%) who were experiencing unresolved grief at the time of the interview, most had not talked about the experience with anyone since the adoptions. In addition, most of those who had indirect contact with the adoptive parents considered the contact unsatisfactory. Dominick also reported that many of these birthmothers had felt pressured to make adoption plans. These findings were similar to those of Winkler and Van Keppel (1984), who suggested that ongoing birthmother grief is related to lack of social supports and lack of opportunities to talk about their feelings about the adoptions.

Contrary to findings from the above two studies, Blanton and Deschner (1990) found greater birthmother grief in open adoptions. In their study of U.S. birthmothers' grief experiences from 1 to more than 5 years (mean = 2.3 years) after placement, birthmothers in open adoptions appeared to be having more difficult grief adjustment than birthmothers in confidential adoptions. In a study of 5 birthmothers who had made adoption plans for their children in open arrangements less than 2 years earlier, Lancette and McClure (1992) found that all 5 were still experiencing unresolved grief that centered around loss fantasies associated with motherhood and parenting the children for whom they made adoption plans. In comparison with the Dominick (1988) and Iwanek (1987) studies, these conflicting findings may be a result of disparate definitions of openness. Blanton and Deschner defined an *open adoption* as one in which the birthmother simply met the adoptive parents; *openness* did not refer to ongoing contact with the adoptive family. Both Iwanek and Dominick deemed that ongoing knowledge or contact was important to birthmother grief resolution. Lancette and McClure determined that all 5 birthmothers in their sample had open adoptions, yet they acknowledged that the degree of openness varied across their participants. Nevertheless, intensification of the grief experience for birthmothers who had met the adoptive parents led Blanton and Deschner to suggest caution in offering open adoptions as standard practice for all birthmothers. Moreover, they called for studies of long-term birthmother adjustment to loss in varying types of adoptions.

To bring further clarification to these varied findings, we examined adoption adjustment and grief resolution for birthmothers in the study. The specific openness coding scheme used here enabled us to discern differences between groups (between time-limited mediated and confidential) that may otherwise be considered similar (no current contact). Although the power of the analyses is greatly reduced when further distinctions between types of adoptions are made, significant and marginally significant findings emerged nonetheless. It is anticipated that further investigation of this type with larger samples would further support these findings. This study revealed the importance of recognizing more permutations of openness in adoptions than the "open" versus "closed" dichotomies of previous studies (e.g., Blanton & Deschner, 1990; Kraft, Palombo, Woods, et al., 1985).

Method

Participants

For this analysis, a subset of the original sample of 169 birthmothers was used; it consisted of 75 of 77 cases (2 cases were dropped because of incomplete information) in which data were gathered from adoptive parents, their adopted child, and the birthmother of that child. By using only the birthmothers who were part of this fully corresponding subset, it was possible to access information from the adoptive parents' interviews as well, which provided further validation of findings (Marshall & Rossman, 1989). In this subsample of 75 birthmothers, 10 had confidential adoptions, 8 had time-limited mediated adoptions, 28 had ongoing mediated adoptions, and 29 had fully disclosed adoptions.

Global Coding of Role
Adjustment and Grief Resolution

Global codes to assess role adjustment and grief resolution of birthmothers were developed. In the process of coding, much of the information in the birthmothers' files was read, including the birthmother interviews, Twenty Statements Tests, interviewer field notes, and adoptive parent and adopted child interviews. Emphasis was placed on the birthmother interview data. The Twenty Statements Test, interviewer field notes, and adoptive parent interviews provided additional data sources for further validation of findings; however, the children's transcripts proved to be less helpful in identifying birth-mother adoption adjustment and grief resolution issues.

Drawing on the literature, as well as a review of the coders' notes on birthmother feelings and behaviors that may be expressions of adoption adjustment or grief, coders developed a list of response categories that were characteristic of each area. Although the composition of indicators was different in each case, evidence of *unresolved grief* included (a) crying during the interview, (b) attempts to deny or repress the past, (c) expressions of regret or guilt, (d) depression, (e) continuing unsubstantiated worries or anxieties about the child, (f) dissatisfaction with the placement, (g) desire to reclaim the child, (h) continuing nightmares about the child, and (i) inability to move beyond the placement decision. Indicators of *good grief resolution* included (a) positive and optimistic feelings about the decision, (b) ongoing positive relationships, (c) acceptance of the decision, (d) ability to separate self from the placed child, (e) demonstration of empathy for the child and the adoptive family, (f) ability to move beyond the placement, and (g) ability to express satisfaction with current life situations.

Evidence of *poor adoption adjustment* included birthmother's (a) inability to separate from the child, (b) regretting the decision to place the child, (c) expression of a need to continue having more children in an attempt to replace the child who was lost, (d) recurring dreams or nightmares in which the birthmother meets the child or some bad fate befalls the child, and (e) lingering family secrets regarding the adoption. Potential *positive adoption adjustment* indicators included (a) feelings of satisfaction with the adoptive placement, (b) positive feelings about or relationship with the adoptive parents, or (c) realistic attitude about the possibility of meeting the child in the future.

As each document was read, evidence of current birthmother adoption adjustment and grief resolution was recorded on coding sheets. After all the information was recorded, coders reread the comments they had included on the coding sheet and decided how well each birthmother had adjusted to her role in the adoption and had resolved her grief. Adoption adjustment and grief resolution scores were assigned on the basis of a 1-to-5 scale (1 = *very poor,* 2 = *poor,* 3 = *fair,* 4 = *good,* and 5 = *very good*) with 0.25-point intervals (these were 17-point scales, which could be coded as 1, 1.25, 1.5, 1.75, . . . 5). Coders were instructed to keep previously coded cases in mind when coding each new file as a means of ranking each birthmother relative to others.

Because coders observed and recorded many different elements of adoption adjustment and grief resolution, actual scores were determined by the frequency, severity, variety, and contextual appropriateness of the evidence recorded. A birthmother who had, or did not have, any one specific indicator would not be automatically placed into a predetermined category; consideration was given to the context from which the evidence came. There was no "typical" profile of characteristics for a birthmother with a particular score. For example, one birthmother who cried once during the interview when recalling her feelings at the time of placement received a higher grief resolution score than another birthmother who cried throughout all areas of the interview and had additional indicators of unresolved grief, such as ongoing unsubstantiated worries about the child. In addition, a birthmother with a score of 1.25 may have had several of the potential indicators of poor adjustment present; another birthmother with the same score may have only had one of the indicators, but it was to such an intensity that it pervaded and negatively affected other areas of her life.

Birthmother files were divided between coders and were coded independently. Reliability was established between each coding team member and the training coder. During the coding process, every fifth case was coded by two coders (the training coder and one of the other three coders) as a reliability check (reliabilities ranged from $r = .83$ to $r = .92$, using intraclass correlation). All disagreements were resolved through consensus. Coders generally coded within 0.5 point of each other in each case. Coders were especially trained to keep their evaluations of role adjustment and grief resolution separate, and different coders rated the two variables whenever possible.

Intercorrelations among ratings of role adjustment, grief resolution, age at placement, years since placement, and age at time of interview are presented in Table 6.2. Role adjustment and grief resolution were correlated .79, which is consistent with both their conceptual similarity and their differences. For example, it is likely that birthmothers with high ratings on grief resolution would be satisfied

TABLE 6.2 Correlations Among Continuous Variables

Variable	1	2	3	4	5
1. Age at Placement	—	-.18*	.79***	.10	.03
2. Years Since Placement		—	.46***	-.07	.03
3. Age at Interview			—	.05	.04
4. Adoption Adjustment				—	.79***
5. Grief Resolution					—

NOTE: For *Adoption Adjustment and Grief Resolution,* the n's range from 67 to 75; for all other variables, from 149 to 160.
*$p \le .05$; ***$p \le .001$.

with their adoption arrangements. It is also possible, however, that those with good grief resolution would wish for structural changes in their adoption arrangements.

Role Adjustment Results

Scores on the dependent measure, adoption adjustment, ranged from 1.0 (poor adjustment) to 4.5 (between good and very good adjustment), with a mean score of 2.9 (slightly below fair adjustment). To assess whether birthmothers in fully disclosed and mediated adoptions had more difficult role adjustments than birthmothers in confidential adoptions, ANOVA of adoption adjustment by openness level was calculated (see Table 6.3). Type of adoption was significantly related to birthmother role adjustment, as indicated by coding of adoption adjustment ($F(3,71) = 5.22, p = .003$). Specifically, analysis revealed that those in the time-limited mediated group were significantly different from the ongoing mediated and fully disclosed participants (Duncan pooled variance estimates[2] $t = -3.57, p = .001$ and $t = -3.74, p = .001$, respectively).[3] In addition, the same analysis revealed that time-limited mediated and confidential birthmothers were marginally different from each other (Duncan pooled variance estimates $t = -2.0, p = .06$). No significant difference was found between confidential and ongoing mediated birthmother adoption adjustment (Duncan pooled variance estimates $t = -1.18, p = .247$), and confidential and fully disclosed birthmother adoption adjustment only approached being significantly different (Duncan pooled variance estimates $t = -1.53$, $p = .13$). Although not all differences were significant, the trend was for a continuum of role adjustment; birthmothers in fully disclosed adoptions, who had the best average outcomes, were at one end of the spectrum, followed by those in ongoing mediated, then by those in confidential, and ultimately by those in time-limited mediated adoptions, who had the poorest average outcomes (see Table 6.3). To determine whether the number of years since the placement was associated with birthmother role adjustment, ANOVA of adoption adjustment by number of years since placement was computed ("number of years since placement" was dichotomized: one group included birthmothers with fewer than 8 years since placement, and the other group included birthmothers with 8 or more years since placement). There was no detected effect on adoption adjustment of having greater versus fewer years since placement ($F(1,72) = 0.172$, $p = .68$).[4] No evidence was found that number of years since placement provided any benefit or detriment to birthmothers in their adoption role adjustment.

To assess whether age of the birthmother at the time of the adoption was related to her role adjustment at the time of the interview, age at the time of placement was also dichotomized (adolescents ≤ 19 years old; non-adolescents ≥ 20 years old). ANOVA revealed no evidence for group differences in adoption adjustment dependent on age at placement ($F(1,72) = 0.09$, $p = .768$).[5]

Summary of Birthmothers' Role Adjustment Findings

We found no evidence that birthmother age at the time of placement was related to later role adjustment, and no support for the hypothesis that role adjustment may be better for birthmothers with more time since the placement. All birthmothers in the study had been in their role for at least 4 years. Perhaps by 4 years after placement, the role is not any more ambiguous than it would be at 6, 8, or 10 years after placement. In addition, by the passage of at least 4 years, birthmothers who were adolescents at the time of placement have grown; as adults, they have likely developed a new understanding of

TABLE 6.3   Adoption Adjustment by Type of Adoption

		Adoption Adjustment			
		Range			
Group	*n*	Low	High	Variance	Mean
Confidential	10	1.25	4	.792	2.68$_{c,d}$
Time-Limited Mediated	8	1	3	.481	1.91$_{a,b,c}$
Ongoing Mediated	28	1	4.5	.661	3.01$_a$
Fully Disclosed	29	1.5	4.5	.777	3.20$_{b,d}$
Group	75	1	4.5	.826	2.92

NOTE: Means with paired subscripts *a* and *b* differ significantly from each other ($p < .05$) by Duncan pooled variance estimates. Means with paired subscripts *c* and *d* approached significant difference from each other ($p < .10$) by Duncan pooled variance estimates.

their decision and its complexities and consequences. In short, perhaps the amount of time since, and age at, placement are only important to role adjustment for a very short time, beyond which role adjustment will be influenced by other factors.

Birthmothers who had adoptions with no ongoing contact had poorer role adjustment than those involved in adoption situations with ongoing contact. Specifically, birthmothers in time-limited mediated adoptions had significantly lower adoption adjustment scores than birthmothers in both ongoing mediated and fully disclosed adoptions. Although not significant, the trend for birthmothers in confidential adoptions was to have lower role adjustment scores than birthmothers in fully disclosed adoptions.

Perhaps having continuing contact with, and access to, information about the adoptive family and adopted child makes the process of role enactment easiest for birthmothers in mediated and fully disclosed adoptions. Because roles are socially defined, modifications and expectations of the birthmother role develop and are established in the process of the relationship with the adoptive family and the adopted child. Birthmothers who have no contact receive no feedback from the adoptive family or adopted child; social exchange from those most essential to the conceptualization of the birthmother role is absent. Those without contact may also remain in an ambiguous situation based on the possibility or hope that a reunion could happen in the future. This may be especially true for birthmothers in time-limited mediated adoptions because the lines of communication have been open in the past; the possibility of reinstating contact may be more salient for them.

One possible interpretation of why birthmothers in time-limited mediated adoptions have significantly more problematic role adjustment than birthmothers in both mediated and fully disclosed adoptions, and marginally more problematic role adjustment than those in confidential adoptions, is based on the dynamic nature of adoption. It has been noted that many birthmothers reported during their interviews that the degree of openness in their adoptions had changed since the initial placement. This raises the issue of self-selection as a possible confound (the possibility that birthmothers who were already having a difficult time adjusting to their adoptions were the ones who were most likely to discontinue the contact and thus selected themselves out of ongoing mediated adoptions and into time-limited mediated adoptions).

To explore the possibility of self-selection as a confound, birthmother transcripts from the eight time-limited mediated adoptions were further reviewed for recurring issues and themes. Only three of these birthmothers, however, felt they were in control of the amount of contact happening at the time of the interview. Two of these three claimed they were very satisfied with their adoptive arrangements; one characterized the discontinuation of contact as a natural conclusion, stating, "There has to be a stopping point." It is noted, however, that two of the three who felt they were in control of the amount of contact they were having also had the two highest adoption adjustment scores within this group (3 and 2.5), suggesting a link between the perception of control and adjustment.

For the five of eight birthmothers in time-limited mediated arrangements who thought the amount of contact was not in their control, self-selection into their type of adoption at this time would be contradictory. Another explanation could be that time-limited mediated birthmothers have a more difficult adjustment to their birthparent role because they are not satisfied with the role they currently have. A majority (five) of time-limited mediated birthmothers mentioned that they wanted *more* contact or information than they had. Most of those who wanted more contact had not initiated it, out of respect for the adoptive parents' wishes and their own desire to not "interfere" in the child's life. One birthmother who requested an updated picture of the adopted child, however, felt "shut out" of the child's life by adoptive parents who feared that she would want to reclaim the child.

Being dissatisfied with the level of contact seems to be part of the reason why time-limited mediated adoptions are resulting in poor birthmother role adjustments; however, dissatisfaction in the role alone does not explain the process that leads to poor adjustment. For those in this group who did not choose to terminate contact, the discontinuation of contact could have triggered feelings of helplessness or a loss of power that may be worsened by other situations or losses in their lives. For example, more than half (five) of the time-limited mediated birthmothers were facing issues related to fertility that could have contributed to their inability to adjust to their role as birthmother. One birthmother whose husband could not have children commented that she would never have placed her child for adoption if she had known that she would never have more children. Another birthmother chose to have a tubal ligation following the birth of her most recent child despite the protests of her husband; another had a difficult miscarriage following placement of the target child. Finally, two birthmothers in this group said they have no desire to have children of their own now; one stated, "I'm 37 years old. I'm not going to start a family now." Perhaps the discontinuation of contact, resulting in unfulfilling roles in the adoptions, makes birthmothers more vulnerable when faced with later losses such as infertility. Reversed, perhaps current losses sensitize birthmothers to be particularly regretful over the loss of a link to the placed child. Birthmothers view their roles in the specific contexts of their lives. The time-limited mediated birthmothers' dissatisfaction with their given role seems to be related, in part, to their suffering of other losses.

The search for patterns also revealed that denial and repression of feelings was a common thread among birthmothers with time-limited mediated arrangements. For some, their own parents or families never knew about the pregnancy or placement, and several of them referred to the "baby" as a "secret." These birthmothers may have poor role adjustment because of their self-imposed isolation from socially constructed conceptions of the role, based on their choice not to discuss their experiences with, or feelings about, the adoptive placement of their birthchildren. These birthmothers, not being active participants in "role enactment," consequently experience more role conflict. It is also possible that birthmothers who still harbor secrets regarding placement are burdened because they have no outlet for their emotions or feelings once contact no longer takes place. The discontinuation of contact may have also meant the loss of a rare confidante for the birthmothers who are unable to talk with their own families about the placement.

Social role theory suggests a possible explanation for the unexpected finding that birthmothers in time-limited mediated adoptions had the poorest role adjustment. These birthmothers may experience the most role strain because their style of adoption is the most ambiguous (see also Fravel, 1995). Unlike birthmothers in confidential adoptions, who have clear roles defined by the confidential nature of the situation, and birthmothers in fully disclosed and mediated adoptions, who have interaction with the adopted child and adoptive parents that facilitates the enactment and development of their roles, the birthmothers in time-limited mediated arrangements currently partake in no interaction with those who have the potential to contribute the most to the social definition of their roles. In addition, they are likely to have the most role conflict because their roles have changed and they currently have no control over the direction of the changes. For these birthmothers, role conflict may be the result of wanting to respect the agreement that was made, but also wanting to return to the role they had before contact was discontinued. This was supported by the finding that the majority of birthmothers in time-limited mediated adoptions were not satisfied with their current roles and, indeed, wanted to have increased contact.

Although no differences were revealed in role adjustment dependent on birthmother age at placement or years since placement (examination of the findings suggested that the time frame of the data may not have been appropriate to evaluate these predictions), significant differences were uncovered in role adjustment dependent on the type of adoption experienced. More interesting, however, is that the finding was not in the anticipated direction. Specifically, we found that birthmothers who had lost or discontinued contact with the adoptive families (the time-limited mediated group) had worse role adjustment on average than their counterparts who had maintained contact (the mediated and fully disclosed groups) and marginally worse role adjustment than those who had never had contact (the confidential group). Patterns within the time-limited mediated group revealed that several issues were involved in current role adjustment, such as secrecy, additional losses, and dissatisfaction with the amount of contact taking place.

Grief Resolution Results

Coded scores on the dependent measure, grief resolution, ranged from 1.0 (very poor resolution) to 4.75 (nearly very good resolution), with a mean score of 2.73 (slightly below fair resolution) and a normal distribution (Kolomogorov D = .944). Although the sample had only eight birthmothers in time-limited mediated adoptions, the normal distribution and similar variance of scores within each group (level of adoption) suggest that significant findings are meaningful, as ANOVA in this case is appropriately, if not overly, conservative (Stevens, 1986). Grief resolution scores were not related to birthmother age at interview ($r = .04$, $p = .74$), age at placement ($r = .03$, $p = .82$), or time since placement ($r = .03$, $p = .82$).

To discern whether grief resolution experienced by a birthmother is related to the type of adoption she has, analysis of variance was conducted for resolution of grief rating by openness level (see Table 6.4). The type of adoption in which birthmothers were involved was significantly related to their grief resolution ($F(3,71) = 3.446$, $p < .05$). Specifically, birthmothers in time-limited mediated adoptions were rated as having poorer resolution of grief than birthmothers in both ongoing mediated (Duncan pooled variance estimates:[6] $t = -2.29$, $p < .05$) and fully disclosed adoptions (Duncan pooled variance estimates: $t = -2.79$, $p < .01$). Although not significantly different from those with confidential adoptions, those in time-limited mediated adoptions had a smaller range of grief resolution; nobody in the time-limited mediated group scored above fair grief resolution. In addition, birthmothers in fully disclosed adoptions had significantly better grief resolution than those in confidential adoptions (Duncan pooled variance estimates: $t = -2.04$, $p < .05$).

TABLE 6.4   Grief Resolution by Type of Adoption

Grief Resolution

Group	n	Range Low	Range High	Variance	Mean
Confidential	10	1	4	.8757	2.33_a
Time-Limited Mediated	8	1	3	.5078	$2.03_{b,c}$
Ongoing Mediated	28	1	4.5	.7410	2.79_b
Fully Disclosed	29	1.25	4.75	.8524	$3.02_{a,c}$
Group	75	1	4.75	.856	2.74

NOTE: Means with paired subscripts *a* and *b* differ significantly from each other ($p < .05$), and means with paired subscripts *c* differ significantly from each other ($p < .01$) by Duncan pooled variance estimates.

Although a significant difference was found for grief resolution between different adoption arrangements, a wide range of birthmother resolution of grief was found within each arrangement (see Table 6.5): 30% of birthmothers in confidential, 38% in time-limited mediated, 10% in ongoing mediated, and 11% in fully disclosed adoptions had very poor grief resolution scores (< 2.0). These birthmothers expressed fantasies, anger, fear, guilt, and anxiety about their children's placements. Within each type of adoption, however, were also birthmothers who experienced fair or better grief resolution scores (≥ 3.0). These birthmothers were more confident that they had made the right decision. The following quotes are illustrative of birthmother expressions categorized as poor to very poor grief resolution and fair to very good grief resolution in varying openness arrangements.

Poor to Very Poor Grief Resolution

I cried the whole day I signed the papers. When I left the hospital, I went to church that Sunday to reconcile what I had done. I still cry about placing the child. It really hurt my husband [the birthfather]. I feel bad on his birthday. I still feel guilty. I couldn't talk about it for 2 or 3 years. I had him right after Easter, so now I hate Easter. (confidential adoption)

TABLE 6.5   Grief Resolution by Type of Adoption: Frequency Distribution

	Grief Resolution Score				
	1–1.75	2–2.75	3–3.75	4–4.75	n
Confidential	3 (30%)	4 (40)	2 (20)	1 (10)	10
Time-Limited Mediated	3 (38%)	3 (38)	2 (25)	0 (0)	8
Ongoing Mediated	3 (10%)	11 (38)	12 (41)	3 (10)	29
Fully Disclosed	3 (11%)	6 (21)	12 (43)	7 (25)	28

NOTE: Percentages may not sum to 100% because of rounding.

I don't know if I could handle the openness. Now, I [crying], now, I wish I could see her. You just get so lonely for her sometimes that I thought that, you know, you get these wild thoughts about wanting to take her. I really wish that I had done some counseling after her relinquishment. (time-limited mediated adoption)

Depression has been a problem since placement. I never really dealt with her placement until after I was carrying my next child . . . Sometimes I find myself crying and don't know why. Later, I have discovered that it was my child's birthday. I was so distraught on one of these occasions that I quit my job. (ongoing mediated adoption)

It's kind of tough sometimes after I talk to him [adopted child] to just jump right back into my life . . . There's a lot of things going on that I wish I could have been a part of. So, yeah, there is disadvantages because of the hurt and because the first time you hear that kid call someone else "Mom," and you say, "Wait, that's my name." (fully disclosed adoption)

Fair to Very Good Grief Resolution

I never regretted the decision. I feel he's happy and probably growing up wonderful, but I always wonder, "What would it have been like if I had raised him?" . . . Every year, I sit back and wonder and say, "Well, he's this many years old, and I wonder what he's doing and how he's grown in the last year." It sounds dumb, but every year on his birthday . . . for a while, I just think about him. (confidential adoption)

I was a little depressed at the time of placement. But it was nothing too big. I sometimes "wonder" what it would be like to have two kids now. That would be the perfect family. I want to leave a letter for her to read when she's 18, but I haven't done this yet because I am anxious about her reaction. (time-limited mediated adoption)

I would say it was much more difficult the first couple of years after placement. I didn't regret my decision, but I was much more in sorrow over it [then]. I missed her [adopted child's] presence in some ways. (ongoing mediated adoption)

Though it took several years for me to get over my depression, I have decided that I did the right thing. My own family and the adoptive family helped me to feel good about my decision . . . thinking about her [adopted child] makes me feel good. (fully disclosed adoption)

Other Influences on Grief Resolution

Because a wide range of grief resolution experiences were noted in each level of openness, it is likely that other factors besides the type of adoption were affecting birthmothers' experiences with grief. Content analyses of the case data revealed several contextual factors related to positive and negative grief resolution. Regardless of openness level, one factor that recurred in several cases was the birthmother's current relationship with the birthfather. Eight birthmothers were in romantic relationships with the birthfathers (six were currently married to birthfathers). Birthmothers who were still in relationships with birthfathers were at greater risk for prolonged grieving. Although the number of birthmothers in romantic relationships with birthfathers was small (three with fully disclosed adoptions, three with mediated, and two with confidential), seven out of eight of these birthmothers had a grief score of 2 or below, indicating poor to very poor grief resolution. It may have been difficult for these birthmothers to reconcile their feelings about continuing relationships with the birthfathers after having chosen to place their birthchildren for adoption. It is possible that these birthmothers experience exaggerated guilt and blame regarding the paradoxical choices they have made. One birthmother who is currently married to the birthfather commented that she thought "giving away" the first child had something to do with her wanting to keep having more children; she already had three children and still desired to have more.

An intensive analysis of the cases of poor grief resolution also revealed that factors such as giving birth to another child, inability to have a child, and religious interpretations sometimes triggered past losses and rekindled old feelings of helplessness, regret, or anger associated with the placement. For example, one birthmother stated, "I now grieve over the loss of not having a chance to love a child." This birthmother, in a time-limited mediated adoption, married a man who is unable to have children. Another birthmother in an ongoing mediated adoption spoke of "moping around" for a few days following contact with the placed child because she wants so much to have a baby of her own. A birthmother in a fully disclosed adoption cried as she speculated about her infertility, "I think God is punishing me for giving up my first child."

Those relatively few birthmothers in confidential adoptions who had positive grief resolution scores were satisfied with their career choices, had used counseling to deal with grief issues, and tended to have emotional support from their families, friends, and spouses. Some indicated they had no regrets because they either harbored no desire to be a parent or had given birth to other children and were satisfied with their current situations.

Summary of Findings on Grief Resolution

Grief is considered a normal, healthy response to loss, but other life events can be complicated if grief issues are not addressed (MacGregor, 1994). Not only did birthmothers in time-limited mediated adoptions have poorer role adjustment, but they also showed significantly worse grief resolution over placing a child than birthmothers in ongoing mediated and fully disclosed adoption arrangements. Those with confidential arrangements also demonstrated significantly worse grief resolution than those in fully disclosed arrangements. Opportunity for contact in ongoing mediated and fully disclosed adoptions seems to help some birthmothers "feel less empty" and be more readily able to see the child in relation to another family. Contact that ceases may be considered an additional loss, which could exacerbate grief associated with making the adoption plan. Within each type of adoption arrangement, however, regardless of time since adoption, some birthmothers were still experiencing problems with grief resolution, and some had resolved their grief issues. Birthmothers should be strongly encouraged to receive postplacement counseling to deal with the inevitable feelings of grief and loss.

These findings of significant differences in grief resolution by type of adoption are consistent with the theoretical literature about interpersonal loss and human relationships. Although adoption is often proposed as an answer to the growing number of pregnant teens, policymakers should note that adoption, too, can be fraught with risks and lifelong concerns for birthparents. This suggests the need for further research to identify factors associated with healthy coping and adjustment for birthmothers who place children for adoption. These research issues are discussed further in Chapter 8.

Limitations

Several limitations should be noted when considering the results. Because birthmothers were not randomly selected to be involved in their adoption arrangements, there may have been mediating factors in the selection process for adoption agency or adoption arrangement that is associated with better birthmother grief resolution. Although many birthmothers noted that they did not think they had a choice about the type of adoption they had, it was noted earlier that type of adoption is not static after the time of placement; some birthmothers are having an opportunity to change their adoption arrangements to include more (or less) contact after the time of placement. In addition, because birthmother temperament and personality were not measured before the time of pregnancy and placement, it is impossible to determine to what extent these factors may also be influencing the birthmothers' grief resolution or to what extent these factors influence the birthmothers' self-selection into the various types of adoptions. Also, this sample does not include birthmothers who did not use an adoption agency for placement. Finally, the number of birthmothers in the sample of confidential and time-limited mediated adoption arrangements was much lower than the number involved in open arrangements. Despite limitations of the study, the findings and observations provide valuable information for clinicians, adoption workers, and birthparent counselors about birthmother experiences after child placement.

CONCLUSIONS

Regardless of type of adoption, birthmothers had adjusted relatively well 4 to 12 years after the placement. However, issues and problems have been identified in each type of adoption. For example, birthmothers in time-limited mediated adoptions and confidential adoptions seemed to have more unresolved grief issues than birthmothers in ongoing mediated and fully disclosed adoptions. Birthmothers in fully disclosed adoptions had some concerns about the impact of contact on their spouses, subsequent children, and how the placed children might compare their lifestyle with that of the adoptive parents. Knowing a great deal of information can prompt anxieties, just as having too little or no information can. Birthparent counselors must consider issues raised in this study as they provide counseling to pregnant women considering adoption. There is no one perfect type of adoption, and each has some different kinds of vulnerabilities and issues. What may be best for one member of the adoptive kinship network at one point in time may not be the best for another. As developmental needs and circumstances change, triad members may have a need for either increased or decreased contact. For example, if birthmothers or adoptive parents move to another location or if adopted children or birthparents become involved in their own personal or family activities, they may find that the network is unable to maintain the same level of contact. How birthparents, adoptive parents, and adopted children interpret these inevitable changes in contact will be extremely important to assess. Moreover, as more and more agencies move toward offering more open options, birthmothers who have been involved in confidential adoptions or mediated adoptions may become less satisfied with their type of adoption. All of these issues must be addressed in future follow-up studies.

NOTES

1. All percentages are based on codable responses.

2. Levine Test for homogeneity of variance revealed no significant differences in variances between any adoption types on the variable of adoption adjustment; therefore, the pooled rather than the separate variance estimates could be used.

3. Kruskal-Wallis One-Way ANOVA (equivalent nonparametric test) also confirmed a significant difference between groups ($\chi^2 = 12.310$, $p = .006$, corrected for ties).

4. Kruskal-Wallis One-Way ANOVA (equivalent nonparametric test) also confirmed this result ($\chi^2 = .2404$, $p = .624$, corrected for ties).

5. Kruskal-Wallis One-Way ANOVA (equivalent nonparametric test) also confirmed this result ($\chi^2 = .003$, $p = .960$, corrected for ties).

6. Levine Test for homogeneity of variance revealed no significant differences in variances between any adoption types on the variable of grief resolution; therefore, the pooled rather than the separate variance estimates could be used.

7

THE ADOPTIVE KINSHIP NETWORK

Putting the Perspectives Together

With Manfred van Dulmen

T his chapter focuses on the dynamics of relationships within the adoptive kinship network, which is composed of the adopted child; his or her adoptive parents, siblings, and extended family members; and birthparents, birthsiblings, and extended birthfamily members. In the first section, we present a descriptive analysis of relationships that involve differing amounts of contact; in the second section, we focus on families in the study in which at least one face-to-face meeting had taken place. Throughout the chapter, our goal is to understand and communicate the perspectives of both adoptive parents and birthmothers, noting points at which their perspectives agree and diverge.

THE DYNAMICS OF OPENNESS IN ADOPTION

Participants in a voluntary relationship interact over time in a way that establishes a degree of closeness or intimacy that works for them. Initial interactions provide opportunities for participants to take stock of each other, to consider whether they would like to know the other person better, to assess how much they might have in common, and to decide whether they would like to become more open or vulnerable to the other by disclosing information or by seeking further inter-action. As this relationship dance proceeds, a "comfort zone" of closeness is established in the relationship.

Concepts from the close relationships model (Kelley et al., 1983) can be used to conceptualize the dynamic process that occurs when strangers such as adoptive parents and birthparents are brought to-gether because of an adoptive placement. The model (Levinger, 1983) considers relationship development in five phases: (a) acquaintance, (b) buildup, (c) consolidation, (d) deterioration, and (e) ending. An adoption may not proceed to an *acquaintance* phase if no information is shared. When identifying or non-identifying information is shared, however, participants have the option to consider whether they should explore the relationship further or to let it remain simply an acquain-tanceship. During the *buildup* phase, relationship partners seek addi-tional information about one another and may increase the frequency with which they interact and the diversity of ways and settings in which they interact. If the relationship proceeds to the *consolidation* phase, it might be quite stable, and partners might become more interde-pendent as their behaviors influence each other. In some cases, the relationship may *deteriorate,* as one or both partners pull away from interaction for various reasons. It may even *end* through death of a partner or termination of contact.

Some features of the relationship development process are unique to the adoption situation. First, we must consider the role of the adoption agency. Through the preplacement counseling process, per-sonnel at the agency have "prepared" both prospective adoptive parents and birthparents to understand the options the agency permits or encourages at placement. They have also framed for both parties a range of reasonable expectations they might have for the future in terms of possible relationships between the child's family of birth and family of rearing. Agency staff exercise considerable control over the options presented to participants and strongly influence their clients' understanding of possible futures for the adoption. For example, the agency may recommend certain types of adoption or frequencies of contact or may facilitate one face-to-face meeting at the agency with agency personnel present but then convey the expectation subtly or overtly that no more meetings will or should occur and/or that no identifying information should be exchanged. Through their process of preparing participants for adoption, agency personnel transmit their values and shape clients' perceptions and expectations.

Second, it is important to acknowledge power asymmetries that exist between birthmothers and adoptive parents as the adoption process unfolds. Prior to placement, the power held by birthmothers in voluntary relinquishments, such as those discussed in this book, presents a paradox: On the one hand, a birthmother typically considers adoption because she feels unable to provide the type of life she would like for her child. On the other hand, the ultimate choice of whether to make an adoption plan or to parent the baby herself belongs, of course, to the birthmother. If the birthfather is identified, he may have a legal role in the decision to place for adoption. Although the birthmother's parents and extended family members do not have legal power with regard to placement decision making, they can exert strong pressure nonetheless. With many agencies, the birthmother also has the opportunity to express preferences with regard to the type of adoptive home into which the child might go (e.g., religion, urban or rural) or to choose the child's adoptive family from among several possibilities presented by the agency.

After the adoption is final and the birthparents legally and permanently relinquish parental rights, power in the relationship shifts into the hands of the adoptive parents. Even though the amount and type of contact may have been mutually negotiated, the final authority to decide about contact rests with the child's adoptive parents.

Thus, the extent of contact, closeness, and interdependence that emerges in the adoptive kinship network develops against the backdrop of the agency's postadoption services and the power asymmetry between adoptive parents and birthmother. When openness arrangements are negotiated informally, either party can refuse to have contact with the other, and neither party can force the other to have contact against their wishes. Agency personnel can be called on to help parties resolve differences.

Relationship development proceeded along very positive lines for some participants in our study. Initial interactions between adoptive parents and birthmother were sometimes tentative, but participants often sensed their liking and concern for the other party. Over time, a relationship between strangers who were brought together by adoption became a relationship between friends. As one birthmother noted,

I went from not knowing them [the adoptive parents] to knowing them, to kind of being a part of their life through their child, to being a part of their life just by being me.

The extent of contact depended on the wishes of the parties involved. When the amount of contact desired by the birthmother and the adoptive parents did not match, the amount that would actually occur tended to be the lower amount desired by either party. The adoptive parents in our study almost never talked about being intruded on by the child's birthmother, but they did sometimes wish for additional contact they thought they could not bring about (see Chapter 5 for further discussion). Birthmothers tended to feel more tentative about what they could ask for. They did have (and occasionally exercised) the right to refuse contact. Sometimes, however, they continued contact out of a sense of obligation to the adoptive parents. In some other cases, they desired more contact but were reluctant to ask for it, not wanting to push the adoptive parents beyond what they were comfortable with. They feared that pushing too much might jeopardize their having any contact (see Chapter 6 for further discussion). In general, however, the comfort zone attained in the relationship tended to be established at the level of contact that was mutually desired or was the lesser of that desired by either the birthmother or the adoptive parents.

In the following case, the birthmother desires less contact than the adoptive parents do at this point in time, and the amount of contact actually occurring is at the lower level considered by the two parties:

The adoptive parents call and ask me to send cards to Sara. They seem to want more contact, and they keep calling and saying that she is asking a lot of questions. They want me to be more involved than I am. But I just don't have the time to just really devote a lot to her now 'cause I've got so much of my own going on. (birthmother, fully disclosed adoption)

The process of negotiating a workable comfort zone can occur in many ways. To illustrate, we looked at the 10 adoptive families in the sample who had the choice between mediated and fully disclosed adoption at placement, chose mediated, but later moved to fully disclosed by the time we interviewed them. Factors initiating the changes differed widely. Among the 10 adoptive families, 2 noted that the change was initiated by the adoption caseworker, who was the person relaying communications between the birthmother and adoptive couple; 3 stated that the birthmother initiated the change; 2 noted that they as adoptive parents initiated the change; 1 stated that the birthgrandmother initiated the change; and 2 stated that the change evolved "naturally" or "mutually" (Mendenhall et al., 1996). Several of these initiatives occurred after the adoptive parents and the birthmother had had several meetings at the adoption agency without knowing each other's full names. After they got to know each other, they chose to share identifying information. One adoptive couple wanted a more open relationship with the child's birthmother after they adopted a second child under a fully open arrangement. Thus, reasons for the initiation of change were quite varied, and most parents noted that the change proceeded mutually even if it was initiated by one party (Mendenhall et al., 1996).

Several cases in the sample had fully disclosed adoptions but had less contact when we interviewed them than they had previously. In most of these cases, the reduction in contact was initiated by the birthmother, rather than by the adoptive parents, especially if she had given birth to another child, married someone who did not encourage the contact, or moved away geographically. When the adoptive parents' contact with the birthmother declined, they sometimes maintained contact with another birthrelative (e.g., aunt, grandmother).

We also had a few cases in which the adoptive parents and the birthmother perceived their openness arrangement differently; these were usually in mediated adoptions, in which contact was being handled by a third party. For example, in one case the adoptive parents originally intended to share information with their child's birthmother through the agency and did send letters for 4 years. The birthmother, however, said she only received one letter, 6 months after placement. She inferred that the adoptive parents did not want to share information with her. Both parties had the intent to share information, but because the agency worker had not transmitted all the information, both parties made incorrect attributions about each other. Mediated arrangements in which a third party was responsible for transmitting information were most vulnerable to problems of this sort, especially if the agency experienced staff turnover, a change in policies, or unmanageable caseloads that made it impossible for staff to follow through with the plan to mediate information exchange. For example, some agencies that participated in the study had closed by the time we interviewed them 5 years later (see Chapter 2), making their role as intermediary impossible to continue.

In general, we noted several factors relating to changes in openness levels. Factors that tended to increase the level of contact between adoptive families and birthmothers (especially in mediated and fully disclosed adoptions) included the following:

- Their mutual concern for the child's well-being

- Emergence of a mutual friendship or satisfying personal relationship

- Unimpeded flow of communication, either directly or through a responsive third party

Factors associated with reduced contact included the following:

- Increased geographic distance

- Major differences in life situations, interests, or values that caused adoptive parents and birthmother to think they have little in common

- Relatives or friends who discouraged contact

- Change in the birthmother's personal situation, such as marriage or the birth of other children

- Inability to negotiate a mutually agreed-on comfort zone of contact

- Adoptive parents' feeling that contact was becoming stressful or confusing for the child

- Agency intermediaries who were not able to keep up the contact to everyone's satisfaction

PERCEPTIONS OF FACE-TO-FACE MEETINGS

In this section, we focus on those families in which there has been direct contact between adoptive parents and birthmother. We are particularly interested in two issues: (a) how the participants evaluated the meetings in which they participated and (b) to what degree the adoptive parents and birthmothers experienced these meetings in a similar way. Specifically, we explore the hypothesis that adoptive parents and birthmothers follow different trajectories over time with regard to their feelings and perceptions about face-to-face contact and that these trajectories may not be in synchrony with one another. Understanding similarities and differences in the perspectives of adoptive parents and birthmothers will provide important information for participants in adoption and for those professionals attempting to facilitate the openness process.

Data for this part of the chapter come from the questions in the adoptive parent and birthmother interviews that addressed feelings about contact from the perspectives of the past, present, and anticipated future. The responses considered here come from the adoptive parents and birthmothers who had had at least one face-to-face meeting; this group comprised 77 adoptive fathers (AFs), 77 adoptive mothers (AMs), and 62 birthmothers (BMOs). Adoptive parents (APs) included 7 (9.1%) with time-limited mediated adoptions, 13 (16.9%) with ongoing mediated adoptions, 2 (2.6%) with time-limited fully disclosed adoptions, and 55 (71.4%) with ongoing fully disclosed adoptions. BMOs included 4 (6.5%) in time-limited mediated adoptions, 18 (29.0%) in ongoing mediated adoptions, and 40 (64.5%) in ongoing fully disclosed adoptions. Confidential adoptions are not discussed in this section because the focus here is on adoptive kinship networks in which contact between adoptive parents and birthmother has occurred.

Variables regarding perceptions about contact were coded from interviews by staff who were intensively trained and for whom inter-rater reliability of at least .80 was maintained. For these variables, coders considered all relevant parts of the transcript and made a judgment about whether perceptions were *negative* (indicating a problem of some kind, e.g., distance in the relationship), *neutral* (e.g., neither positive nor negative, no impact), *positive* (indicating that things were working out satisfactorily, e.g., there was closeness in the relationship), or *mixed* (containing both positive and negative aspects). First, we consider participants' perspectives about their first meeting; second, we consider their assessment of the overall impact of these meetings and the quality of their current relationships; finally, we consider their desire for future meetings.[1]

First Meeting

First meetings between adoptive parents and birthmother took place at different times for different families: Sometimes the first meeting occurred before the child's birth, sometimes at the birth or while the birthmother was still in the hospital, sometimes at a placement ceremony within a few days or weeks of the child's birth, and sometimes when the child was about 6 months old. The timing of the first meeting was often determined by the agency's policies and practices. Coders evaluated participants' statements in terms of how they felt during the first meeting. More than half of the responses of AFs, AMs, and BMOs with regard to how they felt during that meeting were coded as "mixed"; in other words, participants made statements that contained both positive and negative elements (see Figure 7.1). The percentage of AFs whose statements were rated as "negative" was lower than for AMs or BMOs, and the percentage of AFs rated as "positive" was higher than for AMs or BMOs. Almost no one's statements were coded as "neutral." Among fully corresponding sets (for whom coded data were available for all three parties), in 10 cases each party's feelings during the first meeting were coded as "mixed." In no cases were all three parties coded as "positive," "neutral," or "negative." When a discrepancy occurred between adoptive fathers' and adoptive mothers' evaluations, the father was more positive than the mother in 89% of cases.

The mixed feelings of each party were quite clearly articulated in the interviews. Adoptive parents felt joyful to have the child, but they also felt sensitive to the birthmother's loss. In some cases, adoptive parents were nervous about whether the birthmother would like them or how she would evaluate them. Birthmothers also had mixed feelings: They typically felt relieved to meet their children's adoptive

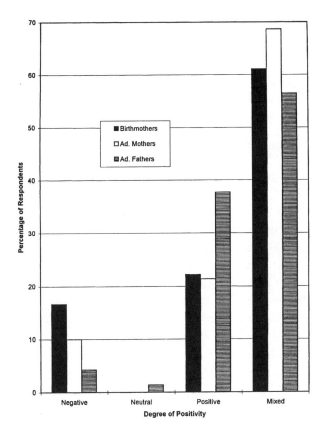

Figure 7.1 Positivity of Own Feelings During First Meeting

parents and felt comfortable with them, but they also felt initially nervous and/or self-conscious. The feelings of nervousness typically abated during the meetings. The following case examples illustrate this mixture of perspectives:

> At their first meeting, Sam (Billy's adoptive father) felt very pleased that Billy's birthmother thought he and his wife would make good adoptive parents for Billy. Billy's adoptive mom was also thrilled at the prospect of the adoption but at the same time felt sad for his birthmother, whose life circumstances were difficult at the time. Billy's birthmother reported feeling very fortunate.

As their first meeting began, Monty (the adoptive father) felt uncomfortable, but as the meeting progressed, he developed a feeling of greater closeness to his daughter's birthmother, Jennifer. Monty's wife, Karen, felt sad for Jennifer and thought she had been asked a lot of questions during the meeting. Jennifer noted that she felt comfortable during the meeting and was relieved to have met Monty and Karen in person.

Participants were also asked what kind of impact the first meeting had on them. The majority of participants (85.4% of BMOs, 68.0% of AMs, and 71.4% of AFs) viewed the impact as positive. Very few saw the impact as negative or neutral; approximately 25% of APs and 10% of BMOs saw its impact as mixed (see Figure 7.2).

When birthmothers were asked what they thought the impact of the first meeting had been on the adoptive parents, almost all of them (97.1%) made statements that were coded as "positive." However, only 68% of adoptive mothers' and 71.4% of adoptive fathers' statements about the perceived impact on them were coded as "positive." In other words, birthmothers overestimated how positive the impact of the meeting was for the adoptive parents ($\chi^2(3) = 13.34, p < .01$; see Figure 7.3).

Darla, the baby's birthmother, thought the impact of the first meeting was quite positive for the adoptive parents, noting, "It wasn't as bad as they thought it would be." The adoptive parents reported experiencing more of a range of feelings; for example, with regard to the meeting, the father commented, "It was happiness and it was sadness." The adoptive mother noted that the meeting "really brought home the pain of what the birthparents had gone through."

When the adoptive parents were asked what they thought the impact of the first meeting had been on the birthmother, AFs thought the impact had been positive (82.6%) or mixed (17.4%); AMs thought the impact had been somewhat less positive: only 56% saw the impact as positive, 24% as mixed, 16% as negative, and 4% as neutral. Among birthmothers, 85.4% viewed the impact as positive. Thus, AMs underestimated how positive the impact of the first meeting had been for the BMO ($\chi^2(1) = 7.00, p < .01$; see Figure 7.4).

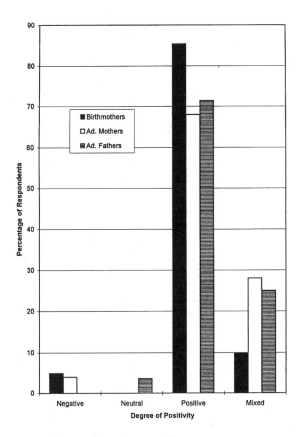

Figure 7.2 Perceived Impact of First Meeting on You

Current Evaluation of Meetings and Relationships

Adoptive parents and birthmothers were asked what kind of impact the meetings had on them overall, up to the current time. The majority of respondents' statements were quite positive (79.4% of AFs, 72.2% of BMOs, and 67.2% of AMs); very few responses were coded as "negative" or "mixed" (see Figure 7.5).

Among families for whom we had data from both adoptive parents and birthmother, perceptions were usually congruent across partici-

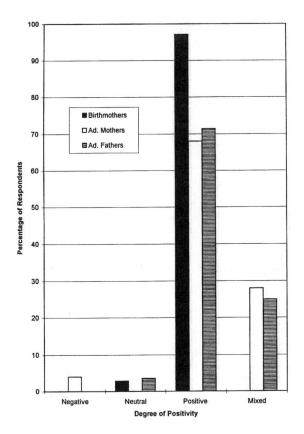

Figure 7.3   Perceived Impact of First Meeting on Adoptive Parents

pants. When perceptions were different, it was typically because one member of the adoptive kinship network saw the relationship in a more complex way that included both positive elements (e.g., being comfortable) and negative elements (e.g., an additional sense of obligation).

Sometimes different perceptions were a result of concerns about the future that had not been discussed among the parties. It appeared that some of these perceptions could be resolved through discussion of their different interpretations and feelings, although such discussions had not yet taken place. For example,

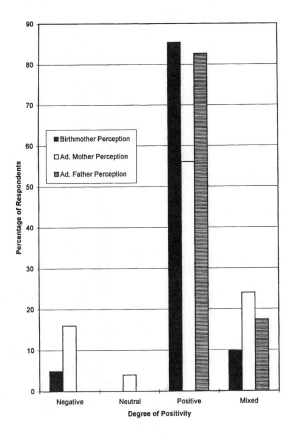

Figure 7.4 Perceived Impact of First Meeting on Birthmother

One adoptive parent stated that the contact had "opened up a whole new world" for him and had made him a strong advocate of openness. His child's birthmother expressed apprehension that the contact might end in the future, although she also stated that she felt welcomed into the process by the child's adoptive parents.

Birthmothers and adoptive parents differed in their overall assessment of the impact of meetings on the adopted child, with BMOs seeing meetings as more positive and APs seeing them as more neutral or mixed ($\chi^2(3) = 8.58$, $p < .05$). Among BMOs, perception of the

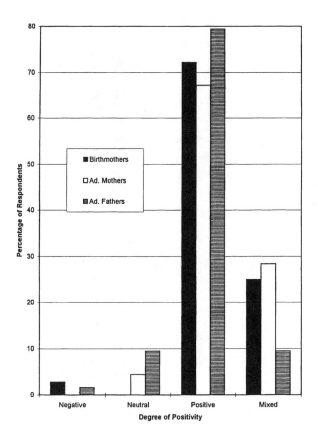

Figure 7.5 Overall Impact of Meetings on You

meetings' impact was positive for 81.8%, neutral for 12.1%, and mixed for 6.1%. Among AMs, perception of the impact was positive for 51.1%, neutral for 23.4%, mixed for 21.3%, and negative for 4.3% (see Figure 7.6).

When the interviews of members of the same adoptive kinship network were coded differently, it was sometimes because one respondent noted no specific impact on the child's behavior and another made inferences about the child's richer understanding of adoption that would result from the meetings. For example, adoptive parents' statements were more likely to be coded as "neutral" when the child

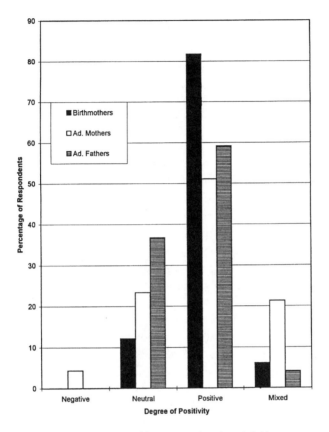

Figure 7.6 Overall Perceived Impact of Meetings on the Adopted Child

was young and they were not sure the child really understood the full meaning of the visits. Birthmothers in those cases often made statements coded as "positive" because of their view that the experience of having the meetings would enhance the child's understanding as he or she grew up.

Barbara, an adoptive mother, noted that her daughter Joanne understands adoption better than children in confidential adoptions and is coming to accept herself as an adopted individual, but there is an added dimension of confusion that her nonadopted friends don't have. Barbara's husband thought the meetings hadn't really had any impact on their daughter. Joanne knows that Sandy is her "birthmother" but may not really understand what that means. Sandy noted that Joanne was very well adjusted, very positive and secure. She recalled that Joanne thinks she's lucky because she has two moms, four sets of grandparents, and gets birthday presents from everywhere.

Although over 80% of adoptive parents felt positive about their current relationship with the birthmothers and vice versa, more birthmothers than adoptive parents felt negative about the current relationship ($\chi^2(1) = 3.96$, $p < .05$; see Figure 7.7). For eight birthmothers, their views of the current relationship with the adoptive parents were coded as "negative," but inspection of their interviews revealed that this meant "distant" or "not very close," rather than hostile. Seven of the eight were in ongoing mediated adoptions in which only one or two meetings had taken place, although some form of communication (typically, exchange of letters) continued. Although most of these birthmothers were not interested in further meetings with the adoptive parents at this time, several of them indicated willingness to meet with the child once he or she was 18 years old if the child wished to meet. Several of these birthmothers thought the single meeting was what had been agreed to and that they did not have the right to ask for anything different. They seemed a bit uncertain about their role in defining the relationship with their adoptive families.

One birthmother commented, "As the years have gone on, I've felt much less close. And I've felt much more . . . distant from them." She had received "a lot of attention" when she was pregnant, but less now.

Asked to describe how close her relationship with the adoptive parents was, another birthmother responded, "Acquaintances . . . There's been some hesitancy on my part to interact with the parents. Again, like I've never sent them a picture. I feel sort of uncomfortable with that. But I've never had the courage to ask them if they ever wanted one . . . I don't know what they expect, and if I did it every year, would they expect that that's too much and that I'm trying to intrude? So I guess there's some uncertainty about what kind of interaction I could have with them."

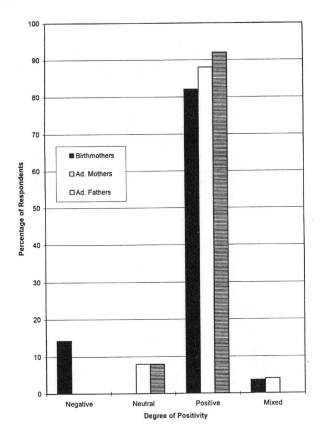

Figure 7.7 Positivity of My Current Relationship With the Other Adult

Desire for Future Meetings

To assess the quality of adoptive parent-birthparent relationships as they are projected into the future, we asked participants whether they wanted to have meetings in the future. Although over 80% of respondents wanted more meetings in the future, the parties stating that they did not want more meetings in the future included 18% of BMOs, 10.4% of AMs, and 7.1% of AFs (see Figure 7.8). The desire for future meetings was also embedded within the adoptive kinship network's search for a comfort zone of relationship involvement, as seen in the following example:

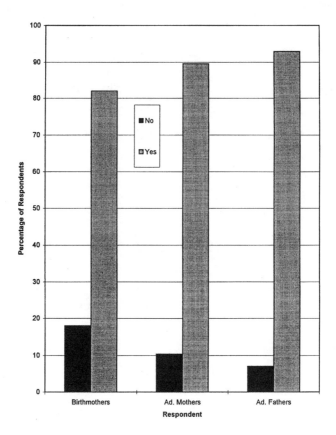

Figure 7.8 Desire for More Meetings in the Future

Emma was placed in a confidential adoption through an agency that only performed confidential adoptions at the time. Emma's parents subsequently adopted another child through an open adoption. Eight years after the placement, Emma's adoptive mother found that she could not answer the many questions that Emma was asking about her birthparents, stimulated by the contact that Emma's brother had with his birthmother. Emma's parents approached the agency to see whether they could begin mediated correspondence with Emma's birthmother, and the birthmother, Ann, was pleased to be involved. They exchanged letters through the agency for about 1 year and then decided that they would have contact directly. For the 1st year of contact, they met many times. As they approached their 2nd year of a fully disclosed adoption, the adoptive parents and birthmother all felt they would probably not meet as frequently. They thought they would be comfortable meeting once or twice a year, supplemented by exchange of letters.

GENERAL DISCUSSION

The data presented in this chapter explore the perceptions of birthmothers and adoptive parents with regard to their first face-to-face meeting, their overall assessment of the meeting and their relationship at the time they were interviewed, and their desire to continue meeting in the future. Several general trends emerged.

During their first meeting, most participants experienced a mixture of positive and negative feelings, frequently combining being "nervous" or "anxious" at first, with being "relieved" and "comfortable" as the meeting progressed. Most respondents thought the impact of that meeting on them and on the other participants was positive. Four to 12 years after the adoption, most participants thought the overall impact of the meetings on them and on the children had been positive and expressed a desire for continued meetings in the future. Furthermore, for most of the participants in our study who had experienced contact of any sort between birthmother and adoptive family, the type of contact (e.g., meetings, telephone calls, letters, gifts) and the frequency of contact changed over time.

Some adoptive kinship network members expressed dissatisfaction with their adoption arrangements. Almost all adoptive parents who were dissatisfied wanted more contact, rather than less. The interviews indicated that dissatisfaction with openness arrangements could originate in several ways. First, network members with little information about the other might want more information, although not necessarily contact. For example, birthmothers in confidential and mediated adoptions typically wanted more information about how their children were doing: Were they healthy? How were they doing in school? Were they happy and well adjusted? Second, there can be a mismatch between the desires of the adoptive parents and those of the birthmothers with regard to the extent of contact and information sharing desired. Third, birthmothers or adoptive parents can make incorrect assumptions about each other's intentions or desires if communication is mediated by a third party, especially if letters seem "cold" or uninformative. Fourth, the transmissions of mediated com-munications were sometimes unreliable, especially if the agency had experienced high staff turnover or unmanageable caseloads. Finally, because of the power differential that exists in the relationship, birthmothers can be reluctant to be fully honest with adoptive parents if they want more contact but sense the adoptive parents might think it is too much, or if they want less contact but do not want to disappoint the adoptive parents or the child.

Within these general trends, however, are some interesting and provocative differences that suggest that adoptive parents and birth-mothers follow different trajectories over time with regard to their feelings about contact. Reflecting on the experience of the first meet-ing, birthmothers thought its impact was more positive for adoptive parents than the adoptive parents did themselves, and adoptive moth-ers underestimated how positive its impact was for the birthmothers. This finding is consistent with the idea that the early meetings are especially valuable and impactful for the birthmother because they allow her to meet the actual people who have adopted or will adopt her child and to be reassured that the child will be well taken care of. Although most adoptive parents also saw the meetings as valuable and important, they also reflected some ambivalence and concern, raising questions such as the following: What if she doesn't like us? How much joy should I really feel or show about something that is causing her so much pain?

As current relationships were evaluated, the impact of the meet-ings on the child was evaluated more positively by birthmothers than by adoptive parents, perhaps reflecting their different views about the child. Birthmothers' responses reflected their views that the meetings would help ensure that their children would have a more complete understanding of adoption, including firsthand knowledge of them as persons and understanding that the birthmothers made the adoption plans out of love and concern for their children. Adoptive parents tended to focus more on the children's behavior during the meetings or on the children's understanding they expressed about the adoption at that time. When perceptions differed, birthmothers tended to evaluate the current relationship more negatively than the adoptive parents (especially fathers). In terms of the desire for meetings in the future, the greatest proportion of negative responses came from birthmothers. These observations are consistent with the notion that, over time, birthmothers may begin to pull away from contact and the relationship with the family, especially if they are satisfied that their children are being well cared for, if they think the adoptive parents understand that the placement decision was made out of love and that they will communicate that to the children, or if their spouses or significant others do not want them to continue contact.

Thus, among adoptive kinship networks in which there is ongoing contact, the relationship between birthmother and adoptive parents is continually renegotiated or fine-tuned. This process reflects the parties' process of finding a workable comfort zone. It also reflects the relationship changes that might be triggered by developmental changes of relationship members or changes in their life circumstances. The lives of birthmothers and adoptive parents develop independently, yet require negotiation to permit continued interdependence at a level that works for all.

NOTE

1. Data in this section come from responses clearly codable as "positive," "neutral," "negative," or "mixed." Data coded as "other" are not considered here.

8

GENERAL CONCLUSIONS AND IMPLICATIONS

T he face of adoption in North America has changed dramatically in the last decade and will likely continue to do so. When we began the pilot work for this study more than a decade ago, opinions in the adoption community were split over the long-term consequences of openness in adoption. Some professionals thought openness was dangerous and harmful; others thought it was more honest and optimal for everyone. Thanks to the willingness of the adoptive parents, birthparents, children, and agency personnel who shared their experiences and insights with us, we have been able to draw some general conclusions.

1. *The movement toward openness in adoption has taken place within the context of broader societal changes.*

   ❖ With the sexual revolution came an associated decrease in stigma associated with childbearing out of wedlock, thus making parenting more attractive than adoption to many young women.

   ❖ The accessibility of birth control and abortion has been associated with a shrinking pool of babies for whom adoptive placements are sought.

❖ The human potential movement in its various forms has made birthparents and adult adopted individuals conscious of kinship connections they have lost in the process of adoption and has spawned support groups of individuals who help one another search for kin from whom they have been separated by adoption.

❖ Society has experienced a general movement toward less secrecy and greater disclosure, as seen in consumer protection laws of all kinds that mandate full and complete disclosure, norms of politics that require careful scrutiny of all aspects of one's personal life, and open access to one's own credit records, accompanied by the right to challenge incorrect entries.

❖ A new model of American society prizing diversity and difference suggests that variations in family structure (e.g., adoptive families or birthparents who have made adoption plans) are valued, rather than considered somehow deficient. The shame of being different is being replaced by pride.

2. *Many of the fears and concerns initially raised about openness in adoption appear to be unfounded.* The data from our study, a snapshot of families taken 4 to 12 years after the adoptive placement, revealed the following:

❖ Parties involved in fully disclosed adoptions are not confused about who has parenting rights and responsibilities.

❖ Fears that birthparents would attempt to reclaim their children or otherwise intrude on adoptive families' lives are not apparent in families with fully disclosed adoptions.

❖ Children in fully disclosed adoptions do not struggle with divided loyalties between adoptive and birthparents, nor are they different from children in other adoption arrangements in terms of self-esteem or degree of curiosity about their backgrounds.

❖ Adoptive parents in fully disclosed adoptions feel more in control of the birthparents' involvement in their lives, are more empathic toward their child and the child's birthparents (with regard to the adoption), sense greater permanence in their relationship with the child, and are less fearful about reclaiming than are adoptive parents in confidential adoptions.

◆ Openness does not interfere with adoptive parents' emerging sense of entitlement.

◆ Birthmothers who have ongoing contact with adoptive families through either ongoing mediated or fully disclosed adoptions show better resolution of grief than do birthmothers whose contact has stopped. Furthermore, birthmothers with fully disclosed adoptions also show better grief resolution than those in confidential adoptions who never had contact.

◆ Developing a trusting, secure relationship with the adoptive family through direct or indirect contact seems to lead a birthmother to the gradual acceptance of the adoptive family's entitlement to the child while allowing her to develop positive feelings about her own role with the adopted child.

◆ Having a fully disclosed adoption does not guarantee successful grief resolution, as is evidenced by the broad range of grief resolution ratings among birthmothers across all adoption arrangements in this study.

3. *The level of openness in adoption should be decided on a case-by-case basis.*

◆ Should these findings be interpreted to mean that open adoption is best for everyone? We think not. No single adoption arrangement is best for everyone.

◆ Each type of adoption arrangement presents distinctive challenges and opportunities.

◆ For those adoptive parents and birthparents who want to establish a fully disclosed adoption, it can work well. Because of the complexity of the relationships, however, it does require ongoing management of family boundaries and the commitment of the parties to continue working on their relationship toward mutual satisfaction. Such management requires communication, flexibility, commitment to the process, respect for the parties involved, and commitment to

meeting the child's needs above all. If these conditions are
not present, the participants may want to consider other
arrangements.

4. *Adoption should be viewed as an ongoing process, rather than
as a discrete event in time.*

   ❖ The importance of viewing adoption as an ongoing process
   became clearly evident as we examined how openness arrangements are negotiated over time.

   ❖ Because adoptions involving openness are relatively new,
   members of the adoptive kinship network are pioneering in
   an area for which relationship norms do not currently exist.
   Thus, there may be some confusion or ambiguity about what
   members' roles actually should be. In particular, because it
   is clear to all that the adoptive parents have the full parenting responsibilities and rights, the roles of birthmothers and
   other birthfamily members are not as clear and will probably
   evolve over time within the adoptive kinship networks as
   relationships develop.

   ❖ Developmental differences contribute to the dynamic nature
   of openness relationships. What may be "best" for one party
   in the adoption triad at one point in time may not be "best"
   for other parties. Furthermore, parties' needs for more or
   less openness may change over time and may not always
   occur in synchrony among triad members. For example, a
   birthmother's need for contact may decrease over time as
   the adoptive family's desire for contact may increase. One
   event that sometimes caused birthmothers to reduce contact
   with adoptive families was marriage, and three reasons were
   noted: (a) involvement in the new relationship and in the
   wedding plans, (b) the husband's lack of enthusiasm for
   maintaining the relationship with the adoptive family at the
   same level, and (c) moving to a location farther away from
   the adoptive family. Once the birthmother is assured of the
   child's well-being in the adoptive family and is comfortable
   that the adoptive parents are the kind of people she wanted
   to raise the child, the birthmother is then able to focus more
   on her own identity and intimacy issues. Factors leading

adoptive parents to desire more contact included (a) increasing questions from the child as she or he matured cognitively and emotionally and (b) the desire to open up one adoption further following the adoption of a younger sibling with a more open adoption than the older child's was originally.

❖ Over time, adoptive kinship networks will develop different relationship solutions as they engage in the process of arriving at a workable comfort zone of contact. This process appears to be facilitated when the parties' relationships can develop gradually so that mutually agreeable levels of intimacy and contact are established. Although this process involves the interaction of adoptive parents, birthmother, and child, power is not equally distributed in this network. The power asymmetry among the individuals may affect the process of negotiating the comfort zone.

❖ One might ask, How "gradual" is best? This question has no simple answer. Each adoption involves a unique set of adoptive parents and birthparents, who bring their individual personalities and relationship histories to the adoption. The pace of the emergence of openness must take these individual and relational differences into account.

5. *Although the role of adoption agencies has changed dramatically in recent years, agency staff have profound effects on the adoptive placements they facilitate.*

❖ During a brief period in history, we have witnessed rapid, unprecedented change in the nature of work conducted through adoption agencies.

❖ Although some agencies have experienced a gradual increase in placements since offering open options, others have not seen such a trend.

❖ Because a birthmother is often viewed as the primary client of the adoption agency, the decision-making power about the initial level of openness in the adoption seems to rest in her hands. Increasingly large numbers of birthmothers seeking agency services are requesting ongoing contact, and agencies are responding by changing their practices to reflect this. Because agencies typically have long waiting lists of prospective adoptive families, it is not too difficult to find a family willing to accommodate the birthmother's wishes in the placement of her child.

❖ Despite the fact that birthmothers and adoptive couples are wanting more control of the adoption process, the personnel at adoption agencies continue to play key roles in the adoption process through preparation of birthparents and adoptive parents, facilitation of the adoption arrangements, and provision of postadoption services.

❖ The practices of adoption agencies are influenced by societal attitudes as they vary across historical time, the population of children available for adoption, and economic factors regarding the agencies' viability.

❖ The shift toward openness practices, especially mediated arrangements in which agency staff serve as a third party for de-identified communication, increases the workload on agency staff during an era of generally shrinking resources and increasing demands on social service providers.

❖ Professionals working with adoptive kinship network members need to be attuned not only to their own philosophy of adoption but also to how to work effectively with clients whose personalities and relationship histories may vary greatly from their own and from those of each other.

❖ Adoption caseworkers participating in the study whose agencies moved toward offering greater openness reported positive experiences with this change. Only two agencies in our sample still preferred confidential adoptions when we interviewed them in 1993.

6. *As families have new experiences with adoption, new questions arise that provoke further consideration.*

   ❖ How can adoptive parents most effectively and successfully express desires for increasing or decreasing contact with birthfamily members?

   ❖ How can birthparents best cope with the impact of open arrangements on their relationships with spouses and other children?

* How can adoptive parents decide how and when to include or exclude their adopted child from the exchange of information or contact with birthfamily members?
* How can the child's worries and anxieties about birthparents best be handled?
* What is the impact on the adopted child of reducing the amount or ceasing contact with birthfamily members?
* What is the impact of openness on other children in the home who have less open adoptions?
* What is the long-term impact of openness for all parties in the adoptive kinship network? Longitudinal research is necessary to answer this question.

STRENGTHS AND LIMITATIONS OF THE RESEARCH

The conclusions noted above must be considered within the context of the strengths and limitations of the research on which they are based. This study is significant because it is national in scope; involves a sample (720 individuals) much larger than other adoption studies that employ interview methods and home visits; and includes the full range of adoptive openness, including cases in which contact has stopped, some in which contact continues, and others in which it has increased or decreased over time, allowing for tracking of trajectories of openness over time. It also includes data from all triad members and about adoption agency practices and policies to contextualize the work. The study links with the investigators' earlier retrospective investigation of emotional disturbance in adopted adolescents, now providing prospective data that can be examined longitudinally to test tentative conclusions drawn earlier (Grotevant & McRoy, 1990; McRoy, Grotevant, & Zurcher, 1988). The sample excludes transracial, international, and special needs adoptions; this is a strength because the complexities involved in such arrangements would make it more difficult for us to draw conclusions about openness. The sample limitations, however, do restrict generalizability of the study to families with similar adoptions.

Other limitations of this study must also be noted when interpreting the results. First, as in virtually any family study, participants were volunteers. We do not know how nonvolunteering families would have responded. We did attempt to sample participants within agencies and not simply ask for families and birthmothers who had the most "interesting" stories to tell. In contrast with other studies, however, one strength of this investigation is that participants were drawn from 35 adoption agencies with diverse philosophies across the United States. Second, it is impossible to make causal statements about the "effects" of different levels of openness because many factors contributed to openness levels, including personalities of the participants (e.g., flexibility, tolerance for ambiguity), their initial comfort level with adoption and with openness, their knowledge of agency practices, birthmothers' interest in having contact, availability of openness options at the agencies they contacted, and agency preadoption counseling about openness options. Furthermore, this study is a cross-sectional one, precluding assessments of causality. Third, because most of our fully disclosed adoptions developed gradually over time, these findings might not be generalizable to adoptions that begin completely open without a period of relationship building. In the United States, a sharp increase has recently occurred in the number of "private" or "independent" adoptions arranged through attorneys or other intermediaries; the applicability of our findings to these situations is unknown if the independent arrangement views adoption as a discrete event in time, rather than as a long-term process that involves both preparation and follow-up. Fourth, the participants in our study were interviewed between 1987 and 1992, when the adopted children were between the ages of 4 and 12. These factors must be considered in contextualizing the study's findings. Finally, the adoptions represented in this study were infant placements. Generalization of these results to placements of older children or children with special needs must be made with caution.

IMPLICATIONS FOR ADOPTION PRACTICE

Perhaps only the participants in individual adoptions can determine how much openness should exist. This approach was suggested by the Child Welfare League of America task force (1987), which recommended that the amount of openness in any adoption should ideally be based on mutual agreement among birthparents, prospective adoptive parents, adoption agency, and adopted child (if age appropriate).

Adoption professionals, as well as members of the adoptive kinship network, are finding that they must be prepared to deal with some inevitable vulnerabilities inherent in each type of adoption. Agencies tend to advocate for their preferred adoption option during the preplacement process. They often find that they must educate some prospective adoptive parents about the advantages of openness and help them overcome their initial fears about contact. They must also be aware, however, that ongoing relationships within the adoptive kinship network may require postadoption services that address the lifelong process of evolving relationships. There is also an increasing need for social workers and other mental health professionals who are knowledgeable about adoption to work with members of adoptive kinship networks involved in openness if issues arise.

When presenting the variety of adoption arrangements available to birthmothers, social workers can help prepare birthmothers for normal grief reactions in placing their children, regardless of the adoption arrangement. Data from this study suggest, however, that 4 to 12 years after placement, there is greater incidence of prolonged grief to this loss in time-limited mediated and confidential adoptions where contact has discontinued or never existed. Absence or loss of contact with a placed child seems to promote fantasies, regrets, anger, and guilt, whereas ongoing contact appears to alleviate some of the loss and facilitates acceptance that the child is also part of another family. In time-limited mediated adoptions, either the agency prearranged for contact to last for a set amount of time (e.g., 6 months, 1 year), or one of the parties no longer wanted to have contact. Birthmothers in confidential and time-limited mediated adoptions reported feeling that they had less control over the level of openness in their adoptions, which could be contributing to their ongoing grief. Thus, birthmothers considering openness options should be informed that grief reactions may vary over time and by type of adoption. In addition, services should be available to facilitate closure and to support birthmothers in time-limited mediated adoptions once contact has ceased. Moreover, continuing close contact with the birthfather also appears to trigger feelings of guilt, blame, and unresolved grief; thus, in addition to individual counseling for birthparents, social workers should offer couples counseling in these situations.

Adoption agencies that arrange time-limited mediated adoptions need to be aware that birthmothers might find it difficult to adjust to the loss of contact once it is established. This suggests that agencies should be extremely careful in their matching process and should attempt to place children in families whose desire for contact is as similar to the birthmothers' as possible. For example, agencies should refrain from trying to appease parties with different ideal birthparent-adoptive parent relationships by arranging a (time-limited) compromise to "satisfy" both.

Every adopted child has a unique set of feelings and reactions to her or his own adoption. Although it is impossible to predict the needs of any one child regarding openness, it is likely that most children desire information about their birthparents, their possible birthsiblings, and their genetic heritage. It is important to take cues from the children to find out whether their questions are being verbalized. If not, discussions should be initiated and information should be offered providing an opportunity for the children to give feedback about readiness to hear information or to meet birthparents. It is also important to be sensitive to the children and to let them provide their input when adoptive parents are making decisions for what is age-appropriate inclusion in the openness.

IMPLICATIONS FOR PUBLIC POLICY

Changing adoption policies have been the source of significant debate in North American and western European countries. Confidentiality policies that were maintained by agencies or by state laws have been challenged by individuals and advocacy groups. National adoption organizations, such as Adoptive Families of America, have formulated policy statements that support, but do not mandate, openness arrangements.

The clearest policy implication of our work is that no single type of adoption is best for everyone. Thus, we believe that a variety of adoption arrangements should be possible by practice and by law. Each type of openness arrangement carries with it strengths, limitations, and challenges. Our research does suggest that open arrangements can work well for adoptive families and birthmothers who desire an open arrangement, who have the commitment to make it work, and who can negotiate a mutually agreeable comfort zone in their relationship. Our data also suggest that some families or birthmothers or both might not be well suited to such arrangements. Each case should be considered on its own merits.

Some states are beginning to mandate mediated contact between adoptive parents and birthparents. The implications of such legislation are as yet unknown; however, such policies appear to be incompatible with our recommendation that openness decisions be made on a case-by-case basis by the persons involved. Successful adoptive placements require consideration of all individuals' needs and styles, with the overriding consideration being the best interests of the child. In other states (e.g., State of Illinois, 1997), legislation has been introduced that would entitle adopted persons over the age of 18 to be given their original birth certificates and all agency records pertaining to their adoptions. Such policies would likely decrease the frequency of confidential or mediated adoptions because parties would know that identifying information could be released when the child was 18.

In addition to best interests considerations, however, other social forces and policies influence adoption practice and policy. Policy changes such as welfare reform limits on public assistance and increased opportunities for contact between birthmother and adopted child may lead more pregnant women to consider adoption in the future. Therefore, it is extremely important for adoption practitioners to have empirical evidence of the long-term outcomes of openness options for birthmothers and adopted children.

Recent years have seen extensive media coverage of such cases as "Baby Jessica" and "Baby Richard," each torn between competing sets of adoptive and birthparents. The parental rights of birthparents and of adoptive parents have been questioned. Partially in response to the issues raised in these court cases, in 1994 the National Conference of Commissioners on Uniform State Laws approved a draft of a Uniform Adoption Act, which is purported to expedite adoption placements, shorten time lines for birthmothers to make relinquishment decisions, further limit birthfathers' rights, and reverse the move toward open adoptions (CUB, 1994). Much debate continues on this proposed legislation in each state, and the findings from our research may be particularly useful in providing empirical data regarding outcomes for families with varying openness arrangements.

IMPLICATIONS FOR FUTURE RESEARCH

Years have passed since the adoptive families, adopted children, and birthmothers in this sample were interviewed. We have begun to visit the families and birthmothers again, now that the children are adolescents; data collection will continue until 1999. What changes will have occurred in the level of openness in the adoptive kinship network, if any? Since the original study, will family composition have changed through parental divorce, death, or birth or adoption of new children? In what ways will the children and the adoptive families have been involved with the extended families of the birthparents? For those families with ongoing contact, we anticipate that, by the time of the children's adolescence, the contact that may have been limited to the birthmothers may now include siblings and half-siblings, birthgrandparents, and other extended birthfamily members. Additionally, now that the children have a more mature understanding of the male's role in human reproduction, we anticipate that more of the adopted children will be expressing interest in finding or learning about their birthfathers.

How does a personal relationship with the family of birth influence an adopted child's struggle with the identity questions that face all adolescents? What kinds of social supports have been most helpful to our participants over the years? What services do they wish they could have had? Will we find the number of agency placements continuing to increase? What new postplacement services will be offered? How are adoptive and birthparents resolving differences? The rapid change in attitudes toward adoption and the changing social policies in our country make it critically important to continue learning from the experiences of the parties involved in all types of adoption.

In this phase of our work, we are especially interested in understanding the adopted adolescent's social construction of self and relationships—that is, her or his sense of identity. We hypothesize that identity mediates the link between quality of family relationships, adoptive family processes, and childhood adjustment on the one hand, and adjustment at adolescence on the other.

Another distinctive feature of this next phase of our work is that we are testing the hypothesis that perceived compatibility of a child with her or his parents provides a key to understanding developmental pathways. Lamb and Gilbride (1985) defined *compatible parent-child relationship* as one in which the behaviors of the partners are well meshed, with communication between them efficient and accurate. Thus, compatibility involves the family members' ability to attain this state and to retain it through interaction over time. Our longitudinal research investigates the contribution of perceived compatibility to outcomes at adolescence. The issue of incompatibility is especially important to examine because it has now emerged as important in our retrospective study of adolescents in residential treatment (Grotevant, McRoy, & Jenkins, 1988) and in the data from the families described in this book (Ross, 1995). Further research should also examine how birthmothers relate to their placed children and their adoptive families during the adolescent years. What happens if the adopted children wish to live with their birthparents?

We are also following birthmothers' development over time, especially with regard to their grief resolution and social relationships with significant others such as spouses, friends, and children. One particular issue needing investigation concerns grief resolution for birthmothers in time-limited mediated arrangements. For example, one key to understanding their adjustment may include the analysis of agency practice regarding when and why a time-limited mediated arrangement, as opposed to an ongoing mediated or confidential adoption, is made. Another clue may be found in additional insights about the birthmothers themselves: Certain personality dimensions (or other unexplored characteristics) may be indicative of both ambivalence at the time of placement, which may lead to a time-limited mediated adoption arrangement, and dissatisfaction at a later time. Further, because it appears that birthmothers in the time-limited mediated group are more likely to be mismatched with adoptive parents on the amount of contact they desire, research needs to look into the possibilities that birthmothers are initially agreeing to time-limited contact in hopes that the adoptive parents will eventually change their minds and that adoptive parents are being encouraged to accept more contact than they desire in their urgency to adopt a healthy baby.

Findings of this study also suggest other areas for future research—for example, How well are openness arrangements negotiated in independent adoptions, when there are no agency personnel to assist before or after placement? What challenges might be involved in openness in international adoptions? What about the placement of older children, who remember relationships they had with their birthparent(s) and other family members? What are the implications regarding openness in cases when parental rights were terminated by the courts? What are the implications of our findings for new techniques in reproductive technology—should sperm or egg donors or surrogate parents be considered the same as birthparents in terms of linking with adoptive families?

The field of adoption provides many exciting opportunities in which social scientists can examine the impact of changing social forces and policies on family dynamics and arrangements and, in turn, the effects of the resulting outcomes on children and families in subsequent generations. We hope this work has contributed to a stronger theoretical and empirical base on which practice and policy decisions can be made, and that it will continue to do so in the future.

REFERENCES

ABIDIN, R. R. (1986). *Parenting Stress Index.* Charlottesville, VA: Pediatric Psychology Press.

ADAMEC, C., & PIERCE, W. (1991). *The encyclopedia of adoption.* New York: Facts on File.

BACHRACH, C. A. (1991). On the path to adoption seeking in the U.S. 1988. *Journal of Marriage and the Family, 53,* 705-718.

BACHRACH, C. A., ADAMS, P. F., SAMBRANO, S., & LONDON, K. (1990). *Adoption in the 1980s.* Hyattsville, MD: U.S. Department of Health and Human Services.

BACHRACH, C. A., LONDON, K., & MAZA, P. L. (1991). On the path to adoption: Adoption seeking in the United States. *Journal of Marriage and the Family, 53,* 705-718.

BACHRACH, C. A., STOLLEY, K. S., & LONDON, K. A. (1992). Relinquishment of premarital births: Evidence from national survey data. *Family Planning Perspectives, 24*(1), 27-32.

BARAN, A., & PANNOR, R. (1990). Open adoption. In D. M. Brodzinsky & M. D. Schechter (Eds.), *The psychology of adoption* (pp. 316-331). New York: Oxford University Press.

BARAN, A., & PANNOR, R. (1993). Perspectives on open adoption. *The Future of Children: Adoption, 3*(1), 119-124.

BARAN, A., PANNOR, R., & SOROSKY, A. D. (1976). Open adoption. *Social Work, 21,* 97-100.

BARTH, R. P. (1987). Adolescent mothers' beliefs about open adoption. *Social Casework, 68,* 323-331.

BELBAS, N. (1987). Staying in touch: Empathy in open adoptions. *Smith College Studies in Social Work, 57,* 184-198.

BENSON, P. L., SHARMA, A. R., & ROEHLKEPARTAIN, E. C. (1994). *Growing up adopted: A portrait of adolescents and their families.* Minneapolis: Search Institute.

BERRY, M. (1991). The effects of open adoption on biological and adoptive parents and children. *Child Welfare, 70,* 637-651.

BERRY, M. (1993a). Adoptive parents' perceptions of, and comfort with, open adoption. *Child Welfare, 77*(3), 231-253.

BERRY, M. (1993b). Risks and benefits of open adoptions. *The Future of Children: Adoption, 3*(1), 125-138.

209

BEVAN, C. S., & PIERCE, W. (1994, November). *Secrecy, privacy, and confidentiality in adoption.* Paper presented at Building Families: Ethical and Policy Issues in Adoption Conference, Minneapolis.

BLANTON, T. L., & DESCHNER, J. (1990). Biological mothers' grief: The postadoptive experience in open versus confidential adoption. *Child Welfare, 69*(6), 525-535.

BOHMAN, M. (1971). A comparative study of adopted children, foster children, and children in their biological environment born after undesired pregnancies. *ACTA Psychiatrica Scandanavica Supplement, 221,* 1-38.

BORGMAN, R. (1982). The consequences of open and closed adoption for older children. *Child Welfare, 61*(4), 217-226.

BRADBURY, S. A., & MARSH, M. R. (1988). Linking families in preadoption counseling: A family systems model. *Child Welfare, 67,* 327-335.

BRINICH, P. (1980). Some potential effects of adoption on self- and object representations. In A. Solnit, R. Eissler, A. Freud, M. Kris, & P. Neubauer (Eds.), *The psychoanalytic study of the child* (pp. 107-131). New Haven, CT: Yale University Press.

BRODZINSKY, A. B. (1990). Surrendering an infant for adoption: The birthmother experience. In D. M Brodzinsky & M. D. Schechter (Eds.), *The psychology of adoption.* New York: Oxford University Press.

BRODZINSKY, D. M. (1987). Adjustment to adoption: A psychosocial perspective. *Clinical Psychology Review, 7,* 25-47.

BRODZINSKY, D. M. (1990). A stress and coping model of adoption adjustment. In D. M. Brodzinsky & M. D. Schechter (Eds.), *The psychology of adoption.* New York: Oxford University Press.

BRODZINSKY, D. M. (1993). Long-term outcomes in adoption. *The Future of Children: Adoption, 3*(1), 153-166.

BRODZINSKY, D. M., PAPPAS, C., SINGER, S. M., & BRAFF, A. M. (1981). Children's conception of adoption: A preliminary investigation. *Journal of Pediatric Psychology, 6,* 177-189.

BRODZINSKY, D. M., SCHECHTER, D. E., BRAFF, A. M., & SINGER, L. M. (1984). Psychological and academic adjustment in adopted children. *Journal of Consulting and Clinical Psychology, 52,* 582-590.

BRODZINSKY, D. M., SINGER, L. M., & BRAFF, A. M. (1984). Children's understanding of adoption. *Child Development, 55,* 869-878.

BURNELL, G. M., & NORFLEET, M. A. (1979). Women who place their infants up for adoption: A pilot study. *Patient Counseling and Health Education, 16,* 169-176.

BUSH, D. M., & SIMMONS, R. G. (1981). Socialization over the life course. In M. Rosenberg & R. H. Turner (Eds.), *Social psychology: Sociological perspectives* (pp. 133-164). New York: Basic Books.

BYRD, A. D. (1988). The case for confidential adoptions. *Public Welfare, 46*(4), 20-23.

CAREY, W. B., LIPTON, W. L., & MYERS, R. A. (1974). Temperament in adopted and foster babies. *Child Welfare, 53,* 352-359.

CARTOOF, V., & KLERMAN, L. (1982). *Adoption: Is it an option for pregnant adolescents?* Waltham, MA: Florence Heller School for Advanced Studies in Social Welfare.

CHAPMAN, C., DORNER, P., SILBER, K., & WINTERBERG, T. (1986). Meeting the needs of the adoption triangle through open adoption: The birthmother. *Child and Adolescent Social Work, 3*(4), 203-213.

CHAPMAN, C., DORNER, P., SILBER, K., & WINTERBERG, T. (1987a). Meeting the needs of the adoption triangle through open adoption: The adoptee. *Child and Adolescent Social Work, 4,* 78-91.

CHAPMAN, C., DORNER, P., SILBER, K., & WINTERBERG, T. (1987b). Meeting the needs of the adoption triangle through open adoption: The adoptive parent. *Child and Adolescent Social Work, 4,* 3-12.

CHILD WELFARE LEAGUE OF AMERICA (CWLA). (1987). *Report of the Child Welfare League of America National Adoption Task Force.* Washington, DC: Author.

CHIRA, S. (1994, August 24). Law proposed to end adoption horror stories. *New York Times,* p. A7.

CHRISTIAN, C. L., McROY, R. G., GROTEVANT, H. D., & BRYANT, C. (1997). Grief resolution of birthmothers in confidential, time-limited mediated, ongoing mediated, and fully disclosed adoptions. *Adoption Quarterly 1*(2), 35-58.

CHURCHMAN, D. (1986). The debate over open adoption. *Public Welfare, 44*(2), 11-14.

COCOZZELLI, C. (1989). Predicting the decision of biological mothers to retain or relinquish their babies for adoption: Implications for open placement. *Child Welfare, 68*(1), 33-44.

COHEN, N. J., COYNE, J., & DUVALL, J. (1993, March). *Preplacement experiences, current family environment, and socioemotional disturbance in adopted children.* Paper presented at the biennial meeting of the Society for Research in Child Development, New Orleans.

COHEN, N. J., DUVALL, J., & COYNE, J. C. (1994). *Characteristics of post-adoptive families presenting for mental health service* (Final report). Newmarket, Ontario: Children's Aid Society of York Region.

CONCERNED UNITED BIRTHPARENTS, INC. (CUB). (1994, May). *CUB action alert.* Des Moines, IA: Author.

COSTIN, L. (1972). *Child welfare: Policies and practices.* New York: McGraw-Hill.

CURTIS, P. (1986). The dialectics of open versus closed adoption of infants. *Child Welfare, 65*(5), 437-445.

DALY, K. J. (1992). Toward a formal theory of interactive resocialization: The case of adoptive parenthood. *Qualitative Sociology, 15,* 395-417.

DEFRIES, J. C., PLOMIN, R., & FULKER, D. W. (1994). *Nature and nurture during middle childhood.* Cambridge, MA: Blackwell.

DEMICK, J. (1993). Adaptation of marital couples to open versus closed adoption: A preliminary investigation. In J. Demick, K. Bursik, & R. DiBiase (Eds.), *Parental development.* Hillsdale, NJ: Lawrence Erlbaum.

DEMICK, J., & WAPNER, S. (1988). Open and closed adoption: A developmental conceptualization. *Family Process, 27,* 229-249.

DESIMONE, M. (1996). Birthmother loss: Contributing factors to unresolved grief. *Clinical Social Work Journal, 24* (1), 65-76.

DEWOODY, M. (1993). Adoption and disclosure of medical and social history: A review of the law. *Child Welfare, 72*(3), 195-218.

DOMINICK, C. (1988). *Early contact in adoption: Contact between birthmothers and adoptive parents at the time of and after the adoption.* Wellington, New Zealand: Department of Social Welfare.

DONNELLY, B. W., & VOYDANOFF, P. (1991). Factors associated with releasing for adoption among adolescent mothers. *Family Relations, 40*(4), 404-410.

EIDUSON, B. N., & LIVERMORE, J. B. (1953). Complications in therapy with adopted children. *American Journal of Orthopsychiatry, 23,* 795-802.

ELONEN, A., & SCHWARTZ, E. (1969). A longitudinal study of emotional, social, and academic functioning of adoptive children. *Child Welfare, 48*(2), 72-78.

ETTER, J. (1993). Levels of cooperation and satisfaction in 56 open adoptions. *Child Welfare, 72,* 257-267.

FISHER, F. (1973). *The search for Anna Fisher.* New York: Ballantine.

FRAVEL, D. L. (1995). *Boundary ambiguity perceptions of adoptive parents experiencing various levels of openness in adoption.* Unpublished doctoral dissertation, University of Minnesota.

GOODE, W. S. (1960). A theory of role strain. *American Sociological Review, 25,* 483-496.

GROSS, H. E. (1993). Open adoption: A research-based literature review and new data. *Child Welfare, 77*(3), 269-284.

GROTEVANT, H. D., & COOPER, C. R. (1981). Assessing adolescent identity in the areas of occupation, religion, politics, friendships, dating, and sex roles: Manual for administration and coding of the interview. *JSAS Catalog of Selected Documents in Psychology, 11,* 52(MS. No. 2295).

GROTEVANT, H. D., FRAVEL, D. L., ELDE, C., ESAU, A., & MCROY, R. G. (1995). *Codebook for rating adoptive parent perspectives on family dynamics.* Unpublished manuscript, University of Minnesota, Minnesota/Texas Adoption Research Project.

GROTEVANT, H. D., & MCROY, R. G. (1990). Adopted adolescents in residential treatment: The role of the family. In D. M. Brodzinsky & M. D. Schechter (Eds.), *The psychology of adoption* (pp. 167-186). New York: Oxford University Press.

GROTEVANT, H. D., & MCROY, R. G. (1997). The Minnesota/Texas Adoption Research Project: Implications of openness in adoption for development and relationships. *Applied Developmental Science, 1,* 166-184.

GROTEVANT, H. D., MCROY, R. G., ELDE, C. L., & FRAVEL, D. L. (1994). Adoptive family system dynamics: Variations by level of openness in adoption. *Family Process, 33,* 125-146.

GROTEVANT, H. D., MCROY, R. G., GUSUKUMA, I., & LOERA, L. (1993). *Intimacy in the close relationships of women who placed children for adoption.* Unpublished manuscript, University of Minnesota.

GROTEVANT, H. D., MCROY, R. G., & JENKINS, V. Y. (1988). Emotionally disturbed adopted adolescents: Early patterns of family adaptation. *Family Process, 27,* 439-457.

GROTEVANT, H. D., VAN DULMEN, M., & MCROY, R. G. (1997, April). Feelings and perceptions about face-to-face contact: Differing trajectories for adoptive parents and birthmothers? In H. D. Grotevant (Chair), *Openness in adoption: Diverging perspectives of adopted children, adoptive parents, and birthmothers.* Symposium presented at the meeting of the Society for Research in Child Development, Washington, DC.

HAJAL, F., & ROSENBERG, E. (1991). The family life cycle in adoptive families. *American Journal of Orthopsychiatry, 61,* 78-85.

HARTER, S. (1983). Developmental perspectives on the self-system. In E. M. Hetherington (Ed.), *Handbook of child psychology: Vol. 4. Socialization, personality, and social development.* New York: John Wiley.

HARTER, S. (1984). Processes underlying the construction, maintenance, and enhancement of the self-concept in children. In J. Suls & A. Greenwald (Eds.), *Psychological perspectives on the self* (Vol. 3). Hillsdale, NJ: Lawrence Erlbaum.

HARTER, S. (1985). *Manual for the Self-Perception Profile for Children.* Denver, CO: University of Denver.

HENNEY, S. M., ONKEN, S. J., MCROY, R. G., & GROTEVANT, H. D. (1998). Changing agency practices toward openness in adoption. *Adoption Quarterly, 1*(3), 45-76.

HOLLINGER, J. H. (1993). Adoption law. *The Future of Children: Adoption, 3*(1), 43-57.

HOOPES, J. L., SHERMAN, E. A., LAWDER, E. A., ANDREWS, R. G., & LOWER, K. D. (1970). *A follow-up study of adoptions: Vol. 2. Postplacement functioning of adopted children.* New York: Child Welfare League of America.

HUMPHREY, J., & OUNSTED, C. (1963). Adoptive families referred for psychiatric advice: Part I. *British Journal of Psychiatry, 109,* 599-608.

HUSTON, A. (1983). Sex typing. In P. H. Mussen (Series Ed.) & E. M. Hetherington (Vol. Ed.), *Handbook of child psychology: Vol. 4. Socialization, personality, and social development* (4th ed., pp. 388-467). New York: John Wiley.

IWANEK, M. (1987). *A study of open adoption placements.* Petone, New Zealand: Iwanek.

KELLEY, H. H., BERSCHEID, E., CHRISTENSEN, A., HARVEY, J. H., HUSTON, T. L., LEVINGER, G., MCCLINTOCK, E., PEPLAU, L. A., & PETERSON, D. R. (1983). *Close relationships.* New York: Freeman.

KIRK, H. D. (1964). *Shared fate: A theory of adoption and mental health.* New York: Free Press of Glencoe.

KIRK, H. D. (1981). *Adoptive kinship: A modern institution in need of reforms.* Toronto: Butterworth.

KIRK, H. D. (1995, July). *Looking back, looking forward.* Keynote address presented at the meeting of Adoptive Families of America, Dallas.

KIRSCHNER, D. (1995). Adoption psychopathology and the "adopted child syndrome." *Directions in Child and Adolescent Therapy, 2*(6).

KRAFT, A., PALOMBO, J., MITCHELL, D., WOODS, P., & SCHMIDT, A. (1985). Some theoretical considerations on confidential adoptions: Part II. The adoptive parent. *Child and Adolescent Social Work,* 69-81.

KRAFT, A., PALOMBO, J., MITCHELL, D., WOODS, P., SCHMIDT, A., & TUCKER, N. (1985). Some theoretical considerations on confidential adoption: Part III. The adopted child. *Child and Adolescent Social Work,* 139-153.

KRAFT, A., PALOMBO, J., WOODS, P., MITCHELL, D., & SCHMIDT, A. (1985). Some theoretical considerations on confidential adoptions: Part I. The birthmother. *Child and Adolescent Social Work,* 13-21.

KUHN, M., & MCPARTLAND, T. (1954). An empirical investigation of self-attitudes. *American Sociological Reviews, 19,* 68-76.

LAMB, M. E., & GILBRIDE, K. E. (1985). Compatibility in parent-infant relationships: Origins and processes. In W. Ickes (Ed.), *Compatible and incompatible relationships* (pp. 33-60). New York: Springer Verlag.

LANCETTE, J., & MCCLURE, B. A. (1992). Birthmothers: Grieving the loss of a dream. *Journal of Mental Health Counseling, 14*(1), 84-96.

LAWDER, E. A. (1970). Postadoption counseling: A professional obligation. *Child Welfare, 49*(8), 435-442.

LEVINGER, G. (1983). Development and change. In H. H. Kelley, E. Berscheid, A. Christensen, J. H. Harvey, T. L. Huston, G. Levinger, E. McClintock, L. A. Peplau, & D. R. Peterson (Eds.), *Close relationships*. New York: Freeman.

LIFSHITZ, M. R., BAUM, R., BALGUR, I., & COHEN, C. (1975). The impact of the social milieu upon the nature of adoptees' emotional difficulties. *Journal of Marriage and the Family, 37,* 221-228.

MACGREGOR, P. (1994). Grief: The unrecognized parental response to mental illness in a child. *Social Work, 39*(2), 160-166.

MARSHALL, C., & ROSSMAN, G. B. (1989). *Designing qualitative research.* Newbury Park, CA: Sage.

MCLAUGHLIN, S. D., PEARCE, S., MANNINEN, D. L., & WINGES, L. D. (1988). To parent or relinquish: Consequences for adolescent mothers. *Social Work, 33,* 320-324.

MCROY, R. G., & GROTEVANT, H. D. (1991). American experience and research on openness. *Adoption & Fostering, 15*(4), 99-110.

MCROY, R. G., GROTEVANT, H. D., & AYERS-LOPEZ, S. (1994). *Changing practices in adoption.* Austin: University of Texas, Hogg Foundation for Mental Health.

MCROY, R. G., GROTEVANT, H. D., AYERS-LOPEZ, S., & FURUTA, A. (1990). Adoption revelation and communication issues: Implications for practice with adoptive families. *Families in Society, 71*(9), 550-558.

MCROY, R. G., GROTEVANT, H. D., & WHITE, K. L. (1988). *Openness in adoption: New practices, new issues.* New York: Praeger.

MCROY, R. G., GROTEVANT, H. D., & ZURCHER, L. A. (1988). *Emotional disturbance in adopted adolescents: Origins and development.* New York: Praeger.

MECH, E. (1986). Pregnant adolescents: Communicating the adoption option. *Child Welfare, 65*(6), 555-567.

MELINA, L. R., & ROSZIA, S. K. (1993). *The open adoption experience.* New York: HarperCollins.

MENDENHALL, T. J., GROTEVANT, H. D., & MCROY, R. G. (1996). Adoptive couples: Communication and changes made in openness levels. *Family Relations, 45,* 223-229.

MENLOVE, F. L. (1965). Aggressive symptoms in emotionally disturbed adopted children. *Child Development, 36,* 512-522.

MESSER, B., & HARTER, S. (1986). *Manual for the Adult Self-Perception Profile.* Denver, CO: University of Denver.

MILLEN, L., & ROLL, S. (1985). Solomon's mothers: A special case of pathological bereavement. *American Journal of Orthopsychiatry, 55*(3), 411-418.

MILLER, N. B. (1987). *Scales and factors of the Child Adaptive Behavior Inventory.* Unpublished manuscript, University of California at Berkeley, Becoming a Family Project.

NATIONAL CENTER FOR HEALTH STATISTICS. (1993). *Births to unmarried teens.* Washington, DC: Author.

NATIONAL COMMITTEE FOR ADOPTION (NCFA). (1989). *Adoption factbook: United States data, issues, regulations, and resources.* Washington, DC: Author.

OFFORD, D. R., APONTE, J. F., & CROSS, L. A. (1969). Presenting symptomatology of adopted children. *Archives of General Psychiatry, 20,* 110-116.

PANNOR, R., & BARAN, A. (1984). Open adoptions as standard practice. *Child Welfare, 43*(3), 245-249.

PARKES, C. M. (1972). *Bereavement: Studies of grief in adult life*. New York: International Universities Press.

PENNEBAKER, J. (1982). *The psychology of physical symptoms*. New York: Springer Verlag.

RAPHAEL, B. (1984). *Scarred by grief: The anatomy of bereavement*. Fayetteville, AR: Hutchinson.

REISS, D. (1992, September). *Preliminary thoughts on the theoretical basis for family assessment*. Paper presented at the meeting of the National Institute of Mental Health Working Group on Methodological Issues in the Study of Family, Washington, DC.

REITZ, M., & WATSON, K. W. (1992). *Adoption and the family system*. New York: Guilford.

RILEY, M. W., FONER, A., HESS, B., & TOBY, M. L. (1973). Socialization for the middle and later years. In D. A. Goslin (Ed.), *Handbook of socialization theory and research* (pp. 951-982). Chicago: Rand-McNally.

ROSENBERG, E. B. (1992). *The adoption life cycle*. New York: Free Press.

ROSS, N. M. (1995). *Adoptive family processes that predict adopted child behavior and self-esteem*. Unpublished master's thesis, University of Minnesota, St. Paul.

RYNEARSON, E. (1982). Relinquishment and its maternal complications: A preliminary study. *American Journal of Psychiatry, 139*(3), 338-340.

SACHDEV, P. (1984). *Adoption: Current issues and trends*. Toronto: Butterworth.

SACHDEV, P. (1989). *Unlocking the adoption files*. Lexington, MA: Lexington.

SANDVEN, K., & EGELAND, B. (1985). *Decision making by black adolescent mothers regarding informal adoption* (Final report). Washington, DC: Office of Adolescent Pregnancy Programs.

SENIOR, N., & HIMADI, E. (1985). Emotionally disturbed, adopted, inpatient adolescents. *Child Psychiatry and Human Development, 15,* 189-197.

SIEGEL, D. H. (1993). Open adoption of infants: Adoptive parents' perceptions of advantages and disadvantages. *Social Work, 38*(1), 15-23.

SILBER, K., & DORNER, P. M. (1990). *Children of open adoptions*. San Antonio, TX: Corona.

SILBER, K., & SPEEDLIN, P. (1982). *Dear birthmother.* San Antonio, TX: Corona.

Silverman, P. R. (1981). *Helping women cope with grief.* Beverly Hills, CA: Sage.

SILVERSTEIN, D. R., & DEMICK, J. (1994). Toward an organizational-relational model of open adoption. *Family Process, 33,* 111-124.

SIMON, N. M., & SENTURIA, A. G. (1966). Adoption and psychiatric illness. *American Journal of Psychiatry, 122,* 858-868.

SINGER, L. M., BRODZINSKY, D. M., & BRAFF, A. M. (1982). Children's beliefs about adoption: A developmental study. *Journal of Applied Developmental Psychology, 3,* 285-294.

SMITH, J. (1991, April). *Attitudes of prospective adoptive parents toward agency adoption practices, particularly open adoption*. Paper presented at the meeting of the National Committee for Adoption, Washington, DC.

SOKOLOFF, B. Z. (1993). Antecedents of American adoption. *The Future of Children: Adoption, 3*(1), 17-25.

SORICH, C., & SIEBERT, R. (1982). Toward humanizing adoption. *Child Welfare, 61*(4), 207-216.

SOROSKY, A. D., BARAN, A., & PANNOR, R. (1978). Adopted children. In D. Cantwell & P. Tanguay (Eds.), *Clinical child psychiatry*. Jamaica, NY: Spectrum.

SOROSKY, A. D., BARAN, A., & PANNOR, R. (1984). *The adoption triangle.* Garden City, NY: Anchor.

STATE OF ILLINOIS. (1997). 90th General Assembly, House Bill 0474, Amending the Adoption Act.

STEVENS, J. (1986). *Applied multivariate statistics for the social sciences.* Hillsdale, NJ: Lawrence Erlbaum.

THOMPSON, S. C. (1981). Will it hurt less if I can control it? A complex answer to a simple question. *Psychological Bulletin, 90,* 89-101.

TOUSSEING, P. W. (1962). Thoughts regarding the etiology of psychological difficulties in adopted children. *Child Welfare, 41*(2), 59-65.

WARD, M. (1979). The relationship between parents and caseworker in adoption. *Social Casework: The Journal of Contemporary Social Work, 60,* 96-103.

WATSON, K. W. (1979). Who is the primary client? *Public Welfare, 37*(3), 11-14.

WATSON, K. W. (1986). Birth families: Living with the adoption decision. *Public Welfare, 44*(2), 5-10.

WHITE, K. M., SPEISMAN, J. C., COSTOS, D., KELLY, R., & BARTIS, S. (1984). *Intimacy scoring manual.* Unpublished manuscript, Boston University.

WIEDER, H. (1978). On being told of adoption. *Psychoanalytic Quarterly, 46,* 1-22.

WIERZBICKI, M. (1993). Psychological adjustment of adoptees: A meta-analysis. *Journal of Clinical Child Psychology, 22,* 447-454.

WINKLER, R., & VAN KEPPEL, M. (1984). *Relinquishing mothers in adoption: Their long-term adjustment.* Melbourne, Australia: Institute of Family Studies.

WORDEN, J. W. (1982). *Grief counseling and grief therapy.* New York: Tavistock.

WROBEL, G. M., AYERS-LOPEZ, S., GROTEVANT, H. D., McROY, R. G., & FRIE-DRICK, M. (1996). Openness in adoption and the level of child participation. *Child Development, 67,* 2358-2374.

ZIATEK, K. (1974). Psychological problems of adoption. *Psychological Wychowawcza (Warsaw), 17,* 63-76.

ZURCHER, L. A. (1983). *Social roles: Conformity, conflict, and creativity.* Beverly Hills, CA: Sage.

Author Index

Subject Index

Adolescent birthmothers, 9-10, 152
Adopted-child syndrome, 12
Adoption:
  defined, 3, 8
  factors stimulating change in, 9-15,
    30, 40-41, 195-196
  family structure changes and, 11
  historical perspective of, 4-9
  identified, 29, 34
  legal issues in, 5, 204-206
  legislation in, 6, 8-9, 41, 204-206
  medical histories in, 5-6
  placement quantity, 41-45
  reasons for, 4-5
  research literature on, 11-15
  sealed records in, 5
  societal changes and, 9-11, 30, 40-
    41, 195-196
  telling children, 5-6, 14, 109-118,
    131
Adoptive family status, 109-117, 120
Adoptive kinship network:
  acquaintance relationship phase, 174
  agency role in, 174-175, 176-177
  buildup relationship phase, 174
  consolidation relationship phase, 174
  current relationship evaluation, 183-
    189, 191-193
  deterioration relationship phase, 174
  determining degree of closeness in,
    173-174
  ending relationship phase, 174
  extent of contact, 175-178
  factors influencing openness level,
    176-178

  first meeting evaluation, 180-183,
    184f, 185f, 191, 192
  future meeting desire, 189-191
  relationship development process,
    174
Adoptive parents:
  adoptive family status and, 109-117,
    120
  agencies and, 29, 34-35, 38-39, 53,
    55-56, 59-61
  birthmother request situation, 29
  birthparent reclaiming and, 109-117,
    122-126, 129
  child's birthparent curiosity, 109-
    117, 120
  confidential adoption, 3-8, 11-13,
    53, 115-129
  control over birthparent involve-
    ment, 109-117, 121-122, 129-
    131
  coparenting, 60-61
  empathy for birthparent, 109-117,
    119-120, 129
  empathy for child, 109-119, 129,
    131-132
  fully disclosed adoption, 59-61, 108,
    115-129, 133
  identified adoption, 29, 34
  mediated adoption, 55-56, 115-129
  narrative coherence of, 109-117,
    128, 131-132
  ongoing mediated adoption and, 115-
    129
  open adoption study and, 109-128
  openness level satisfaction, 83, 87, 90

221

ABOUT THE AUTHORS

Harold D. Grotevant is Professor of Family Social Science and Adjunct Professor of Child Psychology at the University of Minnesota. He completed his B.A. in psychology at the University of Texas at Austin (1970) and his Ph.D. at the University of Minnesota (1977). His publications focus on relationships in adoptive families and on the development of children and adolescents within their families, especially with regard to identity formation. His more than 100 publications include several books: *Adolescent Development in the Family* (with C. R. Cooper, 1982); *Emotional Disturbance in Adopted Adolescents: Origins and Development* (with R. G. McRoy & L. Zurcher, 1988); *Openness in Adoption: New Practices, New Issues* (with R. G. McRoy & K. White, 1988); *Family Assessment: A Guide to Methods and Measures* (with C. I. Carlson, 1989); *Identity and Development: An Interdisciplinary Perspective* (with H. A. Bosma, T. L. Graafsma, & D. deLevita, 1994). He is a Fellow of the American Psychological Association and received the Excellence in Research Award from the College of Human Ecology, University of Minnesota, in 1994.

He has been active in research since the mid-1970s. In the early 1980s, he and Ruth McRoy began their fruitful collaboration, which continues today. Their current project (reported in this volume) examines the consequences of confidential, mediated, and open adoptions for adopted children, their adoptive parents, and their birthparents. They are conducting a longitudinal follow-up of their sample of 190 adoptive families and 169 birthmothers, with funding from the William T. Grant Foundation, the Hogg Foundation for Mental Health, and the Federal Office of Population Affairs. Grotevant's

227

current research also concerns the role of narratives in the regulation of emotion across generations in families.

Grotevant has been actively involved with the Children, Youth, and Family Consortium, a major collaborative effort connecting faculty efforts at the University of Minnesota on behalf of children, youth, and families within the university and linking these resources with those in the community. A special effort has involved creation of AdoptINFO, a Web site for research-based information on adoption available on the Internet through the consortium's electronic clearinghouse (www.cyfc.umn.edu).

Ruth G. McRoy holds the Ruby Lee Piester Centennial Professorship in Services to Children and Families and is the Director of the Center for Social Work Research at the School of Social Work at the University of Texas (U.T.) at Austin. She also holds a joint appointment in the University of Texas Center for African and African American Studies. A teacher of undergraduate and graduate students specializing in practice with children and families, she won the Lora Lee Pederson Teaching Excellence Award in 1984, and in 1990 she was selected as the recipient of the Texas Excellence Teaching Award.

She received her B.A. degree in psychology and sociology and her master's degree in social work from the University of Kansas in Lawrence. She received her Ph.D. in social work from the University of Texas at Austin (1981). Prior to joining the U.T. faculty in 1981, she taught at the University of Kansas School of Social Welfare in Lawrence and at Prairie View A&M University in Prairie View, Texas.

She has been involved in adoptions practice for many years. In the 1970s, she worked as an adoptions and birthparent counselor at the Kansas Children's Service League in Wichita and as the Project Coordinator of the Black Adoption Program and Services in Kansas City. She later was a Technical Assistance Specialist for the Region VI Adoption Resource Center at U.T. at Austin. Currently, she provides consultation on a variety of adoptions practice issues and serves on the boards of several adoption and foster care programs in the Austin area.

She has coauthored three other books and numerous articles and book chapters on adoptions and has presented many invited papers at national and international conferences. Her coauthored books are *Transracial and Inracial Adoptees: The Adolescent Years* (with L. Zurcher, 1983); *Emotional Disturbance in Adopted Adolescents: Origins and Development* (with H. Grotevant & L. Zurcher, 1988); and *Openness in Adoption: New Practices, New Issues* (with H. Grotevant & K. White, 1988). Her other research interests include intercountry adoptions and transracial adoptions; cross-cultural relationships; racial identity development; and African American adoptions, special needs adoptions, and family preservation.